Guillotine in the Wings

Books by Alex Karmel

Mary Ann
Last Words
My Revolution
Guillotine in the Wings

‖ Alex Karmel

Guillotine
in the Wings
A New Look at the
‖ French Revolution
‖ and Its Relevance
‖ to America Today

McGraw-Hill Book Company
New York | St. Louis | San Francisco
Toronto | Mexico | Düsseldorf

*Karmel, Alex,
   Guillotine in the wings.
   1. France—History—Revolution.
   2. Radicalism
—U.S. I. Title.
DC148.K34. 944.04 74-37604
ISBN 0-07-033337-8
First Edition*

for Pepi,
Marianne, and Philippa

‖Contents

Foreword

WILL there be a second American revolution to complete the unfinished business of the first? Americans have asked themselves that question ever since the first days of the republic, sometimes with hope, more often with fear. The fear, in the past, was usually linked to the threat of contagion by foreign revolutionary ideas, as in the Alien and Sedition Acts of 1798, designed to counter the subversive influence of postrevolutionary France. But during the past decade the situation has changed; beginning with the Montgomery boycott and the Berkeley Free Speech movement, this country has seen revolutionary manifestations on such a large scale that even the FBI can no longer blame them all on a Communist plot. Nor have these actions been exclusively the work of blacks and students: witness the post-office strike of 1970 and the wide participation in the peace movement. If there is to be a second American revolution in this century—and some people think it has already begun—it will clearly be a home-grown product, Made in the U.S.A.

If that is so, why bother to take a new look at the French Revolution, the original granddaddy of all the revolutions the world has seen since 1789? The answer, in short, is that the French Revolution is the source of the modern revolutionary tradition and therefore, paradoxically, the only revolution of modern times that was *not* influenced by the tradition it engendered. The French Revolution, like our own, like the one

that may be in progress in this country, was also a grass-roots
movement, neither molded nor limited by any theory of history or revolution, a series of improvised responses to a
national and social crisis. That is enough of an analogy to
lead us to suspect that there are some aspects of those often-
studied events almost two centuries ago that will shed some
new light on our present situation.

Now history is not mathematics, and the lessons to be
learned from history are never equations, either simple or
quadratical. There is a specific character to all historical
events that must be respected if our comparisons and conclusions are not to be false from the start. I have tried to respect the specific character of the events of the French
Revolution while making the comparisons I thought interesting or useful. But in working I discovered that relevance cuts
two ways and that referring to twentieth-century experience
made the men and events of the French Revolution easier to
comprehend. So the result is a kind of dialogue, a new look in
both directions.

Since this is a book for the general public—and I include
myself in that category—I have not hesitated to give a broad
outline of the course of the French Revolution as I went
along. At times, when the story seemed particularly interesting, there is more than an outline. There are also questions and speculations of the sort that scholars usually avoid.
The conclusions are my own, and are intended only as sug-
gestions.

A bibliography of the works consulted in preparing this
book would be nothing more than a list of standard histories
of the Revolution, plus a number of biographies, mono-
graphs, articles, and original sources all known to scholars.
Accordingly, none has been included. But I would like to express my indebtedness to Gérard Walter's biographies of
Marat and Robespierre, and especially to his notes and in-
dexes to the Pléiade edition of Michelet's *Histoire de la révo-*

lution française. Also to Albert Soboul's *Les sans-culottes parisiens en l'an II,* which I have followed closely in the chapter The Pursuit of Happiness. Also to the staffs of the New York Public Library, the New York Society Library, and the Bibliothèque Nationale.

The Most Astonishing...

All circumstances taken together, the French Revolution is the most astonishing that has hitherto happened in the world.
—EDMUND BURKE, *"Reflections on the French Revolution"*

To begin with the guillotine, before the Revolution noblemen convicted of capital crimes were beheaded; commoners sentenced to death were hanged. This class distinction went the way of all others, but not without a certain period of confusion. In January 1790 the marquis de Favas was found guilty of having organized a counterrevolutionary conspiracy to abduct Louis XVI and proclaim his brother, the comte de Provence, regent. On February 18 Favas swung from a gibbet on the place de Grève at the Paris city hall in a well-attended torchlight execution. It was the first time that a nobleman had met his death in this degrading fashion. But a few months later the National Assembly decided to equalize upward instead of downward and decapitation became the lot of even the most common criminal.

Informed of this decree, Sanson, *"Monsieur de Paris,"* the executioner, sent the Assembly a *mémoire* on "the disad-

1

vantages of beheading by the sword." These disadvantages were what one would imagine. The beheading of a nobleman had been a rare event; then as now most of the executioner's clients were drawn from the ranks of the poor. Death was still the penalty for all sorts of ordinary crimes: theft, assault, fraud. If decapitation were to be generalized in the name of equality, some better method was needed.

The hangman's objections had been anticipated by one of the deputies of Paris, Dr. Guillotin, a well-known physician. In December 1789 Dr. Guillotin had proposed that an adaptation of an Italian decapitation machine replace the ax. One of his remarks, somewhat overenthusiastic, revealed his humanitarian intent: "With my machine I cut off your head before you can blink and you don't feel anything!"

The subject caught the popular imagination. Street musicians sang satiric verses about the proposed reform.

> *C'est un coup que l'on reçoit,*
> *Avant qu'on s'en doute;*
> *A peine on s'en aperçoit,*
> *Car on n'y voit goutte.*
> *Un certain ressort caché,*
> *Tout à coup étant laché*
> *Fait tomber, ber, ber,*
> *Fait sauter, ter, ter,*
> *Fait tomber,*
> *Fait sauter,*
> *Fait voler la tête,*
> *C'est bien plus honnête.*

> Suddenly you've got it,
> Before you even know it,
> You just barely feel it,
> You don't even see it.
> A certain hidden spring,
> Suddenly goes ping,
> Cuts it off, off, off,
> Chops it off, off, off,
> Your head flies away,
> It's better that way.

A newspaper parodied the Parisian doctor, "The head will be sliced off so efficiently that for a long time after it has been severed it won't know what has happened. Only the applause of the crowd will convince it of what has taken place."

(As it happened, the question of the survival of consciousness in the severed head worried people even after executions by the guillotine had become a familiar spectacle. When Charlotte Corday was executed in July 1793, one of Sanson's assistants took it on himself to give her head a slap while displaying it to the crowd. Witnesses swore they saw her blush. The man was dismissed.)

Despite the specter of ridicule, the Assembly appointed a commission to study Dr. Guillotin's proposal. The commission returned a favorable report. The first model was built by a piano-maker named Schmidt. It was perfected after being tested on several cadavers taken from the morgue. The machine was used for the first time in April 1792. Its first victim was a mugger who had killed an old woman while stealing her purse. Its first political victim was a royalist conspirator, executed in August 1792.

1792. . . . The Revolution had begun three years before.

We tend to think of the French Revolution as a bolt of lightning streaking across the sky of history. A few stock images are lodged in our minds. Marie-Antoinette, told the people are crying for bread, responds, "Let them eat cake!" A mob storms the Bastille. Heads are carried about on pikes. The women of Paris march on Versailles. Marat is assassinated in his bath. The blade of the guillotine falls as old women knit. Louis XVI is guillotined, Marie-Antoinette is guillotined. Then, for some reason or other, Danton and Robespierre are guillotined. After a while—it is all very confusing—Napoleon becomes emperor and invades Russia, where he is defeated by the snow and Tolstoy. Finally the English capture him at Waterloo, send him off to St. Helena, and it's all over.

True, some of it, but hardly a lightning bolt. From the fall of the Bastille (1789) to Waterloo (1815) is twenty-six years, a quarter of a century. Many of the Bourbons and *emigrés* who returned to power in 1815 had never known the Old Regime. For those who had, it was only a dim memory. Even if we exclude Napoleon, that young general who became the Revolution's unforeseen chief heir in 1799, we are still left with a decade. Even if we restrict the period identified as the French Revolution to the absolute minimum, beginning with the meeting of the Estates (1789) and ending with the fall of Robespierre (1794), it still covers six years. Six years that were not all blood and gore and heads popping into the basket.

It is the Terror that colors the entire period in our imagination; that and the image of bloodthirsty mobs raging through the streets. But the Terror did not begin until March 1793 and lasted only seventeen months. And even during those seventeen months war, inflation, food shortages, and reactionary insurrections dominated the attention of most Frenchmen—which is why the Terror was decreed "the order of the day." As for the bloodthirsty mobs, they existed chiefly in the imagination of Marat, who never ceased berating the people of Paris for their cowardice and *lack* of violence. Also in the imagination of reactionary historians who wrote after the Revolution, men who believed that any resistance to established authority could only be the work of "scum, dregs, and brigands."

But until August 1792 the bloodiest event in Paris for over a century was a riot that occurred *before* the first session of the Estates, the date conventionally chosen as the beginning of the Revolution. In April 1789 hundreds died during the looting and burning of Réveillon's wallpaper factory and the repression that followed. The setting was the faubourg St.-Antoine, a slum as tawdry as any today. As we would expect from our own experience, most of the victims were shot down by the police.

Gouverneur Morris, a rather conservative American living in Paris at the time, observed (in his diary) that "a man must indeed be a great general who with only 1,500 troops, infantry and cavalry, and above all with only two pieces of artillery, could disperse a mob of ten or fifteen thousand, chiefly spectators, but the seditious to the amount of perhaps three thousand, completely armed with sticks and stones."

We must remember that Paris, with 800,000 inhabitants, was a big city for its day and that there was no six o'clock news to inform everyone of what had happened. The day after the event Morris noted in a letter to George Washington (who had asked Morris to buy him a watch), "We have had a little riot here yesterday and the day before and I am told that some men have been killed, but the affair was so distant from the quarter in which I reside that I know nothing of the particulars."

Aside from that April episode, which accomplished nothing, the great changes of the first year of the Revolution took place with relatively little bloodshed. On July 13, with all of Paris in arms, Morris remarked, "It is somewhat whimsical that this day of violence and tumult is the only one in which I have dared to walk the streets, but as no carriages are abroad but the fiacres I do not hazard being crushed and I apprehend nothing from the populace." Paris traffic seemed a greater hazard than the Revolution, at least to a visitor from New York.

The next day the Bastille fell. It was attacked not to free the prisoners but to deliver the arms and ammunition stored within its walls to the Parisian insurgents, who were afraid the city would be attacked by German mercenary troops paid by the king. The siege lasted only a few hours because the commander of the fortress surrendered; the place was, in fact, impregnable. Despite the surrender orders some of the defenders opened fire and ninety-eight of the besiegers were killed. When the fort had been delivered some of the troops

inside were massacred by the assailants, but most were protected by the Bourgeois Militia that had been organized only
the day before. The commander himself was stabbed by a
cook in the rue St.-Antoine as he was being taken to the
Hôtel de Ville (the city hall), headquarters of the rebellion.
The people thought that he had given his troops an order to
open fire.

It was only after the event that the fall of the Bastille became the great symbol of the fall of the monarchy. The
fortress had been built in the Middle Ages as part of the de-
fenses of Paris. By the eighteenth century it was well within
the city limits, surrounded by a densely populated neighborhood (the faubourg St.-Antoine) and useless from a military
point of view. It had been converted into a prison, but even
for that purpose it was antiquated, dilapidated, and expensive to maintain. The day it fell there were only seven prisoners in its cells. Some years before, the administration had
decided that the fortress should be demolished, but the work
had been postponed because the government was short of
money. In short, even if there had been no revolution the
Bastille would have been torn down.

Even if there had been no revolution . . . The words open
a huge abyss of conjecture, remind us of all those tantalizing
questions that can never be answered, the questions that begin, "What if . . ." What if Napoleon had not attacked
Russia? What if Hitler had not attacked Russia? What if
Truman had decided not to drop the atomic bomb on Hiro-
shima and Nagasaki? What if Kennedy had not been assassinated?

Pascal, always dizzied by an abyss, jumped in head first
when he wrote, "Cleopatra's nose, had it been shorter, the
whole aspect of the world would have been changed."

As a rule historians steer clear of Cleopatra's nose. They
are too busy trying to ascertain what actually did happen to
take the time to wonder what might have happened *if*. But

you and I, who are not historians, need not be so prudent.
Besides, there is a teleological fallacy concealed in the historian's insistence on the event as it actually occurred, a
hidden assumption of determinism, all the more tyrannical
for being unconscious. When an historian looks for the
causes of an event, he quite naturally tends to overlook the
conditions and circumstances that would have been the
causes of *some other* outcome, had that, in fact, taken place.
And the better the historian proves his case, the more causa-
tive factors he piles up, the more history comes to seem a
well-oiled machine whose course is fixed in advance.

Perhaps it is. All of the millions of individuals whose
actions taken together make up what we call history may in
fact be playing with loaded dice or dropping the silver dollars of their lives into fixed slot machines. The thesis does
not even require that any individual's actions be predeter-
mined. Millions of random individual decisions can cancel
each other out like the random actions of electrons according to Heisenberg's "Uncertainty Principle" (which is, in fact,
a principle of certainty).* But we are permitted, at least, to
ask the question, "Does the fact that something happened
prove that it was inevitable?" And that validates all our *iffy*
speculations, so long as we remember that they are only
guesses.

Whatever may be the correct procedure for historians,
while an event is in progress the picture is much more con-

* *The position of any single electron can never be determined, much
less predicted. But the total effect of the positions of the billions of
electrons present in the smallest visible speck of matter can be mathe-
matically determined and predicted by the theory of probability. In*
War and Peace, *sixty years before Heisenberg, Tolstoy applied the
same logic to history. It had been claimed that Napoleon lost the battle
of Borodino because he had a cold. Tolstoy maintained that Napoleon's
cold had no more effect on the outcome of the battle than the state of
health of any of the thousands of ordinary soldiers in the French and
Russian armies. For Tolstoy, Napoleon is only a puppet, like all the
other heroes of history.*

fusing than afterwards. For example, if there is a second
American Revolution before the end of this century—and
that is at least a possibility—historians of the future will be
kept very busy explaining why it occurred. No aspect of our
society will be exempt from examination and there will be
oceans of data to be transcribed onto the historians' file cards
—no doubt they will use computers to sort it all out. But if
there is no revolution, only change (that much *is* inevitable),
very few historians will bother to ask why it did not occur.
And right now, in the 1970s, can anyone say for sure that a
second American Revolution will or will not take place?

No event in history has been more meticulously examined
than the French Revolution. This is not an accident; it was
the French Revolution, more than any other episode in the
long, complicated and often horrifying record of the five
thousand years during which men have left written evidence
of their dubious exploits that molded the modern conception
of what is meant by the word "history." There is no event
whose causes have been more relentlessly studied. But sometimes the studies seem to prove *too much*. The more detailed
they are, the more they embrace every aspect of French
society in the eighteenth century, the earlier they discern the
origins of the forces that led to the revolution, the more conclusively they prove that the Revolution was inevitable, the
more—paradoxically—they lead us back to the question,
"Why did there have to be a *revolution*?"

If the monarchy was already weakened, if the nobility was
already superfluous, if the means of production and the
mechanisms of government were already largely in the
hands of the middle class, why did it take a *revolution* to
confirm and legitimize that situation? There are other ways
by which a society can effect change, even fundamental
change. Was it necessary to have a revolution to move from
the France of Louis XVI to the France of Louis Philippe, fifty
years later? Did it really take Mirabeau, Marat, Danton,
Robespierre, and Napoleon to move from the France of

Prime Minister Necker to the France of Prime Minister Guizot, when the net result was to be Guizot's advice to his bourgeois compatriots, "Get rich!"

There are times, as one reads modern studies of the causes and effects of the French Revolution, when the Revolution itself seems to evaporate. Feudalism was dying; it died. The middle class was rising; it rose. Mail was delivered, roads were repaired, bridges built. The administrative bureaucracy that had been expanding since the seventeenth century went on expanding and lost scarcely a day's work. The Bastille was slated to be demolished and it was. What revolution?

And yet there is no doubt that there *was* a French Revolution, whatever the net results. Nor was it one of those events, like the Renaissance, that are named only after they have occurred. In April 1789, before the first session of the Estates, Gouverneur Morris wrote in his diary, "The Revolution that is carrying on in this country is a strange one. A few people who have set it agoing look with astonishment at their own work." In June the still unknown deputy from Arras named Robespierre wrote home to his younger brother, "The present revolution has produced in a few days greater events than the whole previous history of mankind." Edmund Burke in 1790 (three years before the start of the Terror): "All circumstances taken together, the French Revolution is the most astonishing that has hitherto happened in the world."

Astonishing, yes, but not inevitable, at least to those contemporary observers—the very *astonishment* proves that. Burke, the great Whig politician who had been sympathetic to the American Revolution, certainly believed that the French could and should have avoided *theirs*. He advised the French liberals that a revolution was unnecessary, that they ought to have studied the ups and downs of English history and disguised their demand for fundamental reforms as a demand for a *restoration* of neglected medieval liberties:

"You might, if you pleased, have profited of our example

and have given to your recovered freedom a correspondent dignity. . . . But you chose to act as if you had never been moulded into civil society and had every thing to begin anew. You began ill, because you began by despising every thing that belonged to you. . . . The science of constructing a commonwealth, or renovating it, or reforming it, is, like every other experimental science, not to be taught *a priori*."

But that, of course, is precisely what was and remains astonishing about the French Revolution—the unprecedented attempt to remake a commonwealth *a priori*. That attempt and the totally unexpected course of events that were its consequences—not the net results. France might very well, given another cast of characters, have *evolved* from the France of Louis XVI to the France of Louis Philippe without a revolution. But the history of the world would be different if it had.

The very word "revolution" has acquired the meaning of a series of events—and even more, aspirations—comparable to those of the French Revolution. That is how it was used by Marx and Lenin and how it is used today, even by Americans, despite the fact that we have our own revolution to look back to. When we wonder if a "revolutionary" situation exists in the United States, we are not asking if New York or Chicago is comparable to Philadelphia in 1775, but rather if they are comparable to Paris in 1789.

This is not simply perversity or ignorance of our own history. We Americans have, in fact, more reason than anyone else to wonder if we are in Paris in 1789 when we consider the possibility of a revolution. In 1775 the thirteen colonies were a remote, underpopulated outpost of the European world—which is why George III and his ill-advised ministers thought that they could impose their will on the American colonists by fiat. Russia in 1917 was a backward nation, just entering the stage of industrial development, a dinosaur ruled by a despot with a peanut-sized brain. China in 1949 was the debris of a millennial archaic civilization, devastated by a century of imperialist exploitation. Cuba in 1959 was a small, agricultural island, ruled by a vicious, petty dictator, an ex-colony whose wealth, what there was of it, went into the pockets of foreign imperialists (chiefly American). But France in 1789, on the eve of its revolution, was *la grande nation*—the Big Country.

It was, literally, immense. It took ten days to travel from one end of the kingdom to another. And it took only ten days because France had the best system of roads and canals in Europe.

It was rich, even if the government was on the verge of bankruptcy. It had natural resources of all sorts. Except for certain years of poor harvests it produced more than enough food to feed its population. (The persistent shortage of bread in Paris was due to an atrocious system of distribution— which is why it was a *political* issue.) French commerce and industry, if not dominant, at least vied with those of the English and the Dutch, and had created thousands of large private fortunes.

Its culture dominated the European world, with the exception of England. French was the language of diplomacy, the language spoken at the courts of Potsdam and St. Petersburg, the second language of all educated men. (Casanova the Venetian wrote his *Mémoires* in French, so they would be read.) French science, art, architecture, literature, fashions, and manners were models for all of Europe and had held that preeminent position for more than a century.

Above all it was powerful. France had a population of twenty-five million, compared to nine million in England. Spain was poor and decadent; Italy hopelessly divided. Half of Germany was a crazy quilt of petty principalities and the rest was shared by Austria and Prussia. Austria looked big on the map, but the Emperor in Vienna (Marie-Antoinette's brother) governed a collection of peoples who spoke different languages and hated one another cordially. Russia was far off and mostly a wilderness. France was unified and had the largest army in Europe.

If the events that occurred in Paris between 1789 and 1795 had occurred in Stockholm, Budapest, or St. Petersburg they would not have had the same impact on the history of the world. But such events could not have occurred in Stockholm, Budapest, or St. Petersburg. The intellectuals of Sweden, Hungary, or Russia would never have dreamed of "constructing a commonwealth *a priori*." That dream, the dream of remaking society from scratch, the intoxicating notion that all human relations can be reordered by political means, was clearly impossible in all capitals except Paris, "*chef-lieu de l'univers*" (capital of the universe)—which was the phrase that the Prussian visionary and revolutionary Anacharsis Cloots inscribed at the head of his letters.

Now dreams may seem feeble stuff, and they are, until they are believed. To believe them yourself and to get other people to believe them, it is helpful to be a citizen of the most important nation in your part of the world, a nation with immense resources and a powerful army; it is helpful to be part of a culture that is in the forefront of the latest developments in science, art, philosophy, literature, and even fashion. When in 1963 Martin Luther King proclaimed, "I have a dream . . ." it was not only a personal statement but also a political and revolutionary statement, because that dream was articulated before a crowd of two hundred thousand people (plus those watching on television) in Washington, D.C.—*chef-lieu de l'univers* (God help us) of the second half of the twentieth century.

La grande nation today is the United States. It is immense, rich, powerful, and its culture is dominant in at least a third of the world. It is also, and perhaps accordingly, a potential candidate for revolution. Dreams are not to be brushed aside, and nowhere in the world today are men and women dreaming more hopefully and imaginatively than in the United States. If the expression of that hope and imagination is often angry and desperate, it is because the dreams are revolutionary (and sometimes dreams of a revolution). At the end of the eighteenth century the only nation where a revolution could change the history of the human race was France—and the revolution that occurred there did change the history of the human race (more, perhaps, than it changed the history of France). The only nation in a comparable situation in the last third of the twentieth century is the United States.

The revolutionaries of 1789—the men who came to Versailles for the opening of the Estates as well as those who entered the political arena only later—had very few precedents to guide them. No one had tried to renovate a commonwealth *a priori* for eighteen hundred years—aside from some Americans in Philadelphia. When you examine the details of those events that are called the French Revolution, when you read the speeches and the diaries, the letters and the memoirs, what is astonishing and often pathetic is the innocence of the participants—all of them. They knew, right from the start, that they were involved in a revolution, but they didn't know that it would become *the* French Revolution. They came to Versailles determined to do more than consider the tax reforms that Prime Minister Necker would propose in a very boring speech; they were eager to remake society from scratch; but they didn't know that the result would be war, counterrevolution, the Terror, the reaction, Napoleon. The English and American examples were not much help, nor the models offered by the history of ancient Greece and Rome (although they never ceased referring to those examples and models in their speeches, for want of anything better). In fact the whole revolution was improvised as it went along; they were all doing it for the first time.

Afterwards no revolutionary could be that innocent. In fact, the example of the first French Revolution seemed to engender a certain fatalism. The revolution of 1830 was a feeble rerun of 1789. The revolution of 1848—the occasion for the Communist Manifesto—ended with a nephew of the great Napoleon again emperor of the French, a rather ludicrous nephew who pretended to be a socialist. Karl Marx, who decamped to London after that disaster, observed later, "History does repeat itself; first as tragedy, then as farce." Every actor in the Russian revolution kept the French precedent in mind; when the Russian people did not rise to the occasion the Bolsheviks rushed in to push the revolution on to the next obligatory stage. Everyone knew there would have to be a reign of terror sooner or later, which is one of the factors that contributed to the passive acquiescence to Stalinism.

It would be convenient if, before we go on to further speculations about the French Revolution, its causes, course, and consequences—and this whole book, be warned now, is nothing more than that—it would be convenient if we had an authoritative outline, a reliable road map to guide us through the treacherous peaks and swamps of the history of that era. But unfortunately that map does not exist. Or rather there are too many of them, too many definitive outlines that propose sharply contrasting itineraries, all of them marked in red, as the subject demands. Any map is an interpretation, also any history, and no field of historical study has been more diversely mapped and interpreted than the French Revolution.

The problem is hardly a shortage of material but instead its opposite, an *embarras de richesses.* In a certain sense the French Revolution is everything that happened in France between, let us say, 1787 and 1797—plus a great deal that happened elsewhere. When your subject is something as fundamental as a revolution, what is to be excluded as irrelevant? We are not dealing with a period where the evidence consists of pottery shards and legends. During the elections of deputies to the Estates every district in France drew up *cahiers* (notebooks) of grievances and proposals that, taken together, present a comprehensive and detailed portrait of the nation on the eve of the great upheaval. All through the Revolution the proceedings of the various assemblies, clubs, *sections*, and committees were recorded by stenographers; the Buchez and Roux edition of *excerpts* from these records runs to forty volumes. When censorship was abolished in 1789 newspapers of all shades of political opinion proliferated, reporting many of the petty details of daily life as well as the grand events. Many of the leaders of the Revolution wrote their memoirs, sometimes in prison. Afterwards there was a flood of published correspondence and recollections. Even today, almost two hundred years later, scholars continue to discover new documents to add to the pile.

(Nonetheless there are gaps. In 1871 the Communards set fire to the Hôtel de Ville of Paris. The flames consumed the archives of the revolutionary *sections*, those short-lived experiments in local participatory democracy in a troubled urban situation that would be of enormous interest today. The loss is irremediable until someone invents a time machine.)

But *everything* that happens in a decade is a great deal, especially a decade crowded with major events—even more than the documents reveal. People are born, they get married, they have children, they die. Everyone gets older every year. There must have been very few among the twenty-five million Frenchmen who were alive in 1789 whose lives were not in some way affected by the Revolution. So at least twenty-five million lives make up its story. But no one could tell the story of twenty-five million lives, even if the facts were available.

Any selection, no matter how voluminous it may be, implies an interpretation. You find what you look for. The first histories of the Revolution, written by conservative and sometimes reactionary historians, were almost completely negative. These historians did not have to exaggerate—although many of them did—only select the evidence that could enable them to portray the Revolution as the work of a vicious, savage rabble. Carlyle's classic narrative, now in ill repute, represents a more balanced view, yet it suffers from the bias of his sources. (Carlyle added a few touches of his own, such as "*sea-green* Incorruptible" as an oft-repeated sobriquet for Robespierre—"sea-green" is pure invention.) Most of the historians of the Revolution have, of course, been French. In France the Revolution has never been a dead issue, so every interpretation of its history has been and remains a contemporary political statement. In the second half of the nineteenth century the revolutionary tradition became the inspiration for various French political parties, each choosing one of the revolutionary phases or leaders as its inspiration, depending on its ideologic stance. Eventually the left—i.e., the republicans, with a small *r*— proclaimed that "*La Révolution est un bloc*" (the Revolution is a monolith), summarizing the, for then, radical position that you had to be either for or against the Revolution as a whole, without the option to pick or choose among its various stages. In other words, "Take it or leave it!"

In terms of scholarship this had the advantage of permitting historians to study the period without having to take sides, but it also prejudged, for political reasons, the question of whether the Revolution was indeed a *bloc*. In our own century a new factor, or rather a new revolution—the Russian Revolution—radically altered the whole debate. French historians of a leftist bent set out to prove that *their* revolution was the original source of socialism and communism. They rewrote history in the way that it must always be rewritten—not, as is the habit of the Soviet encyclopedia, by making "nonpersons" of inconvenient individuals (like Trotsky or Beria), but rather by reexamining the Revolution, emphasizing its social as opposed to its political aspects. As a result a richer and more fully articulated picture has emerged. (Yes, I am going to provide that road map after all.) *La Révolution* is indeed a *bloc*. It is also a classic tragedy, as defined by Aristotle, with the unities of time, place, and action (also characters). But we can perhaps understand it better if we view it as *two* revolutions, which we will call the revolution of 1789 and the revolution of 1792. And to help us sort out the accomplishments, or at least aspirations, of these two revolutions there is the fact that each produced its own constitution—the first the constitution of 1791 and the second the constitution of 1793.

Dates. Four in two sentences. I know that they are confusing, but unfortunately they are unavoidable—to avoid confusion. If history is an immense jigsaw puzzle with ragged edges it is a puzzle in at least four dimensions, time as well as space. Now there is one very nice thing about time; it moves in only one direction—forward. This is a great help in sorting out the pieces of the jigsaw puzzles of history, which tend to fit together in a dozen different ways. Especially if we are concerned with causes and effects—and if we are not concerned with causes and effects, all we can do is have *fantasies* about history, an activity best left to poets, who do it very well. Because event *a* preceded event *b* does not necessarily imply that *a* was the cause of *b*. But it does make it impossible that *b* is the cause of *a*. It is astonishing how often this bit of elementary logic can be ignored.

There is no period where an indifference to the tyranny of time can be more perilous than that of the French Revolution. So much happened so fast. For most events the year alone will hardly do; you must have the month. At decisive moments you must have the day. And for the important days, like the day the Bastille fell (or rather surrendered), you must have the hour, if you want to avoid making *b* the cause of *a*.

Add to this the question of communications. When something dramatic happens in the world today it is immediately reported by radio and television; sometimes there are films or videotapes transmitted by satellite. But until recently, as history measures time, there was a communications lag, often with serious consequences. The Battle of New Orleans, the last serious engagement of what we call the War of 1812, was fought two weeks *after* the peace treaty was signed in Ghent. In 1814 the Rothschilds were able to make a fortune on the London stock exchange by using carrier pigeons to get the news of the outcome of the Battle of Waterloo a few hours in advance of everyone else, including the British government.

The French Revolution speeded up communications, like everything else. In 1791 an inventor named Chappe devised a machine that he called a *télégraphe*—not, of course, the electric telegraph perfected by Samuel Morse in 1844, but a giant semaphore whose coded messages could be read from a great distance. Chappe's invention (like Dr. Guillotin's) was submitted to the Assembly and eventually approved by the Convention in 1794. A *télégraphe* network was built—a series of Chappe's semaphores transmitting messages by relays—with the result that news of the outcome of battles on the frontiers of France could reach Paris in a matter of hours instead of days.

Three years earlier, when the king had attempted to flee from France and been arrested at the village of Varennes, it took from four to eight days for the news to arrive at the most distant borders of the kingdom—and this rate of diffusion was described by contemporaries as "an electric spark." In some places news of the king's arrest preceded that of his flight. Even Paris, with the best system of communication, did not learn of the king's arrest until twenty-four hours after it had occurred. Paradoxically this hiatus would seem to have accelerated the course of the Revolution. During the hiatus royalists celebrated the king's "successful" flight while antiroyalists called for a republic. The underlying issues that divided France were brought out into the open and the gaps could never be plastered over again.

A year later the September Massacres in Paris were touched off by the rumor that Verdun had been delivered to the Prussians by treason. Verdun did, in fact, surrender to the Prussians on the day the massacres began, but the real news arrived only two days later. That the massacres were provoked by what was as yet only an unfounded rumor is a significant indication of the state of mind of the people of Paris, one that could be overlooked if we forget the communications lag.

But for our own road map of the two revolutions that together constitute the French Revolution, still at least among "the most astonishing that has hitherto happened in the world," we shall stick to years, with a few months thrown in when necessary. But as the itinerary is unavoidably a bit complicated, perhaps it deserves a chapter to itself.

Le Jour
de Gloire . . .

Allons, enfants de la patrie,
Le jour de gloire est arrivé!
—*"La Marseillaise"*

IN the spring of 1792 revolutionary France found itself at war with both Austria and Prussia, which was in itself a singular circumstance in the checkerboard game of international relations as it had been played for over a century. Ever since the rise of Prussia as a military power France had been the ally of one of the two monarchies that dominated the region of Europe called Germany—and, of course, the enemy of the other. First she had been the ally of Prussia and the enemy of Austria, despite the fact that Prussia was a Protestant nation and both France and Austria were Catholic. But eighteenth-century foreign affairs and military actions had no ideologic content; they were pure power politics, which is why the most masterful player on the board was Frederick the Great of Prussia, who was an absolute cynic as well as an absolute monarch. In the middle of the century there had been the Reversal of Alliances; France became the ally of Austria and the enemy of Prussia. One of the results of this was that England became the ally of Prussia—England was *always* the enemy of France. Another result was that Marie-Antoinette, the fourteen-year-old daughter of the Empress Maria-Theresa, was married to the sixteen-year-old grandson of Louis XV, then the dauphin and four years later Louis XVI. The second result was probably more consequential, although at the time it seemed just another of those royal marriages that were a traditional means of sealing alliances.

In April 1792 Rouget de Lisle, a young composer living in Strasbourg, right on the frontier, wrote the words and music of a military song that he called *"Chant des Armées du Rhin."* The song had stirring words and a majestic melody. With all of France intoxicated by patriotic fervor, thousands of young men volunteering to serve in the revolutionary armies, the song immediately became popular.

The following July a regiment of five hundred ardent revolutionaries set off from Marseilles: first to Paris, then to the front. Many of them never got to the front; they were killed in Paris in the attack on the Tuileries palace that resulted in the fall of the monarchy. As they marched they sang Rouget de Lisle's song and, as the regiment became a legend even before it reached Paris, the original title was forgotten and the song became known as *La Marseillaise.*

The anthems adopted by nations or movements are not the most interesting area of musicology, but they are mildly indicative. *God Save the King* is simple and serviceable. *We Shall Overcome* is an expression of faith. *The Star-Spangled Banner* is unsingable and indecipherable, denoting impossible aspirations and pretensions. *La Marseillaise* is very singable, but its words are bloody and ferocious; it is a military hymn, a war song. And that is indicative, alas, of one of the chief legacies of the French Revolution: war, ideologic war, cold war and hot war, guerrilla war and world war, war of liberation and war of conquest—all of them still very much with us today.

The French Revolution—or rather the two revolutions that we call the French Revolution (we *are* getting to our road map)—did not begin with a war. It began with a

financial crisis. In 1788 the government of France was on
the verge of bankruptcy. A financial crisis does not sound
very interesting and it usually escapes the notice of at least
ninety percent of the people of most countries—until they
begin to suffer from its effects. The ten percent who *are*
interested constitute what today we loosely call the "establishment," the people whose wealth or power or position give
them at least the feeling that they are running the country.
To them, a financial crisis is a sign that the "system"
(another loose term), may be breaking down.

And in France, in the years that preceded the Revolution,
the system was collapsing. Everyone in the establishment
knew that it was collapsing, and that meant the monarchy
and the extensive government bureaucracy, the nobility, the
upper echelons of the clergy, the wealthy bourgeoisie
(bankers, merchants, manufacturers), and the intellectuals
(mostly of middle-class origin), many of whom had been
hopefully predicting that the system would break down for
a long time. The remaining ninety percent were mostly
peasants and farmers, plus a few urban workers and artisans
who would later be called the *sans-culottes*.

The government of France was going bankrupt because
(gross oversimplification follows) the Church and the nobility, who owned or controlled much of the real wealth of
France, especially land, paid no taxes. They never had and
they never would, if they could do anything about it, unless
it became absolutely necessary. But by 1788 it had become
clear that it *was* absolutely necessary. If the government
were forced into bankruptcy, the Church and many of the
nobles would also go bankrupt—not to mention thousands
of widows and orphans from good families who depended
on their pensions and who would starve. So the clergy and
the nobility agreed, in principle, to pay *some* taxes—but only
if those taxes were levied by an Estates General, rather than
decreed by royal edict.

The Estates General was a moribund legislature whose

origins, in the distant medieval past, were similar to those of the English Parliament. It had last met in 1614. When Louis XVI agreed to call a new one, his officials choked on the dust that blew off the ancient volumes they consulted to discover just what an Estates General was.

The insistence that only the Estates could impose the necessary taxes was not merely a formal matter. The clergy and the nobility—who were really one class, since all important posts in the church went to noblemen—hoped that an Estates General, once it met, would restore some of the powers and privileges of their orders that had been steadily eroded by a century and a half of royal absolutism.

This *reactionary* reaction to a fundamental crisis of the system should not surprise us. If a second Constitutional Convention were to assemble in Philadelphia tomorrow— and there are people in the United States who are asking for one, most of them on the far right—at least some of the delegates would propose repealing the income tax, outlawing labor unions, abolishing the "welfare state" and nullifying the Bill of Rights. There is always a substantial portion of the establishment that thinks that the cure for all contemporary ills is a return to "normalcy." For the American far right today "normalcy" is pre-1914. For the French far right in 1788 it was pre-1614.

But even before its first session, in May 1789, the Estates General proved a Pandora's box to the reactionaries who had demanded it. The mere fact that the Estates had been resuscitated and that the very complicated process of electing the delegates had begun set the revolution "agoing." Why? Because the reactionaries were, after all, only a minor part of that ten percent of Frenchmen who constituted the establishment.* There was a far larger part made up of men who

---

* The nobility included 350,000 persons, 1.5 percent of the population; they owned 20 percent of the land. The clergy, about 120,000 in all, owned about 10 percent of the land. The bourgeoisie and the peasants each owned about 35 percent of the land—the percentages

could be described as "liberals"—mostly the middle class and the intellectuals, but including a sprinkling of prominent noblemen and churchmen.

These men were fully aware that the "system" was breaking down, but for them the financial crisis was only the visible part of the iceberg. They thought they knew just why the system was breaking down and they were confident that they had the recipe for reforms that would make the system work. More than that, they believed that they knew how to transform France into a modern nation with liberty, justice, and happiness for all. If, as Burke admonished them a year later, they did not profit from the English example and disguise their reforms as a restoration of lost liberties, it was because that was the position of the reactionaries who had demanded that the Estates convene before the king could impose new taxes. If instead they chose to "begin anew" it was because they were sure they knew just how to do it.

At the beginning of 1789 France was still, officially, a monarchy by the Divine Right of Kings, with Catholicism the established and sole permitted religion, the nobility the chief servants of the king, and feudalism the basis of all wealth. But this was only an official myth—just as "free enterprise" is the official myth in the United States today. In fact the monarchy ruled because it was *there*, at the apex of a huge bureaucratic pyramid, the result of a long historical process. There were Protestants, Jews, and, far more numer-

varying in different regions. But the nobility and the clergy had extensive rights to revenues and duties on land they did not own. On the other hand an important segment of the nobility and the clergy was, ideologically, liberal. This summary of course omits the value of urban property, manufacturing and commercial establishments, and colonial property (the lucrative sugar plantations of Martinique and Haiti), all of which were in the hands of the bourgeoisie. The monarchy had large private holdings. Seventy-five percent of the population of France lived on the land. The urban poor and workers (the sans-culottes) *were perhaps 10 percent of the population.*

ous, many freethinkers in France. Most important, France was already a capitalist society, with the power of money dominating its economy. The middle class not only controlled most of the real wealth of France, but they also staffed the government—aside from the upper echelons of the armed forces, the Church, and a few honorary posts at the Court, which were reserved for the nobility.

There was also a strong counterculture, diametrically opposed to the official myth, that had been growing in popularity and influence for almost a century—the often-confused and self-contradictory amalgam of ideas, attitudes, life-styles and works of art known as the Enlightenment. It was because they had read Voltaire and Rousseau, Montesquieu and Diderot, Helvetius and d'Alembert—plus, in translation, Locke, Hume, and Pope—that the liberal, educated, "enlightened" segment of the French establishment believed that they had all the answers. It didn't seem to matter that, for example, Voltaire and Rousseau were fundamentally at variance in their premises and conclusions; the general drift of their works seemed to flow in the same direction. Besides, the American colonists had done it already; just a few months earlier they had completed *their* constitution. Surely enlightened Frenchmen could do as well. (In the early years of the revolution Lafayette owed much of his prestige to being the friend of George Washington—he was known as "the Hero of Two Worlds.") The enlightened liberals of France were imbued with a boundless optimism and confidence that they could transform France in their own image if only they were given the chance. (Some of them retained that optimism even as they mounted the steps to the guillotine a few years later.) And that chance had come with the calling of the Estates General.

So instead of being merely a complicated and archaic way of levying new taxes, the Estates General, even before it met, was awaited as the beginning of a revolution. *That* was interesting enough to filter down to the ninety percent of Frenchmen who couldn't understand anything about a financial crisis—like the workers of the faubourg St.-Antoine, who burned and looted Réveillon's wallpaper factory and mansion just a few days before the Estates was to meet.

The people of France—the ninety percent who weren't part of the establishment—had good reasons to want to see French society transformed. To begin with, many of them were hungry, especially the poor people in the cities. In Paris the price of a four-pound loaf of bread had risen from twelve sous in November 1788 to fourteen and one half sous in February 1789. Bread was the essential nourishment of Parisian workers and their families; whatever meat or vegetables they ate were only condiments. Great resentment had been aroused by the recent establishment of a circle of customs barriers around Paris, which cut Paris off from the rest of France as if it were a foreign country. (As a contemporary slogan put it, "*Le mur qui mur Paris rend Paris murmurant*" —"The wall that walls Paris sets Paris wailing." The customs posts around Paris were burned the night before the storming of the Bastille.) It didn't help that a freak hailstorm the previous July had destroyed most of the crops in the farmlands closest to the capital. It was claimed, and it was probably true, that speculators in the grain market were hoarding stocks of wheat, hoping to profit from rising prices. It also didn't help that the winter of 1788–1789 was the most severe since 1710; the Seine froze solid, preventing the delivery of firewood and other essential supplies.

A hailstorm and a bad winter may seem like nothing more than coincidences, but coincidences can have profound effects in the short term. And the spark that ignites a revolution is a short-term phenomenon.

By the time the Estates finally did meet in Versailles, the "liberal" delegates had the full and active support of the people of Paris, just a few miles away. They needed it. The delegates who hoped to use the Estates as their instrument for the fundamental reform of French society ran into stiff opposition from the reactionaries who had insisted on calling the Estates in the first place. Not only did most of the nobility and clergy insist on retaining their preeminence, but the king, seeing he was not going to get his new taxes in a hurry, decided to call the whole thing off and send everyone home. The liberals responded with the Tennis Court Oath, which was the first and in some ways the essential revolutionary action of the first of our two revolutions (June 20, 1789).

Finding themselves locked out of the palace in Versailles, the liberal delegates walked a few blocks to an indoor tennis court and set up an informal meeting. After some discussion, dominated by Mirabeau's oratory, they declared themselves a National Assembly and vowed that, despite the king's orders, they would not disperse until they had given France a constitution, to be submitted to the people for its approval. Now, monarchs had been defied before. It was the assertion that the *people* must approve the constitution—that the people were the real sovereign power in France—that made the Tennis Court Oath revolutionary.

The king, who did not like trouble, at first seemed to capitulate, then changed his mind. It took the fall of the Bastille (July 1789) to convince him that there really was a revolution taking place in France, and the march of the women of Paris on Versailles (October 1789) to convince him that he must at least pretend to accept its results.

On both of those crucial days the manpower (and womanpower) was supplied by the ordinary people of Paris. Without their support, and the support of peasants during the summer of 1789, the liberal delegates would have been powerless. Some of them, in fact, never wished to acknowledge this dependence; they changed sides and became conservatives. And some radical spokesmen were already saying that the people had been tricked, among them Dr. Jean Paul

Marat, who began publishing his paper, *The Friend of the People*, in September 1789.

But on the whole the liberals who had taken the Tennis Court Oath remained dominant in the Assembly and popular with the people. Their aspirations and ways of thinking were not very different from those of the men who had made the American revolution a decade earlier. They had the full support of Thomas Jefferson, the American ambassador to France, who was invited by the committee charged with drafting the new French constitution to join in its debates. (Jefferson refused, feeling it was inconsistent with his role as ambassador of the United States. But in June 1789 he had not been so prudent; he had given Lafayette a draft of a "Charter of Rights" that he hoped Lafayette could persuade the king to present to the Estates as his own idea. Neither Lafayette nor Louis XVI was interested. Jefferson always believed that if Lafayette and the king had taken his advice there would have been no French Revolution.) Even Gouverneur Morris, much more conservative than Jefferson, was sympathetic.

And yet the *situation* of revolutionary France was very different from that of the revolutionary thirteen colonies from the very beginning. In America there was no powerful Church and privileged nobility who between them owned a third of the land. Above all, for the Americans of 1776 the king was three thousand miles away in London, while for the French of 1789 the king was right there, first in Versailles, then in Paris.

The Constituent Assembly, which was the Estates under its new name, spent almost two years drawing up that first constitution. Of course they were often distracted from their roles as solons by the fact that they were attempting to govern France at the same time, and events did not wait for the new fundamental document to be complete. Eventually they produced the Constitution of 1791, which would have been a radical document in 1789 but seemed like a conservative compromise two years later. (Just as the nobility had not known what it was doing when it demanded an Estates General, so the liberals of 1789 had not anticipated the consequences when they set the revolution agoing.)

The Constitution of 1791 retained the king as chief executive and commander-in-chief of the armies; it gave him a veto power to delay laws passed by the legislature. France was to remain a monarchy, but a limited monarchy, with Louis XVI exercising no more power than George Washington exercised as president of his enlightened nation on the other side of the Atlantic.

But Louis had already demonstrated that he was not meant to be George Washington. Three months before the proclamation of the Constitution of 1791 he had shown his unwillingness to be a constitutional monarch by attempting to leave the country. He had been caught, arrested and brought back to Paris; he had apologized and said it had all been a mistake. And yet it was hardly a good auspice for the success of the new constitution, which went into operation in October 1791.

Thus ended, officially at least, the first of our two revolutions. France had become a constitutional instead of an absolute monarchy; the nobility had been abolished as a privileged class, even their titles suppressed; the Church had, so to speak, been "nationalized," its vast properties confiscated by the state. (*That* was how government bankruptcy had been staved off.) No mean transformation, far more profound, in *social* terms, than what had been effected by the American revolution. France had compressed into two years the changes it had taken England the two centuries from Henry VIII to George III to accomplish. No wonder many of the liberals of 1789 thought the revolution ought to stop there, consolidate its gains, and make the new constitution a working reality.

But that was not to be; the Constitution of 1791 was in operation for less than a year when it was overthrown by the second of our two revolutions. So for our road map we shall draw a dotted line from September 1791 to August 1792 to indicate the at least official hiatus. Not that those eleven months are unimportant—they include the start of the revolutionary war that produced the *Marseillaise,* the war that began with a series of French defeats and in turn provoked the second revolution. We shall come back to the war. For the moment let us follow our sketchy red line. (It is only here, frankly, that things begin to get really interesting.)

The revolution of 1792 began with another Parisian insurrection against the monarchy, this time with the Tuileries palace its target instead of the Bastille. Military defeats had created a state of crisis—the Prussian army had invaded French territory—and the men in power, especially the king, no longer had the confidence of the people. This revolution was led by the men who had not been content with the accomplishments of the Constitution of 1791, men far to the left of the leaders of 1789. Some of them, like Marat, would still be considered radical today. Once in power these men, to everyone's surprise, quickly organized a real war effort, purging the army of former aristocrats so that it became an effective fighting force that not only repulsed the invader from French soil but went on to a series of astounding victories. (Then, as now, radicals were often accused of being only visionaries who would be embarrassed by real power if they ever achieved it.) In fact it was this most radical phase of the French Revolution that laid the foundation for Napoleon's armies.

At the same time these leaders of the far left attempted to remake French society in a more fundamental fashion than had ever been attempted anywhere before. Burke's phrases about beginning everything "anew," remaking a commonwealth "*a priori,*" proved prophetic; they are a far more accurate description of 1793 than of 1789. The men of this second phase of the Revolution attempted to base political power on all the people, not just those with property; they attempted to create a government that would embody the Revolution as a permanent condition, recognizing insurrection as a permanent right; they attempted to promote social equality by redistributing wealth; they also attempted a cultural revolution, giving France a new educational system, a new calendar, new forms of speech, and even a new religion. All this in only two years—which is why most of these attempts remained only attempts.

This second revolution produced the Constitution of 1793, which was republican in form, liberal in principle, and prophetic in its recognition of social and economic rights. But that constitution remained a purely theoretical document. It was never made operative, its application being deferred until the end of the war. And the war was still going strong when this second revolution did an abrupt turnabout with the fall of Robespierre. The turnabout occurred because, along with the military effort and the attempt to remake France *a priori,* those two years also saw the Terror and the pathological phenomenon of "the Revolution devouring its own children." By July 1794, with the death of Robespierre, there was no revolutionary leader of real stature left alive and the pendulum, having swung to the extreme left, now began to swing back to the right.*

* *The terms* left *and* right, *in their political sense, come from the French Revolution. When the Estates first met in May 1789 the nobility and the clergy were seated in the places of honor, to the right of the presiding officer. The Third Estate, or commoners, were on the left. Even after the Estates became the National Assembly and moved to Paris, the delegates remained in their original seats. As most of the leaders demanding reforms were commoners and the delegates who did all they could to resist change were either noblemen or clergy, the position of their seats to the* left *or the* right *of the chairman acquired a political significance.*

The red line on our road map is growing faint—with 1794 we have come to the end of the revolution, aside from a few galvanic twitchings—but it should be noted that the war was still going strong when the never-operative Constitution of 1793 was replaced by the reactionary Constitution of 1795. And that, in turn, lasted only four years until Napoleon became First Consul in 1799. The war, in fact, continued for another fifteen years, although the Revolution was long since over.

This experience of three constitutions in five years explains what seems to us the baffling French habit of founding a new Republic every time there is a national crisis. The way our government actually works today is as different from the way it worked when George Washington was president as the way the French government actually works today is different from the way it worked under the Constitution of 1791. Perhaps more so, since France, even before the Revolution, had a centralized government with a powerful entrenched bureaucracy, while the United States in 1791 was still thirteen ex-colonies, each with its own political structure. But we have had one constitution since 1788—with amendments. The French have had six fundamental laws that were called constitutions, plus a dozen others that served the same function but were called names like Charter, Organic Law, etc. If the United States had been defeated and occupied during World War II, if we had spent four years governed by a Las Vegas regime (the American equivalent of Vichy), we would certainly have returned to our sacred 1788 constitution when we were finally liberated. If an American de Gaulle ever assumes power to save the country from a take-over by the military— and we may need one, soon—he will certainly proclaim that his mission is "to save the Constitution." In France these two occasions led to the Fourth and Fifth Republics.

But we can draw another lesson from those short-lived

constitutions and the work and passion that went into creating them. A *revolution* cannot be a negative action. Men whose sole idea is to destroy the "system," who are interested only in creating a revolutionary "situation," may instigate riots, *jacqueries,* revolts, but never a revolution. Or if they do, by some accident—and history is full of accidents—*their* revolution will be revealed as nothing more consequential than a *coup d'état.* A revolution that remains a revolution in the eye of history creates at the same time it destroys.

With very few exceptions, the men responsible for the French Revolution knew what they wanted—even if history played nasty tricks on them and very little of what they wanted came to pass. It is astonishing how, even in the darkest moments, when not only the Revolution but also the very existence of France as a nation was in doubt, they inscribed on their agenda, discussed, and voted on decrees concerning schools, hospitals, even museums. It was almost as if they wished to prove that the Revolution was a positive act; they all knew that their ultimate audience was posterity. Some of this was sheer bravado, a show—the same bravado that made Napoleon pause in 1812, just before he began his retreat from Russia, to reform the statutes of the Comédie Française. (Napoleon's reform of the Comédie Française, dated "Moscow, October 15, 1812," is still largely operative.) But this very bravado is a sign of the intention, or pretension, to create a new France—and a new humanity—whatever the circumstances.

And yet in the end it was neither the Constitution of 1791 nor the Constitution of 1793 that had the most profound effect on that partial chronicle we call history, but rather the events that created, sustained, continued, and eventually killed the Revolution. Among these, first place must, unfortunately, be granted to the war.

When we think about the French Revolution today we tend to forget the war as a factor in its development. The

war seems only the landscape in the background of the por-
traits of the principal figures, the part of the tale that is only
"history" in the most narrow sense.

But it was the hope of help from abroad that led the king
to decline the role of George Washington, that led him to
attempt the ill-fated "flight to Varennes" which destroyed
his credibility as a constitutional monarch. It was French
defeats that destroyed the weak compromise that the Constitution of 1791 had become by the time it went into operation. It was the war that created the atmosphere of intense
panic that led first to the September Massacres and later to
the Terror. And in the end it was probably the war that,
more than anything else, destroyed the leftist Republic of
the Year II and led to the downfall of Robespierre.

But that war was a new phenomenon on the European
scene—ideologic war.

For a hundred years before 1789, European military
actions had been limited demonstrations of the power of
opposing dynasties. It was true that thousands of men died
in battle, that villages were looted, women raped. But the
major powers generally arranged to fight one another on
some disputed territory—Belgium, the lesser states of Germany, or Poland. Commerce and even civilian travel between the major powers continued with few interruptions.
In the various leading states, only the very poor could not
avoid conscription. Many of the troops and even the officers
of the armies in the field were hired mercenaries, usually
from Germany or Switzerland, like the Hessians employed
by the British during our War of Independence. If a general
happened to be captured, he would surrender his sword and
be invited to dinner by the victorious commander, who was
probably a distant cousin. No one fought during the winter.
Eventually everything was settled by complicated peace
treaties in which bits of European territories and distant
colonies (like Canada) were shifted from ruler to ruler without any regard for the wishes of their inhabitants.

With the French Revolution, all of that changed, probably for the worse (certainly for the worse in terms of casualties). War became ideologic—the Revolution versus the Old Regime. The issue was no longer a dynastic succession or a bit of strategic territory but the triumph or defeat of one system or the other. Armies became immense and the war continued all year round. The territory of the major powers was no longer spared; only England, protected by the Channel, managed to avoid an invasion by foreign troops in the twenty-three years between Valmy and Waterloo. Traditional loyalties and habits were forgotten. An army of French aristocrats in exile, many of them trained officers, called for the invasion of their homeland and looked to Austria, Prussia, and England for support. In Germany, Italy, and the Lowlands groups of local liberals welcomed the invading French armies as liberators. France itself almost dissolved into confused civil war as devout peasants and conservative bourgeois rebelled against the secular, radical Republic.

At the moment of its most acute internal division and greatest foreign peril, the revolutionary Republic mobilized the resources of France on a scale previously unknown in Europe, foreshadowing the "total war" of modern times. Enormous armies were raised, first by calling for volunteers, then by conscription. Property was requisitioned for military supplies; cellars throughout France were scraped for saltpeter to fabricate gunpowder. In 1794 a million men were in uniform out of a nation of twenty-five million—the equivalent of an army of eight million in the United States today. Since many of the prerevolutionary officers were in exile, fighting on the other side, and many of those who remained were purged or sent to the guillotine, men of ability rose from the ranks with meteoric rapidity. Napoleon, who had been an obscure artillery officer in 1793 and commander of the French army in Italy in 1795, continued the tradition; his slogan was "Careers open to talent" and he claimed there was a marshal's baton in every infantryman's knapsack.

But what created this army and kept it going was not, exclusively, the spirit of the Revolution. We return to the *Marseillaise*. It does, to be sure, appeal to revolutionary sentiment. *"Contre nous de la tyrannie l'étendard sanglant est levé"*—the blood-soaked flag of tyranny is raised against us. But remember the first lines, "Let us go, children of the fatherland, the day of glory has come!" And also, "Take arms, citizens! march! march! impure blood will water our fields!" The *Marseillaise* is primarily a patriotic song, a military song—notice all those references to "blood."

No, the prime motivation that made effective fighting forces out of the volunteers of '92 and the draftees of '93 was not the revolutionary spirit, but rather patriotism. These days *patriotism* is rather unfashionable among people who consider themselves the left in England, France, and the United States. But there is another word that means the same thing, *nationalism* (a word that historians prefer, as less emotional)—and that word, in the 1970s, evokes a more equivocal response among the same people. *Nationalism*, if it is British, French, American, or Russian, is imperialist, reactionary. However Black nationalism, Arab nationalism, Cuban nationalism, etc., remain revolutionary. (When Israel won the Six Day War in 1967, Israeli nationalism became "Zionist imperialism" in the lexicon of the New Left.) But what about the nationalism of Biafra or East Bengal? In certain instances even the New Left is confused.

Both nationalism and patriotism imply the very debatable idea that it is a worthwhile and noble use of your life to fight and die for your country. That notion, in the prerevolutionary eighteenth century, was reserved for the nobility, who justified their privileged status by their willingness to serve their king. The French Revolution abolished the nobility and democratized this aristocratic ideal. It was the *élan* of patriotism and nationalism that was responsible for the victories of the revolutionary armies and the subsequent victories of the Napoleonic armies; but it was the same force that was responsible for Napoleon's ultimate defeat.

Because the idea of nationalism, like the idea of revolution, could not be confined to France, the two were linked inextricably, once the Revolution assumed a nationalist stance. After a while, German and Italian "patriots" stopped welcoming French armies as "liberators." Even before Napoleon made the fatal mistake of invading Russia, an army led by his brother Joseph found itself bogged down in Spain, fighting an endless and fruitless campaign in a rugged countryside where the military science that had won the victories of Marengo and Austerlitz proved totally useless. Joseph's most formidable opponents were not the regular army of the Bourbon king of Spain, or even the English expeditionary force, but rather untrained and nonuniformed bands of peasants who melted into the landscape at a show of force and then struck again when they were least expected. These bands of Spanish Viet Cong were called "guerrillas," a new word at the time. (Napoleon dismissed the Spanish disaster with the sour-grapes remark, "Africa begins at the Pyrenees.")

Today, in the era of cold and hot wars, all at least depicted as ideologic, we tend to take for granted the link between revolution and war. Three administrations justified the war in Indochina as a defense against communism, while the New Left calls for "a hundred Vietnams." But when we examine the war that established this whole pattern, we can at least ask—as we did about the revolution itself—was it inevitable? Could there have been a revolution in France at the end of the eighteenth century without its precipitating a general European conflict that, in the end, destroyed the Revolution itself?

The question could hardly be asked if in 1792 France had been attacked without provocation by Austria and Prussia with the design of reversing the Revolution—as Russia was attacked in 1918 or Cuba in 1961. But the stubborn facts of history force us to reject the comparisons. There was no Bay of Pigs in 1792. The French *émigrés* (exiles) in Coblenz (read Miami) complained bitterly that they received very little help from Marie-Antoinette's brother in their attempt to mount an invasion of France. Austria, Prussia, and Russia were much more interested in completing and digesting the partition of Poland than in taking on the most powerful nation in Europe. Leopold of Austria did persuade the King of Prussia to join him in the Declaration of Pillnitz (August 1791) promising to support the *emigrés* in their counter-revolutionary struggle. But the declaration made it clear that Austria and Prussia would actively participate only if harm were done to the French royal family. And in April 1792, when the war began, the royal family was still comfortably installed in the Tuileries palace, with Louis XVI still head of state.

The fact is that it was the French who started the war. But which France? Not, as we might perhaps expect, some hotheaded revolutionaries of the far left, but instead the middle-class liberals who had declared that as far as they were concerned the revolution was over—the men known as the Gironde. They argued that France would be attacked sooner or later and it was preferable to strike first; no doubt they believed it. No doubt also they were sincere in their desire to spread the benefits of the revolution to the "oppressed peoples" of Europe. But the stubborn facts show us a classic instance of men in power seeking to consolidate their position by foreign adventure in order to distract public attention from domestic issues.

And who led the opposition to the war before it was declared? Robespierre. Robespierre, the man who, of all the leaders of the Revolution, most consistently pressed for fundamental social change, the man whose attitudes and actions most completely embody the Revolution as a domes-

tic upheaval. To the plea that the Revolution be spread
abroad, Robespierre opposed the unfinished business of completing the Revolution at home. He predicted that the king
would not support the war, that the officers of the army
would be reluctant soldiers of the Revolution, if not traitors.
He foresaw that the war would be long and costly to France.
But all his objections were overruled by the "moderates" of
the Gironde.

And yet the war, inevitable or not, had the unexpected
effect of speeding up the Revolution within France—because
it began so badly. It was the atmosphere of panic and suspicion caused by French defeats that led to the insurrection
of August 1792, the attack on the Tuileries palace, the fall
of the monarchy, and eventually the execution of the king.
France was declared a republic. The exigencies of mobiliza-
tion for the war led to a partial abandonment of the *laissez-
faire* economic doctrines of the liberals who had begun the
Revolution in 1789. There were wage and price controls and
the decrees of March 1794 ordering that the property of
counterrevolutionaries be confiscated and distributed to the
poor. It is these measures that have led historians to discern
in the "Republic of the Year II" a foreshadowing of a modern
socialist state.

But the foreshadowing is rather dim. The price controls
didn't work; the wage controls were applied for only two
months and they didn't work either; the confiscation of
property and especially its distribution to the poor remained
only theoretical. Because the atmosphere of panic and suspicion, caused by the war, also created the monster that
eventually destroyed the Revolution by devouring all of its
leaders—the Terror.

If we limit our field of vision to Paris for the two years of
the second revolution (August 1792–July 1794) we see a
series of fascinating but pathological events. First the king is
deposed by an insurrection. Then bands of killers slaughter

hundreds of suspects in the prisons while ordinary citizens remain indifferent. Then the king is tried and executed. Then the leaders of the Gironde—the moderates who started the war—are put under arrest. Marat is assassinated. The leaders of the Gironde are tried and executed. Marie-Antoinette is executed. A number of the heroes of 1789 share her fate. But new conspiracies against the Republic are discovered every day. In March 1794 the men who had engineered the attack on the Tuileries palace are executed—by order of the Committee of Public Safety led by Robespierre. Ten days later Danton and Desmoulins, both old associates of Robespierre, are executed—by order of the same Committee. There is a short pause while Robespierre inaugurates a new religion with his Festival of the Supreme Being. The Terror accelerates; fifty, sixty men, women, and children are sent to the guillotine each day. Then suddenly, in July, Robespierre is declared a tyrant and an outlaw and executed, along with ninety of his followers. After that, even though all the men in power are terrorists, the guillotine stops and the reaction sets in.

Odd, to say the least; a peculiar aberration. The left destroys itself, clearing the field for the men of the right. A collective psychosis, worthy of the pen of Dostoevski.

The outline of the drama seems clear. The radicals of 1792, having made France a republic, eliminate the men of 1789 who wanted to stop with a constitutional monarchy. Robespierre becomes preeminent. Trying to keep the Revolution on an even keel, he strikes first to the left, then to the right. Then at the moment of his supreme triumph he is struck down by a cabal of lesser men, jealous of the power he has assumed.

Immediately after the event, the Terror was blamed on the "evil genius" of Robespierre. This was a convenient explanation for the "Thermidorians" who succeeded Robespierre— by making him the scapegoat they absolved themselves of all responsibility for their earlier actions.

But the experience of our own century should awaken our skepticism on this point. Everyone who joined the Nazi party, including many high officials of the Third Reich, later claimed that he had been mesmerized by the "evil genius" of Hitler. Khrushchev, who had been one of Stalin's trusted aides, tried to blame the purges and slave-labor camps of the Soviet Union on the "evil genius" of Stalin. But an "evil genius" is only a madman until people follow him.

Besides, Robespierre was neither a Hitler nor a Stalin. Had he been either he would have remained in power much longer.

The war: we seem to have forgotten the war. It happens every time. The tight Dostoevskian drama in the Parisian cockpit is so much more interesting than the larger picture. And yet in every indictment of every revolutionary leader who went to the guillotine—except for Robespierre—there is the same charge: the man is a traitor, he has been bought by the enemy. In many histories these charges are not even discussed; they seem so palpably false. And yet they are there. Why? Because they were the ultimate justification for any accusation.

If we can bear to pull ourselves away from the political scene in Paris and take a long shot of France in the summer of 1794, what do we see? The armies of the Republic have repulsed the Prussians and Austrians in Belgium and on the Rhine. They are poised on the Italian frontier. At home the rebels of the Vendée, Lyons, and Provence have been defeated. Throughout the immense territory of France, *la grande nation,* competent administrators are mobilizing every resource to continue the war effort.

Meanwhile, in the capital, the politicians go on squabbling about the ideology of the Revolution. The Terror is at its height, the prisons are full of "suspects," but in terms of the number of men involved it is only a minor diversion from the immense activity of the newly created war machine.

Then in July (Thermidor) the Terror suddenly stops with

the fall of Robespierre. The news is sent to all parts of France as fast as possible. The political journals, all full of tributes to the Incorruptible only a few days before, now denounce him as a tyrant and proclaim his fall as yet a new triumph of the Revolution.

But the officers of the victorious armies, the bureaucrats in government offices, the "capitalists" (another new word) who are amassing fortunes selling supplies to the military, all the men getting on with the business of the war—which has become the chief business of France—find themselves yawning as they read about the events in Paris. There have been so many insurrections, so many revolutionary "days," so many impassioned speeches by politicians, so many executions, that it hardly seems worthwhile to bother with the details of the latest "conspiracy." So many of those speechmakers in Paris have been discovered to be traitors that they must all be a rather bad lot. But there is a new breed of men whom you can trust, for example a certain Corsican artillery officer . . .

Even when Robespierre was virtual dictator of France, military affairs never claimed much of his time. Danton went on missions to the French army in Belgium as the emissary of the Convention. St.-Just, Robespierre's young disciple, did the same job at Nancy and Strasbourg. Robespierre stayed in Paris, keeping the fire of the revolution burning at home. Of course he kept his eye on the generals and the bureaucrats directing the war effort; he kept his eye on everyone. But even in the Committee of Public Safety, which had become the chief executive of the Republic, he seems to have been preoccupied with domestic affairs, denouncing traitors, formulating new policies. Because of ill health, the press of other matters, a policy of making himself scarce, he was absent a good deal of the time.

But there was another man on the Committee of Public Safety whose ceaseless activity compensated for Robes-

pierre's absenteeism—a man who survived the fall of
Robespierre, survived the fall of the Thermidorians who
overthrew Robespierre, went on through the Directory to
become Minister of War under Napoleon—a man named
Carnot, the son of a notary, one of the rare commoners to
have been an officer in the army before the Revolution. He
had never been a Jacobin, he had protested the expulsion
of the Girondins from the Convention, and Robespierre detested him. But even Robespierre couldn't get rid of him because he was indispensable; it was Carnot who master-
minded the strategy of the armies and, perhaps more
important, organized their structure and supplies. A methodical, hardworking bureaucrat of genius who never wore a
uniform and staffed his administration with men of compe-
tence and efficiency, paying no attention to their political
opinions. Oh yes, he signed the decree that sent Danton to
the guillotine. He was, in 1793 and 1794, a terrorist. He
supported the Revolution. Also the reaction. Also the Directory. Also Napoleon. Don't you know we're fighting a war?

Carnot knew it and somehow Robespierre didn't. Revolution is much more interesting than war. Robespierre
embodied the Revolution. He went. Carnot embodied the war,
the dull, technical, bureaucratic side of the war. He stayed.

The leftists who survived the fall of Robespierre, the
Thermidorians who in fact engineered the fall of Robespierre, did not intend to put an end to the Revolution; they
wanted it to go on with themselves in charge. Nonetheless
the Revolution was over. There would be a few more Paris
events to be recorded by historians, an attempted insurrection by the workers in 1795, some agitation by a man called
Babeuf who proposed a new radical doctrine called "Plebeian
Equality"—a forerunner of communism. But ideology was
no longer the force that shaped events. Only the forms remained, the new calendar, the slogan on public buildings
proclaiming France a "Republic, one and indivisible." And

even the forms had a short life. Ten years after the fall of
Robespierre, Napoleon became emperor. All that mattered
was the war.

Should it be what matters to us? Not necessarily. It is not
our war. Napoleon has become a pastry and a brandy but the
Revolution lives on.

And yet in their own way, Carnot and his bureaucrats live
on also. They created the first modern military-industrial
complex and their descendants are comfortably ensconced
in the Pentagon and the Kremlin. The descendants of
Robespierre, St.-Just, Danton, Marat, etc., are where? In
the streets.

It is a mistake to take the French Revolution as the necessary model for all revolutions to come—a mistake that has
been made many times. There is no law of nature that says
that the pattern of events in France during the last decade
of the eighteenth century must be repeated everywhere every
time. But it is at least instructive that the first modern revolution was defeated not by its enemies but by the war
machine that was its own spawn. And that that war machine
should be its most enduring legacy.

It Is a Crime
to Be a King

C'est un crime d'être roi.
—*Camille Desmoulins,*
December 1792

La Révolution commence quand le tyran finit.
—*St.-Just, December 1792*

IF there is anything that seems to "date" the French Revolution, it is the importance of the role of Louis XVI and the monarchy as an institution. These days kings and queens are trivial personalities; their names appear more frequently on the society page or in the gossip columns than in editorials. When, in 1969, President Nixon invited a student to the White House to present the student point of view on Vietnam and the "spokesman" turned out to be a *monarchist,* the incident was cited as an instance of inefficiency by the White House staff and proof of the gap between the administration point of view and student sentiment. In America today a monarchist must be some kind of nut.

We forget, because history is unfashionable, how many patriots of the American Revolution wanted to proclaim George Washington king of the United States. We forget, because it seems commonplace, what a daring and revolu-

tionary action it was for our Founding Fathers to constitute
this nation as a republic. We take it for granted because in
our century every new nation is automatically either a republic or a people's republic. (Even the Union of South Africa is,
on paper, a republic.)

When St.-Just, in his second speech on the trial of Louis
XVI, proclaimed that *"La révolution commence quand le
tyran finit"*—which we can roughly translate as "The revolution begins with the death of the king"—he knew perfectly
well that the revolution had begun in 1789, not 1792. But
perhaps 1789 had not seemed to be much of a revolution to
him. In that year he was only twenty-one, studying law at
Rheims, a morose romantic young man who had the walls of
his bedroom covered with black draperies. During his summer vacation, which he spent at his family's small country
estate, he had written a mediocre satiric poem in the style
of Voltaire—six or seven thousand dull verses entitled
Organt. The poem was published in the spring of 1789 and
achieved a certain notoriety because of a few licentious passages.

On the strength of this questionable literary fame, St.-Just
made a short visit to Paris, where he met Camille Desmoulins, the brilliant young journalist who claimed to have
inspired the attack on the Bastille by a speech he made
standing on a café table at the Palais Royal. (In April 1794
St.-Just, as a member of the Committee of Public Safety,
signed Camille's death warrant.) After that visit, St.-Just
abandoned literature for politics. Four years later he was
Robespierre's right-hand man in the Convention, a revolutionary whose rise to prominence had been meteoric, whose
speech on the necessity of bringing the king to trial had been
decisive in determining that fatal judgment. In July 1794
he was guillotined along with Robespierre, just one month
before his twenty-seventh birthday.

St.-Just was the Rimbaud of the French Revolution. In
each of his laconic sentences there is a metaphysical reso-

nance, a hint of a deeper significance that transcends the immediate occasion. When St.-Just said, *"La Révolution commence quand le tyran finit,"* he meant that the death of the king was the beginning of the real, the ultimate, the absolute revolution. That Revolution (with an upper-case *R*) is something far more portentous than Gouverneur Morris's "revolution that is agoing in this country." It is rather the Revolution as we understand the word today, that profound modification of all human relationships of which the French, Russian, Chinese, etc., revolutions are only stages. We all use the word in that sense today, even if we hope that it will never take place—as, for example, when General Westmoreland told the DAR that the original American Revolution had made all further revolutions unnecessary "for all time."

It is lamentable, if not tragic, that we Americans have permitted our own revolution to be appropriated by the right and forgotten that our revolutionary tradition was not completed, "for all time," in 1788. Our Civil War was probably the most important ideologic conflict of the nineteenth century—and the size of the armies in the field exceeded those of the Napoleonic wars. We regard Lincoln's Gettysburg Address as a patriotic piety, appropriately chiseled in marble in that fake Greek temple beside the Potomac, but the revolutionary Hungarians of 1956 broadcast it on Radio Budapest in that short moment of freedom before they were crushed by Russian tanks. The idea of a "new nation, conceived in liberty, and dedicated to the proposition that all men are created equal" is precisely what St.-Just had in mind when he spoke of the death of the king as the beginning of the Revolution.

In relation to that ultimate Revolution, St.-Just's chronology has been proved accurate. If the Constitution of 1791 had been made to work, if France had remained a constitutional monarchy, 1789 would remain an important date in the history of Europe, but not in the history of the world. Using England as a model, one can imagine a series of Reform Bills in the course of the nineteenth century whittling away the power of the throne until the King of France was no more than a figurehead, like Elizabeth II. And that, despite all of Burke's forebodings of 1790, might well have been the outcome—if Louis XVI had agreed to be a constitutional monarch. More than Robespierre, St.-Just, Danton, or Marat it was one man whose actions made the second, violent, tragic phase of the Revolution necessary and inevitable—the king himself.

In the standard Marxist analysis of the French Revolution, the king is barely mentioned. The revolution is seen as a manifestation of the class struggle, the triumph of the bourgeoisie (whose economic base was capitalism) over the decadent aristocracy (whose economic base was feudalism). The monarchy is considered only as a part of the feudal system and the king as the chief of the aristocrats. And, all in all, that is precisely the part that Louis XVI played in the events from which Marx derived his theories.

But was this necessary or even logical? We have seen that it was the prerevolutionary resistance of the *nobility* to the imposition of new taxes that forced Louis XVI to call an Estates General. To equate the monarchy with feudalism is to overlook two centuries of history. During the dramatic, all-night session of August 4th, 1789, the National Assembly abolished many of the special powers and privileges of the nobility. A contemporary newspaper, *Les Révolutions de Paris,* described this as "chopping down the immense tree of feudalism." But by "feudalism" it meant the remnants of an outdated system in a society that otherwise was modern. And the monarchy was an essential part of that modern society as everyone saw it then. Even Robespierre was a royalist in 1789.*

* *In February 1789, when he was a candidate for deputy of the Third Estate of Arras, Robespierre called Louis XVI "the man of providence that the mercy of heaven has sent us," destined "to effectuate the*

There was, although it may surprise us, no reason for him to be anything else. Robespierre was an ambitious young lawyer from Arras, a rather small town in the north of France. For two centuries the growth of the power of the monarchy had been accompanied by the growing wealth and influence of the class to which Robespierre belonged. A hundred years before the Revolution the noblemen at the court of Louis XIV complained bitterly that the Sun King gave all the important posts in the government to commoners. Of course he did; he could hardly trust those proud seventeenth-century aristocrats. As a child Louis XIV had seen France almost destroyed by the Fronde, a series of localized rebellions led by ambitious and irresponsible princes, dukes, and counts. After he assumed power he built the huge palace at Versailles and forced them all to live there where he could keep an eye on them. When Louis XIV asserted, *"L'état, c'est moi!"* he meant that no pretension to aristocratic privilege was going to stand in his way when there was something he wanted done. Middle-class people all over France were delighted.

But the monarch was loved also by the huge mass known as "the people"—the workers and peasants—and not only because of religious sentiments and the legendary prestige attached to the sacred person of the king (although those feelings should not be neglected). It was the monarchy that protected the peasant from the homegrown tyranny of the local nobleman in his château; it was the king's armies that reestablished peace in the towns and villages after a century and a half of civil war. The "silent majority" of ordinary people usually wants nothing more than to be left alone,

---

revolution that Henry IV and Charlemagne had attempted but which was not yet possible in their times." Addressing a direct plea to the king, he wrote, "Ah! Sire, seize this moment; take pity on an illustrious nation that loves you and act so that there will be at least one happy people on this earth!"

wants above all "law and order"—and the monarchy had given them that.

So it would have been in keeping with the traditions of his ancestors for Louis XVI to have taken the side of the middle class and the people *against* the aristocrats. And that was exactly what the liberals of 1789 hoped he could be persuaded to do. When the market women of Paris led the march on Versailles in October of that year and forced the royal family to move to the capital, they were trying to rescue their king from the nefarious influence of his aristocratic court. Of course the shortage of bread was the immediate cause of that unprecedented action. But when the exhausted, rain-drenched, and triumphant "mob" proclaimed that they were returning with "the baker, the baker's wife, and his child" they expressed their certainty that once Louis was in touch with the realities of the hardships suffered by the people of Paris he would use his immense power to alleviate them.

That episode should not seem exotic. We have seen a similar psychological process motivating the impulse to "march on Washington" during the past decade. The President of the United States today has assumed many of the functions of the monarchs of the Old Regime, despite George Washington's refusal to be addressed as "Your Highness." One of these is isolation from the people. When a quarter of a million Americans gathered on the Mall in November 1969 to call for an immediate end to the war in Vietnam and Nixon barricaded himself behind a wall of buses and announced that he would spend the afternoon watching a football game on television, it was as insulting as the remark, "Let them eat cake!"—which even Marie-Antoinette had the good sense never to say. Should the women of Harlem march on Washington to demand that the President move the White House to the Hotel Theresa? The precedent is not encouraging.

Of course 1789 was no longer the reign of the Sun King. Louis XVI could no longer say, *"L'état, c'est moi!"*—not that he ever tried it. But if he had taken the lead in responding to liberal demands (as Jefferson suggested in June 1789), he might have gained more effective power than he had actually had in the years immediately before the revolution. Both Mirabeau and Lafayette wanted a strong monarchy. Two years later the Constitution of 1791 still reserved an important place for the king. Had Louis chosen to accept the role of a constitutional monarch he would have saved the institution he represented. And he would have saved his neck.

The possibility that the king might co-opt the revolution always worried the men of the left. When Mirabeau was dying *Les Révolutions de Paris* expressed relief that Louis had not visited the great orator on his deathbed—it would have made the king too popular. Even after France became a republic, sympathy for Louis remained widespread. When he was put on trial, the Gironde proposed that the sentence, if he were found guilty, be determined by a plebiscite—they knew that a majority of the people would have voted to spare the king's life. His execution made him a martyr in the eyes of many Frenchmen and led to the bloody rebellion in the Vendée two months later.

But even granted the immense prestige and popularity of the monarchy, it would have taken an extraordinary man to have succeeded in riding the tiger of the Revolution. And Louis was a very ordinary man. The great strength of monarchy as a political institution is that it insures continuity. One man is head of state for as long as he lives. His successor is chosen according to rules that are clearly established and he can often be groomed for the role long before he assumes office. "The king is dead! Long live the king!" The catch is that the king is chosen by a genetic lottery.

We are accustomed to the fable that anyone can grow up to be president. But in a monarchy any imbecile can grow up to be king—if he happens to be of the royal blood. During the centuries when monarchy was the usual form of government in Europe there were imbeciles and even certifiable lunatics who became kings and queens. Also a number of extraordinary men and women—in about the proportion that one would expect of a lottery.

Louis XVI was neither an imbecile nor a great man; he was an ordinary man in a very difficult situation and a bit of a bumbler, if fairly intelligent. With the best intentions in the world he bumbled France into a revolution and then he bumbled himself along to the guillotine, veering this way and that, receiving good advice and bad in the usual ratio. His one decisive action, the flight to Varennes, was completely mismanaged and failed. At times he acted with courage and cleverness and at other times he was stubborn and stupid, but it is surprising how often he simply did nothing. In the end he died with dignity, but that was true of almost everyone who went to the guillotine, the great and humble alike. It is much easier to die with dignity than to live successfully.

Because of his powdered wig, double chin, and corpulence we tend to think of Louis as a middle-aged man, if not old. In fact he was only thirty-eight when he died, a contemporary of most of the other figures of the Revolution. It was no generation gap that created his incomprehension of the events he had set in motion, but rather a question of class.

There are amiable, comic, and even grotesque facets of his personality that should neither be neglected nor overemphasized. His two great passions were the hunt and the table. As a Nimrod Louis was only indulging in a royal sport, but there was something pathological about the way he ate that probably had an endocrine basis. A typical light lunch, to be eaten in private—as opposed to state dinners—consisted of four chops, a chicken, six eggs, a slice of ham, and a bottle of wine (not to mention bread, vegetables, and dessert). He ate with such voracity that the naturalist Buffon said the sight reminded him of a monkey in the zoo. Often he would stuff himself until he had to be carried, helpless, to his bed. It is no surprise that he was fat even as a boy and grew ever more obese as he grew older.

To work off his fat, Louis was out on his horse whenever affairs of state permitted, rifle in hand, shooting as many ducks, pheasant, quail, and stags as possible; he got to know every path in the extensive royal forests near Versailles. The celebrated entry in his diary the day the Bastille fell—"July 14, nothing."—means only that he had been unlucky at the hunt that day. (But it does indicate something that he should have been so occupied in that moment of crisis.) When he was forced to move to Paris he had to give up the hunt; his sole exercise during those last years was an occasional stroll in the Tuileries garden, and he grew fatter than ever. Even in his prison, the Temple, he consumed enormous dinners supplied by the Republic and then slept soundly.

Aside from the hunt, his hobby was woodworking and fashioning locks. He had a small workshop set up in the basement of the palace of Versailles and seemed to enjoy the company of the artisans who assisted him more than that of the courtiers. His private life was exemplary. Unlike his predecessors, he was a good family man and never took a mistress—which was probably a mistake; a Mme de Pompadour might have counterbalanced the influence of Marie-Antoinette.* One can see why he has been called a "bour-

---

* *It took Louis seven years to consummate his marriage and produce an heir. The explanation was physiological, a condition known as* phimosis, *in which the prepuce is too tight to permit an erection without pain. It was eventually cured by a minor operation, but in the days before anesthesia any operation could be frightening and it took Louis years to get up his courage. Meanwhile Marie-Antoinette read pornographic novels and had passionate friendships with her ladies-in-waiting. When they were married, Louis was sixteen and Marie-*

geois." But he was not middle-class; he was an aristocrat.
He grew up surrounded by noblemen, some of whom, according to the rigid etiquette of Versailles, performed tasks
that one would expect to be left to servants—such as hand-
ing him his chamber pot. He received a traditional education; he believed, quite simply and sincerely, in the Catholic
religion as it was taught by his tutors and he never doubted
for an instant that he was king by grace of God. How could
such a man begin to comprehend Robespierre?

For all that, Louis took his task as servant of the state very
seriously. He read far more than most monarchs, especially
books on history and science; he was aware of the problems
facing France; he tried to appoint honest and capable men
as his ministers; he was open to the ideas of his time, within
limits. His support of the American War of Independence
exceeded what might have been prompted by the long
English-French colonial rivalry. Ben Franklin made a big hit
at Versailles and the French debt was increased. When the
financial crisis became acute, Louis sent to Switzerland for
Necker, the leading liberal economist of the day, and made
him his chief minister, accepting in advance the idea of substantial reforms. He reduced the court budget as an economy
measure and tried to restrain his wife's penchant for extravagance. He had no dreams of military glory. All in all,
the very model of a modern enlightened monarch. But, as it
happened, that was not enough.

Once the revolution got agoing, Louis seems to have
veered this way and that—unlike his wife, who always knew
where she stood and what she wanted. Marie-Antoinette may
have been wrong all the way, but she was never confused.
She never even flirted with the idea of a constitutional mon-

---

*Antoinette fourteen, so in both cases we are talking about adolescent
behavior. Once cured Louis regretted what he had been missing
and became a doting husband and father who never looked at
another woman.*

archy and she despised the liberal noblemen who tried to persuade Louis to accept his new role—Lafayette and Mirabeau. When Lafayette ran for mayor of Paris, out of pure spite she advised the royalists to vote against him, even though his opponent, Pétion, was an avowed enemy of the throne. She consistently practiced what the French call *la politique du pire*, hoping for the worst, believing that if everything collapsed and there were a civil war the monarchy would come out on top. During the debate on declaring war in the winter of 1792 she told her friends to support the Girondins, who wanted to spread the Revolution throughout Europe (as opposed to Robespierre, who thought France was enough to handle). But her correspondence reveals that she hoped for a French defeat that would destroy the Revolution. She wrote to the Austrian ambassador in Brussels, "The imbeciles! they don't see that . . . if there is war . . . all the monarchs will unite to defend their rights." When the war began she got hold of the secret plans of the French general staff and sent them off to Vienna by diplomatic courier. There has been much loose talk in this country of treason in high places since the start of the Cold War, but no one has yet accused an American First Lady of using the Moscow hot line to disclose Pentagon secrets. That would be the equivalent of Marie-Antoinette's actions. If anyone deserved to be guillotined, it was she.

If Marie-Antoinette had been the monarch, the revolution might have happened sooner or it might have been postponed or it might have gone much faster. But instead it was her husband, earnest, fat, bumbling Louis, who was king.

He convoked the Estates in the hope that they would rubber-stamp Necker's proposed new taxes. But Necker was no politician; even his supporters fell asleep during his long-winded speeches. And before they even began to take up fiscal matters the delegates spent a whole month debating how they should vote. Between hunting expeditions Louis decided that convoking the Estates had been an error; he ordered the delegates to go home. Instead of going home a majority of the delegates responded with the Tennis Court Oath. The report of that action was cheered by wild crowds in Paris and the troops stationed in the capital showed that they sided with the people. After a few tense days of listening to all kinds of advice, Louis gave in. He recognized the National Assembly and ordered the delegates of the nobility and the clergy to take their seats in the new body. It was, after all, only the Estates under another name.

Louis still had no taxes and the new Assembly refused to face the fact that the state was on the verge of bankruptcy; instead it kept talking about a constitution. Marie-Antoinette and her friends convinced Louis that he had made a grave mistake. (The "Queen's Party" had detested Necker all along.) For a second time Louis informed the delegates that their services were no longer needed. He also hustled Necker back to Geneva in a fast coach, at royal expense. Then he went hunting.

While he was hunting—"July 14: Nothing"—the city of Paris rose up in arms and the Bastille fell.

There is an apocryphal story about the king's return from the hunt that evening, a story that has been repeated many times because it ought to have happened even though it didn't. Louis, as usual, went to bed early after an immense supper. The duc de Liancourt, one of those noblemen whose high rank gave them the right to act as domestic servants to the king, took it upon himself to wake Louis up to tell him what had happened in Paris. The king, still groggy, exclaimed, "But that's a revolt!"—"No, Sire," answered Liancourt, "it's a revolution!"

Not prepared for a confrontation and wishing to avoid further bloodshed, Louis capitulated. He recalled Necker from Geneva and reopened the palace at Versailles to the Assembly. On July 17th he went to Paris to confirm his reconciliation with the liberals who had led the Paris revolt. At the Hôtel de Ville he was received by the new mayor, Bailly, and by Lafayette, who had been named general of the five-day-old bourgeois militia, now renamed the National Guard.

An enormous crowd filled the square in front of the Hôtel de Ville and all the streets along the route of the king's carriage. There were repeated cries of "*Vive le roi!*"—even Marie-Antoinette was applauded. Bailly presented the king with the new tricolor revolutionary *cocarde* and Louis stuck it in his hat. As he tried to get back in his carriage a market woman threw her arms around his neck and kissed him. An astute politician would have realized the potential of such universal and heartfelt sentiment. But Louis was no politician. He accepted the duties of his station, even if they included being kissed by a market woman, but he wanted to go hunting.

The leaders of the "Queen's Party"—the Polignacs, Condés, d'Artois—realized which way the wind was blowing and went into exile. They were the first *émigrés*, beginning with the top of the pyramid.

Throughout this crucial month the king's actions were marked by a characteristic lack of resolution. But then the Revolution had just begun and no one as yet knew what the real stakes were.

The stakes were raised by the events in rural France. A collective psychosis known as the "Great Fear" seized many parts of the countryside. There were rumors of foreign invasions, devastations by the king's mercenaries, pillaging bands of brigands, probably based on ancient memories of other times of national crisis. Armed with pitchforks and rakes, troops of peasants gathered to protect their villages. When the mercenaries or brigands failed to materialize, the peasants often set fire to the local château before dispersing —because it contained the documents that recorded their feudal taxes and duties. Meanwhile the Assembly had begun work on the constitution. In the summer of 1789 its two most important accomplishments were the decrees of the night of August 4th and the Declaration of the Rights of Man. These proved, in the end, to be among the most enduring legacies of the Revolution.

The decrees of the night of August 4th, prompted by the "Great Fear," went a long way toward eliminating the vestiges of feudalism as an economic system. Since then French agriculture has been run on capitalist principles, with the peasants stubbornly holding on to their land—even if they often vote Communist to annoy the politicians in Paris.

The Declaration of the Rights of Man is, for France, the equivalent of the first paragraph of our Declaration of Independence plus the Bill of Rights. Its title is significant: not the rights of Frenchmen, but the rights of *Man*. The universal pretensions of the French Revolution are apparent from the very beginning. Every French constitution has had its Declaration of the Rights of Man—as have the constitutions of some of the nations that were formerly French colonies. They have evolved somewhat over the years—for example the Constitution of the Fourth Republic (1946) guarantees equal rights for women and the right to strike—but the document of 1789 remains the "King James Version," whatever the merits of the revised editions.

Louis, with a typical lack of daring, was reluctant to endorse either the decrees of August 4th or the Declaration of the Rights of Man, even though the Assembly pointed the way by declaring him "the restorer of French liberty." When he finally accepted them as a *fait accompli* it was too late to get any of the credit. In September the Assembly took up the king's powers in the proposed constitution. The crucial issue was the *veto*—a power possessed by the president of the United States. In these debates Mirabeau, who had inspired the Tennis Court Oath, emerged as the champion of the throne. In three months everything had changed; the man who had been a radical in the spring was a conservative in the fall.

Much has been made of the fact that Mirabeau was bribed by the court. In 1794 his remains were removed from the Panthéon because it had been proved beyond doubt that he had accepted large sums of money from the royal purse. But as it happened he rendered his most important services to the monarchy before he pocketed a penny. Mirabeau may have dreamed that he would play Richelieu to Louis XVI, becoming the real ruler of France. (As he saw it, his chief obstacle was Marie-Antoinette; "She's the one with balls," he remarked.) When he died, in 1791, he was already out of date. A natural death while his prestige was still intact saved him from the guillotine that would certainly have been his fate two years later.

But despite the bribes, Louis never committed himself to Mirabeau. Nor did he go along with Lafayette, that other popular hero of 1789 who wanted a strong monarchy, even if constitutional. Louis always believed that somehow or other France would go back to 1788, before the Revolution, even if he was less resolute than his wife in insisting on that position.

Lafayette's role in the Revolution was also that of a failure —ultimately a comic failure. In America he is revered for his assistance in our War of Independence. The deputy of General Pershing, landing with the first troops of the American Expeditionary Force in 1917, declared "Lafayette, we are here!" We overlook the fact that in 1793, after trying to stage a military coup, Lafayette deserted his post as commander of a French army and fled to the Austrian lines. Lafayette wanted to be the George Washington of the French Revolution but the French didn't want a George Washington. He lived until 1834 and was buried in the cemetery of Picpus —a very special cemetery, reserved for the relatives of noblemen who were guillotined in the last six weeks of the Terror. His grave is marked by a plaque donated by the Daughters of the American Revolution, which is entirely appropriate.

The debate on the king's veto threatened to go on forever, but then a "second spasm of the Revolution" again raised the stakes. The women of Paris marched on Versailles and returned with the royal family—also the National Assembly. During the hectic night of October 5th, when the queen's life may have been in danger, Louis acted with courage and dignity. The royal family moved into the Tuileries palace, a seventeenth-century extension of the Louvre that was burned down by the Communards in 1871; its site is now lawns, Maillol sculptures, and a favorite stopping place of double-decked sightseeing buses. Louis was compelled, finally, to give up the hunt and enter the revolutionary arena.

Later that month Louis made a gesture of the sort that would have saved his life and the monarchy if there had been more of them. A baker named François was lynched by a mob who thought that he was sneaking his loaves out the back door—to the delegates of the Assembly. Everyone was horrified at this act of "popular justice." The red flag of martial law was flown over the Paris city hall.* In the entire Assembly there was only one delegate who protested that the imposition of martial law was excessive—a still unknown lawyer from Arras, whose name was misspelled in many newspapers as *Robertspierre*. The day that François was strung up on a lamppost his pregnant wife developed a violent fever that threatened her life. The Assembly voted François a state funeral; Louis sent the duc de Liancourt ("No, Sire, it's a revolution!") to give the widow six thou-

* *The red flag was first used as a symbol of revolt in July 1792 when it was carried in a demonstration at the site of the Bastille with the inscription, "Martial law of the sovereign people against the executive power."*

sand livres and the promise that he and Marie-Antoinette would stand as godparents for the unborn child.

A few more such gestures and the Revolution would have been over—if they had been sincere. Louis would have saved the monarchy in France the way FDR saved capitalism in the United States during the Great Depression. (But it is hard to imagine Marie-Antoinette playing Eleanor Roosevelt.)

For the next year and a half Louis veered this way and that, sometimes declaring his faith in the still-unfinished constitution, sometimes declaring his opposition to this or that measure that had been decreed by the Assembly. His conduct during this period can be ascribed either to indecision or Machiavellianism. During his trial in 1792 it was the Machiavellian interpretation that became official. All his actions that seemed to support the Revolution were interpreted as shams, devices to mislead the people as to his true intentions. But if Louis was acting, he was a very bad actor. The record of those twenty months makes much more sense if we assume that he was confused. Like everyone else involved in the Revolution, he miscalculated again and again, underestimating the gravity of the ultimate ante.

We must put aside the image of the French Revolution derived from *A Tale of Two Cities* and remember that in 1790 and 1791 Paris was the brilliant and prosperous capital of the most powerful nation in Europe. Because the events of 1789 had, in part, been incited by food shortages, the authorities made extraordinary efforts to assure that bread was cheap and plentiful. A score of theaters played to full houses every night. The cafés and restaurants did a roaring business. Gambling and prostitution flourished. Society was brilliant, far more exciting (because more open) than it had been for a long time. The hostesses who welcomed the members of the Assembly and distinguished journals to their salons found that their invitations had never been more desired. Foreigners came from all over Europe to enjoy the excitement of the "City of Light"—a pun, *les lumières* meaning both the frequent illuminations for holidays and the Enlightenment of the *philosophes,* now embodied in the Revolution.

Of course politics dominated everything, even fashion. *Coiffures à la liberté* were the rage—extravagant mountains of curls decorated with tricolor ribbons. The political leaders spent their evenings meeting in *clubs* (a word imported from England)—the Jacobins, largely upper-middle-class, where Robespierre was a frequent speaker; and the Cordeliers, a bit more plebeian, where another orator named Danton could often be heard. A ticket to the visitors' gallery of these clubs, above all that of the Jacobins, was more difficult to obtain than the best seat for a hit play, but every tourist made a try and many succeeded, as their letters attest.

Paris in those years was Paris at its best, the Paris of intelligence, intrigue, sophistication, love, fashion, theater, and the excitement of being alive. There was nothing to match it anywhere in the world. (The guillotine and the Terror came later. Not much later, but later.)

But this was a Paris that Louis never knew, just as he had never known Paris before the Revolution. He and his family were stuck in the Tuileries palace, one of the dullest spots in the capital. Louis never attended a session of the Jacobin Club, that very serious society of respectable citizens. He never went to the Feuillants, a more aristocratic, right-of-center club whose membership included Mirabeau and Lafayette. He never had a chance to stroll in the streets, to see the newsstands at every corner and the bright new fashions. He remained a prisoner in his palace, where the antique etiquette of the court was still enforced, where wigs were still powdered and shoes still sported silver buckles instead of tricolor rosettes.

Because Louis and his family were virtual prisoners everyone thought they would try to escape. The royalist press told
him that he must try to escape. During this period the reactionaries were as violent in their rhetoric as the most radical
of the revolutionaries. They demanded an end to the "anarchy" that prevailed in France; they called for a massacre
of everyone opposed to the throne and the Church. In February 1791 an assemblage of noblemen at the Tuileries was
disarmed and dispersed by the National Guard on the orders
of Lafayette. These "Knights of the Dagger" were accused of
trying to kidnap the king. Louis protested his good intentions
and ignorance of any such plot. That April a well-organized
demonstration prevented the royal family from departing for
Saint-Cloud, a palace not far from Versailles. Again Louis
protested that his only plans were to spend Easter in the
country. He stayed in Paris instead, announcing that "If it
should cost one drop of blood I shall not go."

At that time there were still many liberals who believed
that the king would be faithful to the oath he had taken to
abide by the still-unfinished constitution, even if he objected
to certain of its provisions, especially those concerning the
Church. They may have been right—in April. But two
months later all the suspicions of the far left were confirmed. On June 20th Louis attempted the incredibly mismanaged flight to Belgium that got only as far as Varennes.
Frenchmen would never trust one another again; they would
never fully trust their leaders; the example of supreme du-
plicity had been set by their king.

The attempted evasion was a masterpiece of ineptitude. A
huge, lumbering coach had been constructed especially for
the occasion. It was painted yellow and brown and could
not fail to be noticed as an unusual vehicle. The royalist
troops who were supposed to provide relays and protection
along the route got their signals crossed, arriving either too
early or too late. The very fact of so much military activity

aroused suspicions; bands of peasants gathered to watch the strange carriage go by. Crucial hours were lost waiting for escorts that never arrived. Finally, at Varennes, at eleven-thirty at night, the royal family was forced to descend from their berline. They carried false passports identifying them as the family and servants of a Russian Baroness de Kroff (played by Mme de Tourzel, governess of the royal children) —Louis was assigned the role of valet. But the king was recognized immediately; indeed he had been recognized at the preceding stop by the son of the postmaster, who had galloped to Varennes by a back road to alert the authorities there about the identity of the voyagers in the strange yellow-and-brown coach. Even so the berline might have passed through Varennes safely if it had not paused for half an hour to pick up an escort that was awaiting its arrival at the other end of the town. The escort—German mercenaries—finally joined with the royal coach in the center of the town but by then it was too late; the entire countryside was in arms, the National Guard had been called out, and to have attempted the final twenty-five miles to the frontier would have put Louis, Marie-Antoinette, and their children in danger. At 2:00 A.M. Louis admitted that he was who he was and agreed to return to Paris. His brother, the comte de Provence, who left Paris at the same time as the king, got to Belgium without difficulty, but then he traveled alone and swiftly.

The worst thing about the attempted royal evasion was that it failed. In the three days that Paris was without news of the king's whereabouts, knowing only that he had disappeared, the word "royal" was effaced from all signs and public buildings, the fleur-de-lis was painted over wherever it appeared as a decoration, and someone stuck up a notice on one of the doors of the Tuileries palace reading, "FOR RENT, A LARGE HOUSE, FURNISHED." There were petitions and demonstrations. In short, it is likely that if Louis had been successful in his aborted flight, France would have become a republic in 1791 instead of 1793.

The "scenario," to borrow a word from the Rand Institute, is not hard to imagine. Louis would have set up a "government in exile" and declared the Assembly in Paris illegitimate. He would be recognized by Austria, Prussia, and Russia, but probably not by England and the United States, which would hedge and not recognize the government in Paris either, at least for a while. The Pope would remind all good Catholics in France of their allegiance to their king and there would be royalist rebellions in those regions of France where they occurred, in fact, two years later. But the support of Austria and Prussia for the expatriate Bourbon would be halfhearted and carry a high price in the way of territorial concessions. After a few months of confusion it would become clear that the cause of the Republic was that of France, a national issue, and most Frenchmen would support the government in Paris. The Constitution of 1791 would be modified on the American model so that a president, chosen by an electoral college, would be chief executive instead of the king.

Beyond that my crystal ball grows cloudy. But two things are clear. Had bumbling Louis made it those few twenty-five miles to the frontier, the first French Republic would have been the republic of the whole spectrum of revolutionary opinion—the men of 1789 as well as the men of 1792, the moderates as well as the radicals, the rich as well as the poor—everyone who did not wish to return to the Old Regime. The Terror might not have been inevitable; the revolution might not have devoured its own children. And the Republic would have been spared the stain of regicide.

Regicide? What an old-fashioned word. But we return to St.-Just: "*La Révolution commence quand le tyran finit.*" The moment that Louis was, in effect, put under arrest in the little provincial town of Varennes, his execution became at least probable. Death is, after all, the usual penalty for high treason. In fact his execution was deferred for nineteen months, most of them occupied by a mammoth attempt to pretend that the flight to Varennes had never happened, a sham that led, eventually, to the Terror.

If Louis had made it those extra twenty-five miles to the Abbaye d'Orval where he expected to spend the night of June 21, 1791, if he had made it to Belgium and then lived out the rest of his days as an obese pensioner of his wife's nephew (the Austrian emperor), housed in some palace or other, complaining about his allowance, overlooking Marie-Antoinette's infidelities, eating more than ever and going hunting whenever his servants could shove him up on a horse, the first French Republic would have owed its birth to his *treason*. Instead, because Louis bumbled his flight the way he bumbled everything else, the first decisive act of the Republic was cutting off his head. The Revolution—the big one, with a capital *R*—began with the death of the king.

The immediate consequence, important enough, was that England and Spain joined the coalition united against France, ideology triumphing over power politics. And that unprecedented situation set the stage for Napoleon.

But the long-term consequences were even more grave. Because the Revolution began with the death of the king, it marked an irremediable break with the principle of *legitimacy* in political affairs. A thousand years of history were ignored. Nothing was left but seven hundred delegates meeting in Paris with the most powerful nation in the world a blank slate.

(Well, not quite blank. There were all those bureaucrats running the country and organizing the war machine. But it wasn't until the middle of the twentieth century that anyone began to recognize the bureaucracy as a political class.)

Poor Louis. For all his good intentions he made a mess of everything. He wanted reforms and got a revolution instead.

He was declared the "restorer of French liberty" but he missed his chance to become a revolutionary hero. He bungled his one attempt at a decisive action and never made it to Belgium. He was conscientious about his duties and faithful to his principles but all he ever wanted was a happy family life, a good dinner, and the chance to go hunting. He became a martyr in spite of himself. The moment the guillotine severed his head from his body he suddenly became more important and more powerful than he ever had been while he was alive. His death was the most important moment of the thirty-eight years of his life.

We can wonder about Marie-Antoinette, that narrow-minded and unyielding woman; we can wonder what she thought about her ineffectual husband when she, in turn, was forced to offer her neck to the guillotine. But those thoughts were hers alone and so excluded from that imperfect record that we call history.

‖The Incorruptible

FIRST of all we must put aside our own ideologic categories and prejudices, our current notions of the left and the right, revolutionaries and reactionaries, militants and moderates. Let us imagine a senator named McCarthy from a Midwestern state, but in the French fashion let us give him two first names, Joseph and Eugene. This Senator Joseph-Eugene McCarthy has acquired a huge following all over the country, composed of men and women of all ages who are convinced that the men in power have betrayed the Constitution, deceived the people, and undertaken actions that are opposed to the fundamental interests of the nation. One of Senator McCarthy's chief targets is the Secretary of State, to whom, again in the French fashion, we will give a hyphenated last name: Secretary Dean Rusk-Acheson. Again and again Senator Joseph-Eugene McCarthy accuses Secretary Dean Rusk-Acheson of having sponsored a foreign policy that is ill-considered, immoral, and disastrous. The senator strongly hints that Secretary Rusk-Acheson is a traitor, or at least someone beguiled by a foreign power. He also claims that the defeats and casualties American forces have suffered have been due to treason, treason protected and encouraged in high places. He promises that when the time comes he will name names, expose the enemies of the people. "I have in my hand a list . . ."

Let us add that Senator Joseph-Eugene McCarthy is a fairly young man, only in his thirties; also that he is a lawyer who, like Ralph Nader, has acquired his reputation by fearlessly taking the people's side in battles with the establishment. He has many enemies but, despite numerous personal attacks, he has always been proved to be uncorrupted and incorruptible. He lives modestly and devotes himself night and day to the service of the people, assisted by a growing band of devoted supporters.

We begin to have the portrait of a twentieth-century Robespierre, at least in the early stages of his career.

Certainly the most important figure of the Revolution, Robespierre has always been something of an enigma, even to the French. He doesn't seem very French; he wasn't interested in the good life, he wasn't witty, he had no amorous adventures. He wasn't even swayed by fashion; he wore the same respectable silk suits throughout the Revolution that he would have worn if there had been no revolution and he had remained a provincial lawyer. It is hard to find anything quotable in his speeches without quoting the whole speech. There are books that temptingly purport to reveal "the private life of Robespierre." Of necessity they are limited to letters to his brother and sister, letters from feminine admirers (all of which went unanswered), and speculations that he was in love with the daughter of the Duplay family. (The Duplays were a middle-class family whose modest fortune was derived from real estate and furniture-making; they offered Robespierre their hospitality during the last two years of his life.) No one has even bothered to suggest that he was homosexual, even though he had a male secretary for a few months. It would seem that he kept a discreet mistress during the first years of the Revolution, so discreet that no one knows her name. If he did they spent very little time together and she never talked about it—which would make *her* unique also.

He was one of the deputies to the original Estates, where he was naturally a supporter of Mirabeau, who said of him, "He will go a long way; he believes everything he says." But then Mirabeau was an aristocrat of the old school, with a *mot* for every occasion; what he said about forgotten men is also forgotten. After the Estates became the National Assembly, Robespierre's positions tended to differ from those of the great orator (Robespierre was never a great orator), especially on questions concerning the power of the throne. He managed to acquire a certain celebrity as the spokesman for the people, so that in August 1790 St.-Just, still an unknown law student in Rheims, wrote to him, "You, whom I know only as I know God, by his marvels . . ." And yet he remained distinctly in the second rank of the luminaries of the first years of the Revolution. In February 1791 Camille Desmoulins wrote of him, "Who has not heard of our dear Robespierre, his pure patriotism unmotivated by any personal ambition? . . . He is the living embodiment of the Declaration of Rights and good sense itself. And yet I don't believe that one of the proposals he has made has been voted into law."

In May 1791 one of his proposals was finally voted into law. The Assembly had almost completed its task of writing the constitution. Robespierre made a brilliant speech, full of allusions to "the great legislators of antiquity," proposing that a clause be added to the constitution making all the members of the Assembly that had drafted it ineligible to stand for election to the incoming Legislature. It was, we can say by hindsight, a characteristic tactic, apparently so disinterested that it was hard to vote against it. (Characteristic also in that it was supported by the deputies of the *right*, who were delighted to see the men who had made the Revolution of 1789 excluded from continuing their political careers.) Robespierre was apparently doing himself out of a job, the only job he had, but at the same time he was making life difficult for the enemies he had acquired in the two years since the Estates first met. In fact it is doubtful that Robespierre would have been reelected by his home town of Arras if he had been eligible to run. Too many respectable people in that provincial center had been shocked by the radical views of their representative—and the electoral law of the new constitution limited the vote to men of property. But Robespierre, unlike many of his enemies and rivals, both conservatives and liberals, knew that there was another arena in which he could continue his political career—he was by then one of the leaders of the Jacobin Club.

The Jacobin Club merits an explanation. By 1791 it was more like a political party than a club. Later it became something of a church. Exclusion from the Jacobins became the equivalent of excommunication and, at the high point of the Terror, had the same consequences as excommunication by the Spanish Inquisition. The society had been founded in the spring of 1789 as the *Club Breton,* a sort of planning committee of the liberal delegates to the Estates, many of whom came from Brittany, whence its name. When the Estates, by then the Assembly, moved to Paris in October, the club expanded, admitting members who were not delegates and changing its name to the "Friends of the Constitution." But because it met in what had been the chapel of a Jacobite monastery on the rue St.-Honoré, it became known as the *Jacobins.*

In that first year of the Revolution patriotic clubs, mostly middle-class in membership, were formed in towns and cities all over France. The "Friends of the Constitution" in Paris— already recognized as the revolutionary elite (those two words did not then seem contradictory)—set up a correspondence with the provincial clubs. Those found worthy of the high principles of the Paris group were granted the title of affiliates. The Jacobins of Paris thus became the "Mother Society" of a vast network of subordinate clubs all over France.

These origins explain the peculiar power that the Jacobins

acquired. The Paris club counted among its members many of the most celebrated delegates to the various assemblies as well as journalists, businessmen, and political leaders temporarily out of office—like Robespierre in September 1791. Its provincial affiliates attracted the most articulate and well-placed supporters of the Revolution. In Paris the Assembly would meet during the day and often waste its time listening to speeches by delegates with no political clout, or perhaps by receiving and applauding some group of middle-class women who were donating their jewelry and silverware to the nation. In the evening the important delegates of the Assembly would speak at the Jacobin Club on the important matters that the Assembly had to face. The debates at the Jacobins were thus often more decisive in determining policy than those in the Assembly.

An intense system of correspondence between the "Mother Society" and its affiliates kept the provincial clubs up to date, often more up to date than government officials in the same towns. The Jacobins thus became a sort of shadow government, with a bureaucratic efficiency that surpassed that of the official bureaucracy. No wonder its enemies feared that it would become the government itself—as the Communist Party is the real government in Eastern Europe today; the possibility was always there.

During the year that Robespierre was out of office (September 1791 to September 1792) he was able to devote most of his time to the Jacobins. He became the uncontested leader of the apparatus and acquired a following of influential men all over France personally devoted to him. In effect he became the boss of a well-oiled political machine. But the analogy should not be pushed too far. Robespierre remained incorruptible. The ultimate basis of his authority was his idealism, improbable as that may seem for the boss of a political machine. Although Robespierre himself was a middle-class lawyer and never made any attempt to disguise

the fact—he was never seen sporting a red "Liberty cap"—
he considered himself above all as the representative of *"la
classe laborieuse,"* the working class, which, in fact, was not
represented in the Assembly. "I am attached to its interests
by that urgent sentiment that has always drawn me to the
cause of those who are unfortunate. . . . I defend, above all,
the poor."

This idealistic identification with the poor, unmarred by
any affectation of lower-class *style,* gives dignity to Robespierre's otherwise ludicrous statement (October 28, 1792),
"Nous sommes les sans-culottes et la canaille!—We are the
lower class and the scum!"

But Robespierre was not all idealism and selfless devotion
to the people. There is another side to his personality, evi-
dent in his speeches from the very beginning: an obsession
with plots and conspiracies, with betrayal and treason.* It is
a theme that becomes amplified as the Revolution progresses
and often assumes a personal tone; any betrayal of the Revolution is an insult to Robespierre and any attack on Robespierre is a betrayal of the Revolution. It was a note that was
all the more effective because Robespierre was always chary
of naming names, claiming he wished to accuse as *few*
individuals as possible, and then only the ringleaders of the
plots he had discovered. At times the very men he was accusing, exasperated by his lengthy and vague denunciations,
would force him to "get to the point" by interruptions, catcalls and hooting—which, in effect, put the blame on *them*
when their names were mentioned. Then, after making an
accusation, Robespierre might suddenly turn magnanimous.

---

* *An example from the spring of 1790, the palmiest, most optimistic
phase of the Revolution: "The guilty maneuvers of the enemies of
the Revolution take place daily before our eyes. . . . The friends of despotism and the aristocracy are weaving their deadly plots with an
indefatigable confidence. . . . The secret of the most shameful, the
most extravagant, of conspiracies, that venality and tyranny have ever
mounted against liberty and the nation is coming to light . . . etc."*

For example (November 5, 1792), after a ferocious attack on the Girondins: "But if possible let us bury these miserable machinations in an eternal forgetfulness. Let us turn the attention of posterity from these shameful days of our history when the representatives of the people, led astray by miserable intrigues, appeared to forget the great destiny to which they were called." Followed by (note the personal tone), "I renounce the just vengeance that I might take on those who insult me; I ask for nothing more than a return to concord and the triumph of liberty."

As Robespierre's position as the leader of the Revolution was solidified, this magnanimity made him even more powerful. It was also a sign of his power; mercy is, after all, a royal prerogative. The whole technique—vague accusations, naming a few names, occasional forgiveness—was, of course, at its most effective later, during the feverish atmosphere of the Terror. Robespierre would speak for hours of the shadowy machinations of the enemies of the people, until every delegate to the Convention became afraid that he might somehow be implicated in the latest plot to be uncovered, no matter how innocuous his actual activities might have been. When a few names finally were mentioned it came as a great relief to everyone except those directly accused, and a decree putting the accused under arrest would be voted unanimously. It was a technique that failed Robespierre only once—on the 9th of Thermidor, the day of his fall, when he was shouted down by his opponents before he could name names and was declared an outlaw by the terrorized Convention.

But we are getting ahead of ourselves. If the obsession with "plots and machinations" had been nothing more than a personal quirk of Robespierre's there would not have been a Terror. In fact it was shared by many of his contemporaries. There is one word that tolls like a bell throughout the history of the Revolution—*treason*. Harmonizing with it are others

—*faction, corruption,* and especially *conspiracy.* These notes were sounded first in the press; Marat discovered the tone in the very first issues of his journal. The royalist papers were quick to imitate their adversaries and until the king was deposed in August 1792 there were as many violent voices on the right as on the left, all informing their readers that every misfortune was the work of subversive groups bent on destroying either the Revolution or the fabric of society. Only rhetoric, perhaps, but a rhetoric that began to creep into the speeches at the Jacobin Club and even those at the tribune of the Assembly. And not just the speeches of Robespierre.

Of course the conspiracy theory of history has always been popular; it appeals to everyone's desire for a simple and rational explanation for complicated and often irrational events. The fake "Protocols of the Elders of Zion" still turn up in some pro-Arab propaganda as evidence of a Jewish plot for world domination. Joseph McCarthy got a lot of mileage out of blaming the Chinese Revolution on traitors in the State Department, as if the Chinese had nothing to do with the event. Millions of people still believe that both Kennedy assassinations were the work of some shadowy organization protected by the authorities for reasons that are hard to fathom. Spiro Agnew and J. Edgar Hoover mutter darkly about subversive groups, refusing to believe that American blacks and youth spontaneously reject the kind of society those two gentlemen represent.

But if conspiracy is, in general, an untenable theory of history—and I believe it is—there are, nonetheless, such things as conspiracies, plots, betrayals, and treason. The men and women of the French Revolution had more reason than most to be suspicious of them. From 1791 to 1793 a series of major events convinced them that the rhetoric of the newspapers corresponded to the facts.

The first of these was the king's mismanaged flight

abroad, which obviously must have been planned. As soon as
it was known that the royal family had disappeared, everyone wondered who was in on the plot. The National Guard,
commanded by Lafayette, was responsible for the security of
the Tuileries palace. Had Lafayette given orders that the
king be permitted to escape? He denied it, of course, but the
suspicion remained that not only the king but many men in
high places had been lying to the people of France for
months. (The impact of the royal deception should not seem
distant to Americans who have lived with the credibility gap
of the Johnson and Nixon presidencies, especially since the
publication of the Pentagon papers.)

Worse yet, in the eyes of many Frenchmen, were the
events that followed the king's arrest. By the end of June
1791, the constitution that had been in the works for two
years was almost complete. If now, as common sense would
suppose, the king were no longer to be trusted, the delegates
would have to rewrite the whole document. But in those
two years the social issues, glossed over in the heady days of
1789, had become sharply defined. The conservatives, who
were a majority, felt things had gone far enough. "The question," as Barnave put it, "is do we want to terminate the
Revolution or do we want to begin all over again?"

(Poor man, he didn't realize that revolutions are not to be
terminated on command. Barnave was one of the three
deputies sent to accompany the royal family on their return
from Varennes—their presence was thought necessary to
prevent violence. During three days while the berline lum-
bered slowly back to the capital Barnave had long conversa-
tions with the queen. He arrived in Paris convinced that he
had persuaded Marie-Antoinette that her best interests lay
in accepting the new constitution. She encouraged him in
this illusion but her correspondence shows that she was only
leading him on, thinking he could be useful to the court. He
was, for a while.)

To patch things up the Assembly declared that Louis had been "abducted" and blamed it all on Bouillé, the general in command of the army of French noblemen in exile, the *émigrés*. (The existence of that army, poised on the frontier, was another factor that led reasonable men to credit accusations of conspiracy.) This legal fiction was believed by no one. Louis announced that what he had seen in the course of his "voyage" had convinced him that the people of France were attached to the Revolution and that henceforth he would bow to their sentiments. No one believed *that* either, but the men running France all pretended that they did.

Three weeks later this whole legalistic house of cards was threatened by a petition of the Cordeliers Club—the left-bank club of Danton and Marat—calling for a republic. The city government tried to prevent this petition from being presented to the people of Paris. But on Sunday, July 17, tables were set up at the Champ de Mars to collect signatures.

The Champ de Mars is still there in a modified form; it is the site of the Eiffel Tower. In 1791 it was a parade ground at the western edge of Paris that was still occupied by the remains of the constructions that had been erected for the *Fédération* of 1790, a grandiose ceremony that had marked the first anniversary of the fall of the Bastille. These were a large amphitheater and an "Altar of the Fatherland"—part earthworks, part scaffolding. The ceremony of 1791 had been less impressive, the king's flight having dampened people's spirits. But the Champ de Mars remained a holy place of the Revolution, as well as a favorite destination for a Sunday afternoon stroll for Paris families.

This particular Sunday began badly. As the Cordeliers were setting up their tables, a lemonade peddler who was watching from the grandstand let out a scream; she had felt the point of a drill pierce the wood under her foot. Men came running, tore up the planks and discovered an unemployed wigmaker and an invalid soldier, two "dirty old men" who

were hidden in the scaffolding and drilling holes in the
boards so they could peep up under girls' skirts that afternoon. These two individuals were taken to the nearest
section, where they were lynched by an angry crowd, indignant at the insult to the women of Paris and the Altar of the
Fatherland.

By the time the news of this unsavory incident got to the
City Hall at the other end of Paris it was reported as a sign
that a bloodthirsty insurrection was about to take place.
Lafayette galloped up with the National Guard and a sniper
took a potshot at him, but the pistol misfired. Lafayette
galloped off again. The Assembly was in session as well as
the municipal council; throughout the afternoon they received scattered reports of the situation at the Champ de
Mars, most of them inaccurate. At six o'clock Paris was declared under martial law and the red flag flown at the City
Hall.

Meanwhile, at the Champ de Mars a revised petition was
being presented—revised because the Jacobins, taking the
advice of Robespierre, had disavowed the initiative of the
Cordeliers as untimely. The crowd had swelled with the
arrival of demonstrators who knew nothing of the events
of the morning as well as many nonpolitical Parisians out for
a Sunday stroll, some of whom were resting on the grandstand. The scene was peaceful; there was no sign of a riot,
much less an insurrection. Six thousand men had signed the
petition.

At seven, as the crowd was beginning to go home, the
National Guard arrived, ready to put down the revolt against
the government. The regulations prescribed that an unlaw-
ful assembly be given three orders to disperse before any
action was taken. This formality was, apparently, omitted.
In any event, 1791 was long before the advent of the bull-
horn and the Champ de Mars is a big open space. A few
hotheads in the crowd shouted insults at the troops. The

Guard, greatly outnumbered, panicked and opened fire. The crowd panicked in turn and fled. At least twelve and at most fifty remained behind, dead.

A report on the incident states that the National Guard fired first into the air, then into the crowd, *because some of the demonstrators were throwing stones.* (The words should be familiar.)

Afterwards at least two hundred of the demonstrators were arrested, and Robespierre, even though he had opposed the Cordeliers' petition, decided that changing his address would be a prudent action.

This Sunday's events, known as the Massacre of the Champ de Mars, have been described in some detail because they marked a turning point in the sentiments of the people of Paris and of the supporters of the Revolution all over France toward the early heros of the Revolution, the liberals of 1789, especially Lafayette and Bailly. It is cited again and again in the accusations that two years later sent many of them to the guillotine. The National Guard had been a creation of the Revolution in July 1789; it had replaced the hated and feared police of the Old Regime; now it had slaughtered innocent men and women in the course of a peaceful demonstration. It is not surprising that many revolutionaries felt betrayed.

And yet the Massacre of the Champ de Mars was, after all, only a minor incident. It might have been forgotten, even the flight to Varennes (a major incident) might have been forgotten, if Louis had really allied himself with the liberals of 1789 and the moderates of 1791 to make the new constitution a working reality. In the winter of 1791–1792 it seemed that France had settled down to a new kind of normalcy. The Revolution, it had been declared, was over. The new Assembly, largely conservative and middle-class, tried to consolidate the achievements of 1789 without attempting any new reforms. But this normalcy was an illusion. The group that held a majority in the legislature—the group of delegates known as the Gironde*—knew it was an illusion. They were aware that in trying to make France a constitutional monarchy dominated by the upper middle class they were walking a tightrope. The equilibrium might be upset at any moment by the threat from the right or the threat from the left.

The threat from the right consisted of the court and the aristocrats, especially those aristocrats who had gone into exile. It may be epitomized by the attitudes revealed in the correspondence of Marie-Antoinette, who never despaired of turning the clock back to the grand old days when the court of Versailles was the most resplendent in Europe but who was not too proud to dissemble, to lie, to *use* the politicians of the Gironde who thought that they were using her.

The threat from the left consisted of everyone who wanted more from the revolution than a constitution that restricted the vote to men of property, that gave political power to men whose fortunes were based on sugar plantations in the colonies and the slave trade, that left the people as poor and as hungry as they had been before. In practical terms this meant the opposition of the left-wing press (writers like Marat, Desmoulins, and Hébert), of left-wing clubs like the Cordeliers, and especially of the dissatisfied Jacobins, the members of that powerful society to which Robespierre now devoted all of his time.

To defuse these threats the Girondins turned to the classic distraction from domestic issues—foreign affairs. In the Assembly and the clubs and the press they mounted a campaign for a declaration of war on the powers that had declared they would support the ever-growing army of

---

* *The name comes from the region around Bordeaux, the rich commercial port, whose delegates formed an influential* bloc *in the Legislative Assembly. Actually many of the leaders of the Gironde—Brissot, Roland, Pétion—were* Girondins *only by political persuasion; they came from all over France.*

émigrés, camped in various small towns along the Rhine, against Austria and Prussia. They were careful to exclude England—the traditional enemy of France—a nation they both feared and admired. In public they said that the war was necessary to protect the Revolution in France and also justified as a way of spreading the benefits of liberty to the other peoples of Europe, still groaning under the heel of "tyrants." In private they said that the war would force the king to abandon all hope of aid from abroad, force him to fulfill his role as the leader of France.

Was this purely a political maneuver? Certainly not. There had been voices calling for a revolutionary war since 1790. It is difficult to gauge the attitude of the "people" (there was no Gallup poll in 1791), but the people certainly supported the war once it was declared. What is important is that the Girondins, like almost all the leaders of the Revolution, believed what they said, even when they contradicted themselves. The Girondins were sincere, which is often a liability, even during a revolution.

We must remember that the French revolutionaries of 1789 were called "patriots," just like the American revolutionaries of 1776. Of course France was not a colony; it was an imperialist nation. But the relation of European monarchies in the eighteenth century to their own subjects was not unlike that of imperialist governments to colonies.* So *patriotism* became an antonym to *monarchy*. The revolutionary press, in addition to calling Marie-Antoinette a spendthrift, a strumpet, and a Messalina, referred to her as

---

* *Catherine the Great of Russia was a German baroness. The reigning dynasty of England was also German. The Habsburgs of Austria ruled an empire most of whose peoples were Hungarian, Czech, Slovene, Serbian, etc. The Bourbon king of Spain was a descendant of Louis XIV of France. Those monarchs fought one another in bloody wars—Aramco vies with Shell for the rights to some new oil strike in an Arab desert—but when the peace was signed it was sealed by an international royal marriage. So it is not too far-fetched to regard the monarchies of the eighteenth century as a number of interlocking international imperialist cartels.*

"the Austrian." The last epithet was perhaps the most effective since it needed no proof.

The Girondin leaders, as well as many of their opponents on the left, were imbued with this "patriotic" *nationalist* sentiment. But, as intelligent politicians, they also saw the advantages they could reap from exploiting it. A war would rally the workers and the peasants to the Constitution of 1791, distracting them from social issues. And in political terms, at least for the moment, they were right. What opposition there was to the war came chiefly from the far right. But there was one exception—Robespierre.

In the winter of 1792 Robespierre fought a single-handed and losing battle against the proposed declaration of war. The arena was the Jacobin Club, his home territory. But the chief warmonger of the Gironde, Brissot, was also a Jacobin, and he utilized the forum of the Mother Society to present his views, usually brilliantly. It was, in many ways, Robespierre's finest moment, even if he lost. (Lost causes have often been the occasion for finest moments.) Some of Robespierre's arguments were so soon and so conclusively proved right that he appeared to be clairvoyant. But it was superior intelligence, not ESP, that was responsible.

Robespierre, in this Eugene McCarthy phase of his short career, was not a pacifist. He opposed the war because he refused to accept the idea that the Revolution had gone as far as it ought to go. He had voted for the Constitution of 1791 as a working compromise, but only as that; he had hoped that the new Assembly would continue the Revolution by legislation. Now that the Girondins proposed war as a way of spreading the Revolution all over Europe, Robespierre insisted that it was more important to get on with the Revolution in France.

The debate, in some ways, foreshadows the conflict between Trotsky and Stalin in the 1920s. Trotsky wanted the revolution to spread to the rest of Europe; he wanted the

Bolsheviks to give active support to Communist revolutionaries in France, Germany, Italy, etc. Stalin insisted that
priority be given to "building socialism in one country"—the
Soviet Union. Stalin's desire to keep Russia out of war led
eventually to the Nazi-Soviet pact of 1939. But the parallel
should not be pushed further than the facts allow. If Trotsky,
like the Gironde, was "internationalist," he also, more like
Robespierre, demanded more immediate revolutionary
measures within the Soviet Union; he accused Stalin of being "rightist." Like Robespierre, Stalin later presided over a
Reign of Terror, but again the parallels are only partial.

In addition to giving priority to the Revolution "in one
country," Robespierre argued that the army could not be
trusted. He predicted that the generals and officers, most of
them former noblemen, would betray the nation, even try to
use the war as an excuse to mount a counterrevolutionary
coup. He predicted that the king might try to sabotage the
war effort, since the interests of the court would be better
served by a French defeat than a victory.

All in vain. The warmongering campaign of the Gironde
and their supporters carried the day. Robespierre's position
was made especially difficult by the fact that there were
many vocal men on the left who argued for war. (Many of
them were later guillotined, along with the Girondins.) War
was declared in April 1792 with overwhelming popular support. Robespierre's finest moment was the only phase of his
career when he was unpopular.

But it took only a few months for all of Robespierre's pre-
dictions to come true. French generals refused to attack the
enemy. Fortresses were delivered from within by royalists.
Lafayette, who had been appointed commander of the
armies of the Rhine, seemed more interested in marching
his troops on Paris "to restore order" than in attacking the
Prussians.

Robespierre was too clever to say, "I told you so!" Instead

he supported the war effort while muttering darkly about plots, conspiracies, and treason. In the circumstances talk about plots, conspiracies, and treason seemed quite reasonable.

The Girondins, who were, after all, revolutionaries, had sponsored two laws whose object was to consolidate the achievements of 1789, one cutting off the income of priests who refused to swear fidelity to the constitution, and another declaring that the *émigrés* were traitors. The king, as was his right under the constitution, had vetoed these laws, but they remained a controversial subject in the press and in the Assembly. In June, apparently made bold by the defeats of his armies, Louis dismissed the Girondin ministers who continued to ask him to sign these controversial laws.

This had the paradoxical effect of making the Girondins the heroes of the hour. But it also made it plain that the Girondin attempt to force Louis to support the Revolution by means of the war had failed—indeed that their whole policy of compromise was a failure.

Lafayette chose this moment (the end of June 1792) to return to Paris and propose that, in effect, he be made dictator. No one was interested.* The court also found its hopes that French defeats would lead to a counterrevolution belied by the event. Instead, the revolutionary ardor of 1789 was rekindled. An invasion seemed imminent; again it was the people versus the king with German armies threatening the revolution—only this time the German armies were not hired mercenaries but Prussian troops. The Assembly declared that the nation was "in danger" and volunteers were recruited all over France to meet the threat. In Paris radical leaders began to prepare the people for another insurrection that everyone knew would be more dangerous than the storming of the Bastille.

---

* *Lafayette returned to his command with the Army of the Rhine. On August 19th he deserted to the Austrians, who put him in prison for a while, as a revolutionary.*

On July 14th, at the Champ de Mars, Louis again took a
solemn oath to support the constitution. But by then it was
too late; no one believed him. He and Marie-Antoinette had
become powerless hostages whose lives were useful only as
bargaining points in eventual negotiations with the invading
armies. Even that minor importance was nullified when the
Prussian commander, the Duke of Brunswick, issued a
manifesto proclaiming that anyone who had *ever* supported
the Revolution would be put to death when his armies
arrived. This not only pulled the rug out from under the
royal family but also made even the most reluctant liberals
rally to support the government. (The Germans have always
made incredibly stupid occupying armies.)

It was in these circumstances that the house of cards constructed after the flight to Varennes finally collapsed. The
expected insurrection took place on August 10th. Armed
groups from the radical districts of Paris, volunteers on their
way to the front (including the Marseilles regiment) and
several detachments of the National Guard attacked the
Tuileries palace. The king and his family fled across the
garden to the hall where the Assembly was meeting and
asked the delegates for protection. At this early hour, 8:30
A.M., there had as yet been no shooting, only a show of force.

Before leaving, Louis had neglected to give his Swiss
Guards, the defenders of the palace, any orders—he didn't
even inform them that he was going. Perhaps he hoped
that they would win the battle or perhaps it was simply a
characteristic bumble. At 9:00 A.M. the shooting began. As
always in violent situations, accounts differ as to who fired
the first shots. In any event, fire from the palace killed four
hundred of the attackers as well as a number of innocent
bystanders. (Noblemen who had camped in the palace to
defend the king apparently fled for their lives by the Grand
Galerie of the Louvre, pausing to shoot at civilians on the
quay and in the streets from the high windows.) Finally the
king sent a cease-fire order from the Assembly. Afterwards,

in revenge, six hundred of the Swiss Guards were slaughtered, their bodies stacked like firewood in the Place du Carrousel and the Tuileries gardens.

The actual details of what happened that day matter less than what was believed at the time. The story that gained credence was that Louis had given the Swiss orders to slaughter the people of Paris and that this had been planned in advance. Again conspiracy and betrayal.

Robespierre took no direct part in the events of August 10th or in the planning of the insurrection. That fact is significant in several respects. Robespierre was never a man of direct action, an insurrectionary, a proponent of unstructured violence. (His chief apologist, Mathiez, attributes his ultimate downfall two years later to his reluctance to lead an insurrection of the forces loyal to him against the Convention.) Robespierre had a curiously legalistic concept of revolution; he believed in a "revolutionary order," recognizing that such an "order" would imply actions that would be illegal by ordinary standards.

On July 29th, knowing what was going to happen, Robespierre spoke at the Jacobins, proposing a *legal* way out of the crisis. He asked that the legislature dissolve itself and call for new elections by universal suffrage, to elect a Convention that would write a new constitution. This Convention, Robespierre argued, would have a legal right to depose the king, since it would be based on the sovereignty of the people.

That, in fact, is just what the legislature did, but only *after* the insurrection of August 10th. Once that had happened, Robespierre decided that the events of August 10th were fully justified, *because of the results they had achieved.*

Three months later (November 5th), in a speech defending not only the insurrection but some of the violent events of September, as well as the summary actions of the Paris Commune, Robespierre reminded his critics that the attack on the Bastille had also been illegal when it occurred. "Is it by consulting the criminal code that one should evaluate the necessary precautions demanded for the security of the people in a time of crisis created by the impotence of legality? ... All these things were illegal, as illegal as the Revolution, as the fall of the throne and of the Bastille, *as illegal as liberty itself*" (italics Robespierre's). "Citizens, are you asking for a revolution without a revolution?"

"*As illegal as liberty itself . . . are you asking for a revolution without a revolution?*" The words, out of context, sound incendiary, almost anarchistic. But Robespierre, the lawyer from Arras in his silk suit, was certainly no anarchist. The type of revolutionary action he preferred can be observed during the period when he was the undisputed leader of the Revolution—the trial of the king by the Convention; the exclusion of the Girondins, accomplished with a show of force but without bloodshed; and, of course, the Terror in which revolutionary violence was channeled through an *institution*.

Robespierre's actions in August 1792, or rather his inaction, shows another side of his character. He always preferred to remain at the edge of events, uncompromised by personal participation (which may mean making mistakes), ready to resume his role as conscience and guide of the Revolution when the dust had settled.

Immediately after the insurrection of August 10th, the lame-duck legislature created a Revolutionary Tribune to deal with everyone suspected of royalism, treason, or conspiring against the Revolution. Robespierre was offered the post of chief justice of this extraordinary court. The choice was natural; not only had Robespierre been demanding as early as October 1789 that such a court be created, but he had been denouncing traitors and conspirators ever since. Robespierre declined the honor, explaining later that just because he had so often been an accuser he was unfit to be a judge. Another instance, perhaps, of legalistic scruples, but more likely a desire to avoid responsibility. There is at least a chance that if Robespierre had accepted the post and made the new Tribunal effective, the September Massacres—the most violent and repulsive incident of the whole Revolution —might have been avoided.

Skipping ahead we can note that when the Committee of Public Safety had become the chief executive of France, Robespierre was again reluctant to become a member. He did not join the Committee until July 1793. In the six weeks that preceded Thermidor, he rarely showed up at committee meetings. This preference for indirect action, as well as his insistence on legality, was undoubtedly a factor in his ultimate downfall.

Among the charges most frequently aimed at Robespierre was that he wanted to be a dictator. After his death he was execrated as a "tyrant." Robespierre always denied these accusations and his reluctance to assume official responsibilities shows that his denial was not hypocritical. For all that he had created his own political machine, his short period of dominance can be ascribed more to the lack of any other commanding revolutionary leader than to his own efforts. Once the compromise of 1791 fell apart, once the Gironde was discredited by French defeats, once the king was deposed, there was no one else who so clearly embodied the Revolution, who so clearly embodied, at that moment, France. But unlike another perennial gadfly, Winston Churchill, also called to power at a moment of national crisis, unlike de Gaulle, who also was a gadfly and who also preferred to remain aloof, Robespierre never quite made the grade as the leader of a nation when his moment came. He never assumed command of the war machine—and the war, during those two years, was the dominant factor in the life of France. His character was much better suited to the role of leader of the opposition than to that of statesman, and he never made the transition.

And yet, on the domestic scene—and furthering the Revolution within France was Robespierre's real interest—he did occupy the classic position of the middle of the road. The words may seem strange when applied to the man whose name is identified with the Terror, but in the political climate of the high crest of the Revolution they make sense. There were still many royalists and aristocrats in France, but royalism and aristocratic pretensions had been excluded from the political sphere as treasonous. After the king had been deposed, Robespierre still had the Girondins on his right, but there were also the radicals who had engineered the insurrection of August 10th on his left. Many of his actions can be explained only by his attempt to remain true to his own ideals while at the same time appearing to be as "militant" as any of the new radicals of 1792.

This middle-of-the-road stance can best be observed in Robespierre's attitude toward religion. Of course Robespierre had favored the confiscation and sale of land owned by the Church, the dissolution of monasteries and convents, the decrees that demanded an oath of fidelity to the constitution of all priests whose salary was paid by the government. But with that much accomplished he felt that it was not the role of the state to dictate religious beliefs; he felt that Frenchmen should be free to practice whatever religion they chose, even to the extent of permitting the nonjuring priests to say Mass in private for those Catholics who did not believe in the efficacy of the sacraments proffered by the "constitutional clergy." This relative indulgence has often been ascribed to his Jesuit schooling, but Robespierre himself gave a *political* explanation for his attitude. In November 1791, opposing a recommendation at the Jacobins that confession be abolished, Robespierre declared, "I think that the Society cannot entertain this motion without danger. We must not attack directly those religious prejudices that are adored by the people; we must let the people mature with the passage of time until they are gradually elevated above these prejudices."

The radicals to Robespierre's left were much more dogmatic. Many of them were confirmed atheists who wanted to convert everyone to their beliefs, by force if necessary; they considered all religious sentiment to be counterrevolutionary, all priests to be suspect unless they had renounced the cloth. It was the leaders of the Commune who organized the rather ludicrous *"Fête de la Raison"* at Notre-Dame in November 1793 where an actress in a white robe represented Liberty; it was their followers all over France who vandalized so many churches, cutting off the heads of statues of saints and breaking stained glass windows. These actions aroused Robespierre's fury—and in the fall of 1793 that was dangerous in the extreme. He declared that atheism was "aristocratic" and that God was on the side of the people. It followed—and this is characteristic of Robespierre's psychology —that the *"Fête de la Raison"* must be the work of a conspiracy. "We will bring to light the counterrevolutionary activities of these men who have no other merit than that of displaying an antireligious zeal. We will tear the mask of patriotism from their hideous faces. . . ." The radicals paid for their opposition to Robespierre's position at the guillotine.

But again we are getting ahead of ourselves. After August 1792 Robespierre is so deeply involved in every aspect of the Revolution—except, perhaps, the war—that it is impossible to consider him apart from the events. And, conversely, many of the events of those twenty-two months can be explained only by Robespierre's preeminence, his identification with the Revolution both in his own mind and those of others; they are molded in the image of Robespierre's personality. But twenty-two months is a very short time, and ten of them were occupied with disposing of the losers of the insurrection of August 10th, the king and the Gironde. Unlike Lenin, Mao, or Castro, Robespierre was supreme master of his revolution for only one year. His failure as a leader, statesman, or dictator (whatever you want to call him) can—in the classic pattern of the tragic hero—be

attributed to a fatal flaw, his myopic tendency to see an
enemy in everyone who opposed him in any detail, until
there was almost no one left who was not an enemy. But it
can also be attributed to his idealism, an idealism that
proved more *impractical* than the Terror and had far fewer
supporters. Robespierre the Terrorist was quite acceptable
to the hardheaded businessmen and bureaucrats who sent
him to the guillotine in Thermidor; they were Terrorists
themselves. It was Robespierre the idealist who got in their
way, because his ideals threatened the war effort, and
especially because they threatened the reign of the newly
rich who by the summer of 1794 were ruling revolutionary
France. We shall see in the next chapter where those ideals
led the Incorruptible.

Virtue Has Always Been in the Minority . . .

*La vertu ne fut-elle pas toujours
en minorité sur la terre?*
—*Robespierre*

FORTY days after the insurrection that finally deposed the king, the Convention assembled for the first time in the Manège, the former riding academy that had been used as a meeting hall by both the Constituent Assembly and the Legislative Assembly. The date is September 21st, the autumnal equinox of the year 1792. There are seven hundred forty-nine deputies who have been elected by universal male suffrage and who have, collectively, unlimited and undefined powers. They are to be the government of France—a France at war with both Prussia and Austria—and they are to continue the Revolution by writing a new constitution. There is no longer a king, there are no provincial assemblies, there are no independent courts. In the immense territory of France with its twenty-five million inhabitants these seven hundred forty-nine men are the only recognized, legitimate power. They can use that power as they decide, limited only

[92]

by the *realities* of their situation, not by any inherited structures. France, for them, is a blank slate. Burke's vision of remaking a commonwealth *a priori* has become a *legal* fact.

I underline the words *legal* and *realities* because their opposition is the essence of much of the history of revolutions. Because revolutions begin with the actions of men who oppose existing governments, men who call themselves "revolutionaries," the word "revolution" seems to be the opposite of "legality." But a revolution, until it succeeds, is only a rebellion. And revolutionaries, until they are successful, are only rebels. Louis XVI: "But that's a revolt!" The duc de Liancourt: "No, Sire, it's a revolution."

Once that happens—once a revolt becomes a revolution— the revolution becomes *legal* and the actions of the revolutionaries are legal actions, be they good, bad, or indifferent in their results. This apparent paradox is resolved when we remember that legality is, ultimately, nothing more than the power that certain men have over other men. Most of the time, for better or worse, legality is much more than that— it is tradition, it is inertia, it is an unspoken agreement to conduct a nation's affairs by preestablished rules and with a minimum of violence. But revolutions expose the ultimate nature of legality, which is raw power.

A revolutionary of sorts from an earlier troubled time when the established political authority was disintegrating described the essence of the process. Writing in the fifth century, soon after the first sack of Rome by the barbarians, St. Augustine posed the hypothetical case of a province infested with bands of brigands. As the legal authority—the government—grows weaker, the brigands find it to their advantage to divvy up the turf instead of fighting one another. Eventually they choose a leader to settle disputes among themselves. This arrangement makes them so strong that the government ceases to have any power; the brigands are now in complete control. But how, St. Augustine asks, is the rule of this established Mafia to be distinguished from that of any other principality, aside from the fact that its origins are more recent?

Of course the Convention did not consider itself a band of brigands, although it was just that in the eyes of the remaining royalists. Louis XVI had not thought of himself as a remote descendant of the chieftains of the barbarian Frankish tribes who invaded the northern reaches of the province of Gaul as the Roman Empire disintegrated, but he was just that, in fact, as the revolutionaries reminded everyone by calling him "Capet." Louis considered himself king by grace of God, his sovereignty sanctified by the holy oil with which he had been anointed during his coronation. The Convention considered itself the legitimate ruler of France because it had been elected by the people in whom, by *its* lights, true sovereignty resided.

Theories aside, the Convention was the government of France because the seven hundred forty-nine deputies concentrated in themselves collectively what political power there was in France in September 1792. This is the ultimate test of what constitutes a government—although our State Department is often slow in admitting it. The delegates to the Convention could write any constitution they wanted, pass any laws, decrees, or edicts that might occur to them; it would all be *legal.*

The effectiveness of legal power should not be exaggerated—and yet it is exaggerated all the time whenever anyone, suddenly aware of an injustice, exclaims, "There ought to be a law!" Perhaps there ought to be a law. Perhaps also a law would accomplish nothing. Implicit in St. Augustine's cynical description of government as a band of brigands who have seized power is a recognition of the limitations of the power of any government, however absolute. Even the most efficient Mafia cannot increase the annual rate of rainfall in a locality. By his analogy St. Augustine sought to discredit

the Roman state, which had its own theories proving that it
was the legitimate ruler of the world; he wanted to convince
Christians that true justice would never be found in the City
of Man, only in the City of God.

But revolutionaries are not interested in the City of God.
They want justice here on this earth and they want it now.
There is no one with greater faith in the power of government than a revolutionary—especially a would-be revolutionary. He believes that if only he and his brothers and
sisters are able to seize power the world will not have to wait
for the millennium. Men with the experience of political
power are much less optimistic; they know its limitations
(and sometimes that seems to be all they know).

Karl Marx, the most influential revolutionary in history,
would seem to have avoided the trap of putting undue faith
in political power by regarding government as only a "super-
structure" with a class base, by regarding the transfer of
power from one *class* to another as the essence of revolution.
The Marxist millennium, to follow the acquisition of power
by the proletariat, includes the "withering away of the state"
as true justice comes to rule all human affairs. But at least
so far all Marxist revolutions have followed the pattern of a
group of revolutionaries seizing political power and attempting to change the class structure by governmental action.
The state, far from withering away where Marxists have
been successful, has grown ever more powerful. (And yet
the annual rainfall still escapes political control.)

But Marx had not yet been born in 1792 when the Convention first met at the Manège, determined to overcome all
obstacles and possessing unlimited power to enact the Revolution into law. The deputies include almost every revolutionary personality who had become celebrated since 1789.
There are the *philosophes*, Sieyès and Condorcet. Many of
the leaders of the two previous assemblies. The spokesmen
of the Jacobin Club (Robespierre) and the Cordeliers Club

(Danton). Many journalists, including two whose papers have already had a great influence on the course of the Revolution (Camille Desmoulins and Marat). Not a royalist in the lot, unless we count as such the *ci-devant* duc d'Orléans, soon to be renamed Philippe Egalité, the "liberal" brother of the king who will vote that Louis be executed and who perhaps, on the morning of this first meeting, still secretly hopes that he will be asked to take his brother's place.

If so that hope is shattered in a matter of hours. The first action of the Convention is to declare France a republic, unanimously.

Three years later when the Convention disbands, forty-eight of the seven hundred forty-nine will be dead of unnatural causes—two by assassination, one by suicide, the rest by *legal* means, their heads lopped off by the guillotine. More than a hundred others will have spent months in prison or in hiding, expecting that each new day may prove their last. Among these victims will be almost all the leaders of the Revolution, the men who were best known on that September day when this extraordinary body first met.

This extreme rate of unnatural mortality would be completely understandable if in those three years the war had been lost, the counterrevolution had triumphed, France had been occupied by the armies of Prussia and Austria, and Louis XVI were back on his throne. But instead, during those three years Prussia and Austria were defeated, counterrevolutionary rebellions in various parts of France had been successfully repressed, and Louis had been executed.

The apparent paradox is somewhat overstated, since the unanimity of that September 21st was illusory. It was like the unanimity we see in Congress in moments of extreme national crisis, such as the votes on a declaration of war back in the days when presidents still paid enough attention to the Constitution to ask Congress to declare war. The abolition of the monarchy was already a *fait accompli*. But many of the delegates of the Convention had, in the past, hoped for a different resolution of the revolutionary crisis. After Varennes, Brissot and the other Girondins had done all they could to preserve the monarchy and, along with it, the preeminence of the upper middle class they represented. Their opponents, the group of prominent leftists who became known as the "Mountain," had not forgotten that effort. If a thousand years of history were wiped out by the proclamation of the Republic, the three years since 1789 were still very much alive.

For a comparison we could imagine that an unusual series of events in this country leads to the result that the Black Nationalists have won their point—the United States is to be two nations, one black, one white. Black voters go to the polls to elect a Black Constitutional Convention. Every black leader finds a district to elect him or her a delegate—Thurgood Marshall, Shirley Chisholm, Julian Bond, Roy Wilkins, Charles Evers, Mrs. King, Bayard Rustin, etc. Also James Baldwin, Leroi Jones, etc. Also Eldridge Cleaver, Muhammad Ali, Angela Davis, etc. The first session of the Convention unanimously proclaims the independence of the Black Afro-American Nation—even though half the delegates had, in the past, worked long and hard for integration. That would be the equivalent of the unanimity of the Convention in proclaiming France a republic in September 1792.

The seven hundred forty-nine delegates met in extraordinary circumstances. The forty days since August 10th had been occupied with far more than just elections; it is a proof of the democratic faith of the revolutionaries that there were elections at all instead of some kind of emergency, provisional government. Lafayette had gone over to the enemy; the border fortresses of Longwy and Verdun had been delivered by treason. There was nothing between the Prussians and Paris but an untried army of ill-equipped and untrained volunteers. Fortifications were hastily erected on the heights of Montmartre, to the north of the capital, but it didn't seem likely that anything could stop the invaders.

Within Paris the Commune, led by Robespierre, Danton, and Marat, had assumed total power. There was a house-to-house search for royalists and priests in hiding, conducted, as one would guess, with little regard for due process. The prisons were filled with "suspects" who expected to be freed when the Prussians arrived. On September 2nd, in circumstances that remain unclear, gangs of armed thugs went to the prisons, forced the guards to open the cells, and with a mere semblance of a trial slaughtered everyone they decided must be an enemy of the people.

In four days over 1,100 were killed. When the butchery finally stopped everyone was appalled at what had happened. The news spread throughout Europe and confirmed everyone's worst fears of the anarchy to which a revolution might lead. Even the radical leaders of the Commune were appalled. They wanted a revolutionary government, but slaughtering men and women without trial was not any kind of government at all.

There were accusations and counteraccusations about who was responsible. But the responsibility was never fixed on anyone, not even *falsely* fixed on anyone, as is usually the case. It was as if the earth had suddenly gaped open, offering a vision of the Inferno, and then as inexplicably closed up again. But the threat of a repetition of these "September Massacres" became a determining component of the psychology that led, six months later, to the Terror.

Then, on the eve of the first session of the Convention, the French won the Battle of Valmy.

The Battle of Valmy was not much of a battle as battles go. It was above all a moral victory for the untried army of French volunteers—which is why Goethe, present in a minor post in the Prussian camp, is reported to have said, "From this place and day will be dated a new era in the history of the world." What happened is that the Prussians laid down a massive artillery barrage, expecting that the raw recruits facing them—all "tramps, tailors, and cobblers" according to the *émigrés*—would turn tail and run at the sound of the cannon. Instead they stood their ground, responded with shouts of *"Vive la nation!,"* and even managed a few attacks on the Prussian lines. Brunswick, whose army was outnumbered, decided it would be more prudent to try again another day instead of advancing immediately. While he was waiting for that other day his troops were harassed by the peasants of the region, who were not eager to have the *émigré* aristocrats return to their burnt-out châteaus. It began to rain steadily and many of the Prussians came down with dysentery which was attributed to drinking too much raw Champagne wine in the cellars they had raided. Brunswick eventually persuaded the king of Prussia to postpone the offensive until the spring. France and the Revolution were saved, in part by a microbe.

Given this breathing space, the deputies to the Convention immediately turned to what would prove their most absorbing activity—accusing one another of betraying the Revolution, now and in the past.

A portent of this insistence on revolutionary purity can be seen during the elections even before the Convention met. The system for choosing delegates varied from place to place. In Paris ordinary voters first met in the forty-eight *sections* to chose nine hundred and ninety electors who in turn were to choose the twenty-two Paris delegates. No secret ballots—the *sections* chose their electors by voice vote. The electors also voted openly and could (and did) choose delegates from their own numbers. All in all a system open to undue influence by the majority, especially during a moment of crisis and high emotions. (This electoral process had been proposed by Robespierre.)

The nine hundred Parisian electors first met on September 2nd—the day the massacres began. Robespierre immediately took the floor to suggest that, before getting down to business, the electors first eliminate anyone who had ever belonged to an "anticivic" club or signed a rightist petition. Immediately adopted. (Notice that it was *past* affiliations that were to be examined—an illustration of the Joe McCarthy side of Robespierre's character.) The electors were then called one by one to give account of themselves. Many did not even bother to take the floor but simply slipped away. In all over two hundred were purged, men who had been elected to represent their *sections* just a few days before.

The first deputy chosen by the remaining electors was, of course, Robespierre. Pétion, who had been mayor of Paris but was associated with the Gironde, saw which way the wind was blowing; he sent an urgent message to his home town of Chartres, where his friends got him elected as a deputy of *that* city. In the end every delegate elected to represent Paris had the personal approval of Robespierre.

But such tactics were not confined to the left. In the Convention the ideologic battle began on September 25th, just four days after the proclamation of the Republic. The news of the victory at Valmy had just arrived in Paris, but the Prussians had not yet retreated and the threat of an enemy offensive remained imminent.

We must remember that of the seven hundred and forty-nine delegates, only about two hundred were definitely committed to either faction. Many of the remaining five hundred were new to politics. These five hundred freshmen were to become known as the Plain (because they occupied the flat center benches of the amphitheater) and sometimes, pejoratively, the Swamp. Their votes, motivated sometimes by reason, sometimes by enthusiasm, sometimes by fear, were decisive. That is why so much of the (literally) life-and-death struggle between the Gironde and the Mountain

was conducted by speechmaking from the Convention's tribune.*

The Gironde had an initial majority, as was demonstrated
in the votes that chose the first Chairman (*Président*) and
secretaries of the Convention. Confident of their strength,
the leaders of the Gironde accused the "triumvirat" of the
Parisian Commune—Robespierre, Danton, Marat—of aspiring to a collective dictatorship. If those three could be
discredited, or better yet purged, the left would be leaderless.

Danton was the first to reply to the accusation, but he
avoided the issue. Robespierre, caught unprepared (which
would not happen again), tried to defend his actions. For
over a year he had been the oracle of the Jacobins, his
speeches listened to in a religious silence, broken only by
applause. Now he found himself interrupted by catcalls and
questions. He reacted with a typical phrase, *"Eh bien, je
m'en vais donc vous forcer à m'écouter!"* ("Very well, I will
force you to listen to me!")—followed by a vehement attack
on the leaders of the Gironde.

Then came the turn of Marat.

Marat was a special case. There was very little chance
that either Danton or Robespierre could be expelled; they
were too powerful. But Marat had never held any public
office; he was only a journalist, the most radical, unre-
strained, incendiary journalist of the hundreds who had
been scribbling away since censorship had been abolished.
(Incendiary is not just a metaphor: the previous spring he
had advised his readers that the best thing to do with the
Legislative Assembly would be to lock the doors and set fire

---

* *The Mountain took its name from the seats high up in the back of
the hall taken by the leaders of the radical left after the Girondins had
grabbed all the best seats. Later, when the Mountain had taken over, its
name became associated with the "Mountain of the Fatherland" at the
Champ de Mars, still used for patriotic ceremonies.*

to the hall.) Even his personal appearance seemed an insult to the dignity of the Convention—his ragged clothes, sickly complexion, and cadaverous face.

This specter climbs up to the podium for his maiden speech as a delegate. There are shouts, "To the guillotine!" Marat grins and observes, "I see I have many enemies in this assembly . . ." The shouts continue, "All of us!" Enduring the chorus of jeers and insults, Marat comments ironically, "May I remind you of decency. . . ."

He goes on to admit that he is guilty of having called for a dictator to lead the Revolution in its moment of extreme peril. At the same time he absolves Danton and Robespierre, insisting that both of them had rejected this suggestion. He mentions that the most recent numbers of his paper have called for a reconciliation. But if his earlier views are to be considered a crime, he will execute the will of the Convention immediately.

With which he pulls a pistol out of his pocket and puts it to his head. No one laughed, which was too bad; the pistol wasn't loaded. But if the Convention had had a sense of humor the Terror would never have happened.

Finally the curtain is rung down on the comedy when a delegate proposes that these personal quarrels be put aside. The dispute is plastered over as the Convention decrees that, "The Republic is one and indivisible." The Gironde has failed, for the moment, but the battle lines have been clearly drawn.

The ultimate crunch was postponed by the trial of the king. The Prussian army having retreated and the news generally good on all fronts, the leaders of the Mountain used the opportunity to push the Revolution irrevocably into its ultimate phase. The leaders of the Gironde warned that in terms of international politics the trial made no sense at all and this time they were right; the immediate result of the execution of the king would be that England, Holland, Spain, and Russia joined Austria and Prussia as belligerent enemies of revolutionary France. But it was less than a year since the Girondins had pushed France into the war, predicting immediate victory, and their objections were dismissed. The real issue was ideological. On November 13th St.-Just made his sensational debut as an orator at the Convention. His command of logic and the language would have been astonishing in any freshman speaker; the effect was even more pronounced since he was only twenty-five. St.-Just argued that putting the king on trial was above all a political act. Louis could not be tried as monarch, since as monarch he was inviolable; he could not be tried as a citizen, since he had never been a citizen; he must be tried as "a foreign enemy." There was no middle ground; the era of compromise had ended on August 10th. "That man must either reign or die."

So in December and January we see the Convention use its absolute power to become a High Court. Even as revolutionary trials go—and our own century has seen some fine examples—the trial of Louis XVI had its singular aspects. The Convention was prosecutor, judge and jury all in one; it formulated the charges, decided on guilt or innocence, and passed sentence. In the course of the trial the factional dispute between the Gironde and the Mountain continued, if on a somewhat more elevated level than that of the session of September 25th. Each delegate was forced to declare his position, not once but many times. There were votes on whether the sentence ought to be decided by the people, whether it was to be death or life imprisonment, whether it was to be immediate death or death with a reprieve. (That Louis would be found guilty was never in doubt—as one deputy said, the people had judged that issue on August 10th.)

But the Mountain got more than it expected when it first pressed the issue of the trial. Robespierre and St.-Just were pushed into positions that were extreme and extremely revealing, not just about the left in France in 1792 but about the revolutionary left everywhere since.

From an ideologic point of view the most interesting issue was that raised by the Girondins when they proposed that after the king had been judged and sentenced the verdict should be ratified by a national referendum. Turnabout. The left insists that the sentence, as well as the determination of guilt, be decided solely by the Convention. The right insists that the people of France—the ultimate sovereign according to revolutionary doctrine—must participate in the ultimate decision. (In fact the Gironde was counting on the "silent majority" not only to save the king's neck, but to save their own.)

St.-Just, for once not a revolutionary mystic, observed, "What other language would be used if the intention were to spare the king?" Which is to say that he recognized a political reality—a majority of Frenchmen would have found the king guilty, but not of a capital crime.

The left had been forced to acknowledge that, at least on this issue, they were at odds with the "people" whose cause they championed, whose ultimate wisdom they had so often proclaimed. Of course they did not acknowledge it explicitly; they talked instead of aristocratic maneuvers, counterrevolutionary plots, bribes by foreign powers; they accused the Girondins of being royalists at heart; they warned of civil war if the sentence were delayed; they said it would be attaching too much importance to the person of the "last king of the French" to regard his sentence as a special case; they even claimed that such a vote would not really represent the people since peasants and workers would be too busy to go to the polls.

Robespierre, in his speech of December 28th, utilized all these arguments. And yet he did not avoid the ideologic issue, although he approached it in an oblique fashion, first

accusing the Gironde of promoting discord by their proposal.
Then he came to the point:

"The minority has in all places an eternal right: that of
expressing the voice of truth, or what it regards as such.
Virtue has always been in the minority on this earth. Otherwise why would the world be peopled by tyrants and slaves?"

After that a number of historical examples to prove his
point. Socrates was in the minority and had to drink the
hemlock. Cato was in the minority. Caesar was in the majority but Brutus was in the minority.

All in all, a weak argument, even if brilliantly stated. The
Girondin leader, Verniaud, answered Robespierre the next
day. He said it was an insult to the people of France to say
that they would be influenced by aristocratic intrigue. The
reactionary nobility and clergy had been in the minority in
the first Assembly, and if *that* minority had not been defeated, France would still be a monarchy. "Kings also are a
minority on this earth, and to enslave the people they also
maintain that virtue is in the minority, they also say that the
majority of the people is composed of conspirators who must
be silenced by terror. . . ."

As it happened it was Robespierre whose advice was followed, not because he had won the ideologic debate—such
debates are neither won nor lost—but because the Plain, the
uncommitted deputies, were convinced by his arguments
about the practical difficulties of a referendum, especially the
argument that such a procedure would weaken the authority
of the Convention. (After all, if this issue were to be submitted to the people, why not every important issue that
arose in the future?)

Louis was guillotined on January 21, 1793, with all the
streets of Paris heavily patrolled by the National Guard. His
body was buried in an unmarked grave behind the Made-
leine, not far from the spot occupied by the offices of the
American Express Company today. On January 24th the

French ambassador was ordered to leave England. On February 1st France declared war on England and Holland, which were about to declare war on France. The stage was set for the final, violent years of the Revolution—and for Napoleon.

But we should return to Robespierre's statement, "Virtue has always been in the minority on this earth," because its implications go far beyond the particular circumstances of the trial of Louis XVI.

A year earlier, speaking at the Jacobins, Robespierre had defined the role of the revolutionary leader in these words: "The true means of demonstrating one's respect for the people is to alert them as to their own mistakes, for even the people make mistakes." He had quoted Rousseau: "The people always desire what is good, but they do not always see it."

Well then, who does see it? Robespierre, of course. Or perhaps Lenin, who had the same conception of a revolutionary leader. Or perhaps Mao. Or perhaps . . . ?

"Virtue has always been in the minority on this earth." A very appealing, even seductive statement that was greeted with such wild applause when Robespierre made it that the speaker was forced to put on his hat to reestablish silence in the hall. Robespierre mentioned Cato and Socrates as examples. Whom shall we add—Gandhi, Thoreau, Jesus?

The well-camouflaged trap, disguised by the political context, is the word *virtue*. Of course virtue has always been in the minority, even if the etymologic root of the word is simply Latin for *man*. You don't have to believe in original sin to subscribe to Robespierre's statement—it is sufficient only to look around, whatever your definition of virtue. But is the ultimate aim of the Revolution (with a capital *R*) the reign of virtue? Many revolutionaries, of all persuasions, would deny it. Since 1789, with a few exceptions (Gandhi), most revolutions have been antireligious, or at least anti-established-religion. But on the other hand they have also been puritanical—witness present-day Russia, China, and (to everyone's surprise) Cuba. Robespierre himself had no doubts on this score. The ultimate aim of the Revolution, as he saw it, was certainly the reign of virtue.

To return to politics, if virtue is in the minority, if the role of the political leader is to instruct the people when they make mistakes, what has become of democracy as a political ideal? It has flown out the window.

In 1791 Robespierre had spoken eloquently in favor of extending the right to vote to every Frenchman, without property qualifications. In September 1792, when the Paris Commune was trying to impose its will on the lame-duck Legislature, he had used the phrase "power to the people" to legitimize the demands of the revolutionary *sections* that had organized the insurrection of August 10th. He had spoken in favor of what we would call "participatory democracy"—local assemblies of ordinary citizens who would debate the issues of the day and whose decisions would be followed by their elected representatives. Now in December he opposed the national referendum suggested by the Gironde. And later, when he became a virtual dictator (even if he did not exercise all the power at his command), he turned on the men of August 10th, the proponents of popular democracy, and sent them to the guillotine.

This apparent contradiction and reversal was justified, for Robespierre, by the teaching of his favorite political scientist, the philosopher he had adored in his youth, Jean-Jacques Rousseau. When Robespierre said "Virtue has always been in the minority" he was restating Rousseau's concept of the General Will, one of those abstract ideas tucked away in philosophical works that can be dynamite with a long fuse.

At first glance the concept of the General Will can seem like nothing more than common sense. However much we

believe in democracy, we must admit that there are times
when the majority, silent or otherwise, makes dreadful mistakes. An overwhelming majority of the United States Senate
voted for the Tonkin Gulf Resolution, including Senator Ful-
bright, who was one of its sponsors. Of course they did not
know that the facts on which they based their judgments
were lies and they could not know that they were voting for
defoliation, the bombing of North Vietnam, free-fire zones
and the My Lai massacre. A plurality of the voters in Germany made Hitler premier in 1933 and a majority supported
him when he became *der Führer,* but they did not know that
their votes and support would lead to the Germany of 1945,
occupied by foreign armies and with many of its cities
leveled by bombing.

And yet, even when the majority is mistaken, there are
always a few men of clear vision who see where the *real*
interest of the people lies, who see the direction and policies
the nation must take to assure, at the very least, its survival.
For example, Winston Churchill, who resigned in 1938 because of the Munich Pact but was called to become prime
minister in 1940 and lead England through the ordeal of the
Battle of Britain. These men of clear vision represent the
General Will.

What Rousseau never explained, and what Robespierre
may have thought he had explained by basing it all on
virtue, is just how these prescient individuals are to be
recognized. The General Will is embodied in that course of
action that is ultimately in the interest of the people, even
if it is opposed by a majority of the people at any given moment. But Churchill was not the only minority leader in
England in 1938; there was also Oswald Mosley, who had a
good-sized following, and wanted to turn England into a
fascist state.

What person or persons embody the General Will in the
United States today? The President, Congress, the Supreme

Court? State governments or local governments? General Motors, General Electric, the Pentagon, or the AFL–CIO? The Black Panthers, the SDS, the John Birch Society? They all do, of course, in their own minds, and who can dispute it? Virtue has always been in the minority.

Robespierre was never bothered by this problem. The General Will was virtue, the General Will was fidelity to the Revolution—as defined by Robespierre. The changing course of events might demand different policies at different moments, but the General Will remained clear and unchanging. And so Robespierre could examine anyone's actions and attitudes at every stage of the Revolution and determine whether or not they were in accord with the General Will. If not, the man was "suspect." Royalism in 1789 was forgivable, since Robespierre was a royalist in 1789. But republicanism in 1791 might be suspect, since Robespierre, with a true understanding of the situation, had opposed those who demanded a republic in 1791. Aristocracy was always suspect; allegiance to the pope was always suspect. But an excess of anticlericalism might also be suspect; atheism was certainly suspect. At any given moment there was a certain position that was revolutionary; consequently all other positions were counterrevolutionary. It was all perfectly clear. Moreover, if you investigated a man with counterrevolutionary attitudes, whatever "mask of patriotism" he might assume you would usually find that the man was dissolute and a traitor. Nor was it surprising that there were so many plots, intrigues, conspiracies, to overthrow the Revolution; it was not surprising that so many men who had at first seemed to be revolutionaries later proved to be enemies of the people. Virtue has always been in the minority.

Lenin also had no doubts about the General Will, only he called it the proletarian revolution. For Lenin also the role of revolutionary leaders, i.e., the Communist Party, was to "alert the people to their own mistakes"—for example to break the habit of religion, "the opium of the people," to instill class consciousness. For Lenin the General Will was also revolutionary virtue and fidelity to the revolution, which meant Marxism, as revised by Lenin. For Stalin it was again virtue and Marxism, as revised by Stalin. For Mao it is virtue and Marxism-Leninism, as revised by Mao. And all along there have been many zigzags of the party line in different circumstances, with only one correct attitude at any time— also many "enemies of the people" who, when unmasked, were discovered in the ranks of the most ardent revolutionaries.

Louis XVI has been dead a long time. Indeed everyone who took part in the trial of the king in 1792 has been dead a long time. But the ideologic issues raised during that trial are still with us. The concept of the General Will served as a justification of the Terror and it has served to justify things since that make the Terror seem like child's play.

And yet, and yet . . . Virtue remains in the minority. How many of the most committed believers in democracy will not occasionally waver when they are sure that a position or policy supported by the people is obviously wrong? Perhaps democratic procedures should be suspended for a short while until the people have been made aware of their mistakes by responsible leaders? Especially in a moment of grave danger that will not wait for the people to be educated about the true facts of the situation.

(Suppose, for example, that you are a Greek colonel in 1967. Or perhaps Lyndon Johnson in 1964 and you want the Congress to vote for your legislation for the Great Society and you think that can be done only by concealing your plans for escalating American involvement in Vietnam.)

It will, after all, be in the interest of the people as you see it. It will be the General Will. What you and I believe will always be the General Will, no matter how many others oppose us. We may have to sacrifice some of our best friends, but that will only prove our devotion to the cause. (In fact, some of the things *you* have said are a bit suspicious, but let it pass, for the moment.) We believe that history will justify our actions in the end—especially if we have the passionate courage of our convictions displayed by Robespierre.

‖ Violence

Liberty must be established by
violence.   —*Marat*

Examine the history of nations,
none has broken its chains except
by choking its oppressors in blood.
            —*Marat*

The tree of liberty must be
refreshed from time to time with
the blood of patriots and tyrants.
            —*Jefferson*

IN February 1777, twelve years before the start of
the Revolution, the *Gazette de Berne* announced that a
"friend of humanity" was sponsoring a literary competition
on the subject of criminal law. The prize was to be fifty
louis, a healthy sum, and entries were to be submitted by
July 1779. The anonymous "friend of humanity" was probably Voltaire and the prize money was probably donated by
Frederick the Great. The notice caught the eye of a physician
attached to the service of the comte d'Artois in Paris, Dr.
Jean-Paul Marat. In 1779 he submitted his *Plan de Législation Criminelle* to the jury in Bern. The prize was awarded
jointly to two German jurists, both now forgotten. Marat
then had his work printed in Neuchâtel. But before the
volumes arrived in Paris they were seized by the censor, who
tore out many "subversive" pages. Marat had the mutilated

books destroyed. It was only three years later that he managed to get the work reprinted and distributed, without his name on the title page.

In 1777 Marat was thirty-four. Born in Switzerland, he had moved to France when he was sixteen. Six years later he moved to England for an eleven-year stay. In 1775, with the help of some friends, he was awarded the degree of Doctor of Medicine by the University of St. Andrews in Scotland, a school which had then the reputation of being a diploma mill. Armed with his new title he returned to Paris, where he was lucky enough to cure a few rich clients and be hired by the comte d'Artois, a younger brother of Louis XVI, a member of Marie-Antoinette's intimate circle, and the future king Charles X. His services for the count included some pimping and were rewarded by a large salary, a comfortable apartment in Paris, and the right to wear a sword.

Despite his employ as a physician, Marat had always been, primarily, a writer. He did publish a number of scientific papers, most of them on optics and electricity and their medical application; also *An Essay on Gleets* (gonorrhea) whose aim was "to diminish as much as possible the number of unfortunate victims" of the clap. But his chief interest was political science. During his eleven years in Great Britain he had written a novel, *The Adventures of Count Potowski*, with diatribes against all monarchs interspersed in the intrigue. Also *A Philosophical Essay on Man*, a work that was reviewed and reviled by Voltaire when it was published in Paris. Also *The Chains of Slavery*, an attack on monarchy ("In the beginning kings and princes were all bandit chiefs"), on religion ("whose powers is used by princes to enslave us"), and on the rich. (Marx made detailed notes in the margins of his copy of this work.)

When Marat sent his *Outline of Criminal Legislation* to the jury in Bern, it is doubtful that he really hoped to win the prize. That the censor removed only some pages is astonishing; the entire work is a call for revolution, with the insistence that the revolution must be violent if it is to succeed.

For Marat the law has no moral standing; it is only an instrument used by the rich and privileged to preserve the unjust distribution of wealth. The rule of law "is nothing but the tyranny of the few against the many . . . nothing but the orders of an insolent master." Of course the rich preach respect for the law as a virtue—"What is surprising about that?"—but for the poor it is only a trap. He imagines a revolutionary saying, "You accuse me of undermining the social order. Why should I care about an order that has always hurt me?" The poor have the right to use force to demand justice and when they do, "any authority that stands in their way is tyranny and the judge who condemns them to death is a cowardly assassin."

Not only revolutionary action but even ordinary theft is justified in Marat's eyes if the thief has no other way to stay alive. "Self-preservation is the first duty of man. . . . He who steals when he has no other way to live is only exercising his rights." In a *Discours du Voleur* whose tone anticipates Camus's *L'Étranger* and the *Prison Letters of George Jackson,* Marat imagines a mugger awaiting his execution addressing the men who have condemned him:

"Clothed in rags and sleeping in the street, each day I displayed the painful spectacle of my sores. I pleaded for help in vain; no charitable hand came to my aid. Made desperate by your obstinacy, lacking everything, driven by hunger, I took advantage of the darkness of the night to seize from a passer-by the scanty help that his hard heart had refused me. Because I asserted my rights as a human being you send me to the scaffold. Unjust judges! Remember that humanity is the first virtue and justice the first law. Even savages would tremble with horror if told of your cruelty; it is you who are savage! Bathe in my blood if you must to keep your ill-gained possessions; in the midst of the torments I endure my sole consolation will be to damn heaven for having me born among you!"*

(Marat would have understood—and applauded—the prison revolt at Attica. He would also have anticipated its outcome.)

Ten years later, when he started his paper *L'Ami du Peuple,* Marat would reiterate the same ideas for a wider audience than the jury of the *Gazette de Berne.* It was their originality that set him apart from the swarm of revolutionary journalists who rushed in to fill the vacuum created by the abolition of censorship. In 1791 he wrote: "According to my principles, a poor man without other resources has the right to steal to stay alive." In his essay on the constitution (1789) he pushed his logic to the extreme, without, however, becoming absurd. "When a man lacks everything he has the right to take by force the superfluities on which another is feasting. What have I said? he has the right to seize another's necessities, and instead of dying of hunger he has the right to kill the other man and devour his palpitating flesh. . . . Whatever violent crimes such a man commits, whatever destruction he wreaks on his fellow men, he troubles the order of nature no more than a wolf when he pounces on a sheep."

If Marat was annotated by Marx he was also a precursor of the neo-Darwinists of the end of the nineteenth century for whom the survival of the fittest was the first law of nature. At times his rhetoric sounded the discordant tones that would later be amplified by Nietzsche, as, for example: "Pity is a false sentiment, bred by society. . . . Neglect to indoctrinate a man with the ideas of goodness, kindness, charity,

---

* *The passage is modeled on a similar page in the* Essay on Crimes and Punishments *by the eighteenth-century Italian jurist Beccaria. Marat was, in his own underground way, a man of letters, even if he is remembered chiefly for his journalism, his political role during the revolution—and for his lurid assassination.*

and he will spend his entire life ignorant of even the notion of pity."

Rhetoric. It was the violence of Marat's *rhetoric* that earned him the title of the Apostle of Violence, and rightly so. Rhetoric is much more effective than our disparaging use of the adjective "rhetorical" would indicate. But the substance behind Marat's rhetoric was his pre- or proto-Marxist conviction that the *sine qua non* of a real revolution was the war of the have-nots against the haves—the class struggle. Consequently the Revolution, like the rhetoric, must be violent.

Why violent? Because the men at the top of the social pyramid will never surrender their privileges and possessions except by force. "It is the height of folly to think that these men, in power for ten centuries, who have deceived us, stolen from us, oppressed us without constraint, will suddenly decide that they will be nothing more than our equals. . . . Examine the history of nations, none has broken its chains except by choking its oppressors in blood, without slaughtering them in battle, without executing them in the course of an insurrection." If you want a real revolution, stop wasting time discussing tactics; there is "only one" that gets results, "the one I've recommended so many times, a general insurrection and executions by the people. . . . Begin by capturing the king, the dauphin, and the royal family; put them in a well-guarded prison and hold them hostage. . . . Then, without hesitation, cut off the heads of the general (Lafayette), the counterrevolutionary ministers and ex-ministers; slaughter the whole Paris establishment, all reactionaries and moderates in the National Assembly, all known supporters of despotism. I repeat, there is no other way to save the nation."

The citations in the preceding paragraph are all taken from issues of *L'Ami du Peuple* of 1790—the year when most Frenchmen thought that the reforms of the first stage of the revolution had inaugurated a new era. They seemed only outrageous words even to the thousands of lower-class Parisians who bought Marat's paper, who disrupted the trial when a partisan of Lafayette took Marat to court (Marat had written that Lafayette should be castrated). The "friend of the people" decided that the Parisians were a cowardly, corrupted lot, and began to put his faith in patriots in the provinces.

Curiously enough the other journalist whose name is still known by the general public also began as an apologist of violence. In August 1789, Camille Desmoulins published his *Discours de la Lanterne aux Parisiens*, a defense of what was euphemistically called "popular justice," i.e., lynchings. The *lanterne* of the pamphlet was the one across from the Hôtel de Ville that had served as a gallows for several prominent officials of the Old Regime accused of plotting to starve Paris into submission. The pamphlet earned Desmoulins the nickname "Attorney General of the Lamppost" and a reputation as a radical. In October 1789 Desmoulins started his own journal, *Les Révolutions de France et de Brabant*, which was an instant success. Marat at first saw in Desmoulins a potential ally, especially as several flattering references to *L'Ami du Peuple* had appeared in Camille's paper. In June 1790 Marat sent Desmoulins a draft of a manifesto attacking the Assembly and its proposed constitution as nothing more than "a posthumous child of despotism"—Marat suggested that the piece be published simultaneously in both their journals.

But Desmoulins was no Marat. He did not see the Revolution as a class struggle and he must have been perplexed if not horrified when Marat proposed that taxation be used to redistribute wealth, when Marat condemned the Declaration of the Rights of Man as "a derisible trap to amuse fools." Desmoulins had no theories; his arms were his wit and his personal charm, a charm so well communicated in his prose that everyone who writes about him sooner or later succumbs to the temptation to call him Camille, as if he were a personal friend. A lawyer from Picardy, he had attended the same college in Paris as Robespierre—he often refers to the Incorruptible as "my classmate" although they were several years apart. Of course they became friends—even Robespierre couldn't resist his "classmate's" charm; Robespierre was a witness at Camille's wedding in 1790.

Desmoulins turned down Marat's manifesto, which Marat published on his own. Marat kept his feelings about the matter to himself. One can only speculate about the personal relations of the two journalists. They lived only a few blocks from each other on the Left Bank; both belonged to the Cordeliers Club. In *his* paper, Camille continued to treat Marat as an ally, but occasionally his tone was bantering. In December 1790 Marat said that six hundred heads must fall if the Revolution were to continue; in the next issue of *l'Ami du Peuple* the figure was raised to twenty thousand. Desmoulins asked, "My dear friend, to be serious, of those nineteen thousand four hundred heads you added to the six hundred, can't one be spared? Are they all really indispensable?" (Later Marat would call for 500,000 deaths.)

Camille always seemed to consider Marat the *nec plus ultra* of the Revolution, even after Marat's assassination. In December 1793 he would write that "beyond Marat there can be only delirium and extravagance . . . beyond his notions we must inscribe, like the geographers of antiquity at the edge of their maps, 'There we find no more cities, no more dwellings; only deserts and savages, ice or volcanos.' " But those words were written at the height of the Terror when men had appeared whose ideas went "beyond Marat," and Desmoulins was invoking the authority of the Friend of the People to oppose them. At the end of his short career the Attorney General of the Lamppost was ironically revealed a humanitarian; it was his appeal for a Committee of Clemency, his statement that "mercy is also a revolutionary measure" that led to his breach with Robespierre and soon after led him to the guillotine. It is hard to imagine Marat at the same period calling for anything other than *more* executions—and perhaps being sent to the guillotine for *that*.

Violence. It is a word everyone uses, but only occasionally does a Marat appear who will admit that he believes in it. Society is usually far more shocked by a Marat who preaches violence than it is by men who actually commit it—perhaps because society itself has always been the chief "perpetrator of violence" (to use the phrase of one of the rare apostles of nonviolence, Martin Luther King). There are at least three kinds of violence that human beings can perpetrate on one another: violence against property (theft, arson, looting, vandalism), violence against persons (assault, injury, rape), and murder (criminal murder, warfare, executions, assassinations, etc.). The violence that results in death is clearly the most extreme, but even there some confusion remains. Coroners make a distinction between natural and unnatural deaths, but being struck by lightning or drowned in a flood is considered an "unnatural death" for some reason. Insurance policies call these last two "Acts of God" as distinguished from damage, injury, or death caused by "rebellion, riot, insurrection, civil war, revolution, etc."—usually not covered by the policy. (When the governor of a state calls out the National Guard, he has to choose his words carefully in describing the situation if property owners are not to lose their coverage.)

What distinguishes Marat from Camille Desmoulins in his defense of violence is that he does not limit his apology to political violence. Marat recognizes that political violence takes place within the context of the society it is trying to change, in the context of the level of violence that is considered normal. In a society where the punishment for stealing a loaf of bread may be death (as was the case in the

France of the Old Regime), lynching a man for hoarding flour while people are hungry will have a different significance than the same act in a society that has no death penalty, even for murder.

This point was forcefully expressed by Babeuf, another proto-Marxist of the French Revolution. Babeuf was to be executed in 1797, three years after the fall of Robespierre, for having inspired the "Conspiration des Égaux," a rather feeble conspiracy that aimed at starting the Revolution all over again but accomplished little more than writing slogans on walls. In July 1789 he was only an unemployed surveyor who had written a book on agrarian reform that no one would publish. He had witnessed the post-script to the double lynching of Foulon and Berthier, two officials of the monarchy who were accused of trying to starve the people of Paris. (These lynchings were among those defended by Desmoulins in his *Discours de la Lanterne*.) The next day, Babeuf wrote his wife:

"I saw the heads of the father and the son-in-law go by accompanied by a thousand armed men. This parade, a show for the people, went the whole length of the rue St.-Martin, watched by two hundred thousand spectators who were shouting and rejoicing along with the marchers, who stepped to the sound of a drum. Oh! this joy made me uneasy. I was both glad and downcast; I said, 'So much for the better' and 'So much for the worse.' I understand that the people takes justice into its own hands; I approve that justice that can be satisfied only by eradicating those who are guilty—but why must it be so cruel? Public ordeals of all sorts—drawing and quartering, torture, the wheel, burning at the stake, gibbets, a multiplicity of executioners everywhere—have given us such bad standards! Our masters, instead of civilizing us, have made us savages because they are savages themselves. They reap what they have sown; for all this, my dear little wife, will have terrible consequences; this is only the beginning."

But the *norm* of acceptable violence can and does change in every society, and in both directions. Everyone knows about certain lowerings of the level of acceptable violence in Western societies; they are part of the myth of "progress." Thieves are no longer sent to the gallows. In England and other countries the death penalty has been abolished. Even Governor Wallace does not condone lynching as a way of dealing with "uppitty nigras." But this change is not a one-way street. During the past decade in the United States we have seen a rise in the level of "normal" violence in many respects. A riot in which a few innocent bystanders are felled by police bullets may be of only local interest. A policeman killed by a sniper or a Black Panther descendant of Marat shot in his bed by a policeman is no longer a startling event. To call such incidents "normal" does not imply approval; it is merely a statement of fact.

During the French Revolution we see a society altering its norms of acceptable violence in both directions under the pressure of political events. The guillotine was a humanitarian innovation. The laws relating to ordinary crimes that were eventually frozen in the Code Napoleon were far more humanitarian than the laws of the Old Regime. But there were those lynchings and the September Massacres. Also the Terror, which was an institutionalization of violence, responding to the escalation of violence as an acceptable and accepted means of political action.

The Réveillon riot of April 1789—the one Morris reported in his letter to Washington—took hundreds of lives, but at the time it had little political impact. Modern historians see in the event a portent of the conflict between the *sans-culottes* and the bourgeoisie that took political form only four years later. We can speculate that it contributed to a subconscious apprehension of the perils of disturbing the social order, but if so the incident was effectively repressed by the collective unconscious; the polemicists of the Revolution hardly mention it. Perhaps we should conclude that violence does not become political until it is interpreted as such. If Marat had been publishing *l'Ami du Peuple* in April 1789 the Réveillon riot would have been a political issue.

A hundred men were killed during the storming of the Bastille, but even conservatives acknowledged that on the whole the Paris revolt was a disciplined and orderly affair. The lynchings that followed the fall of the Bastille aroused far greater fears, because they were the work of spontaneous mobs. But what really raised the level of rhetoric (even if it inaugurated a period of relative calm) was the march of the women of Paris on Versailles with the important result that the royal family and the Assembly moved to the capital (October 1789). From then onward, with the king and the Assembly surrounded by the people of Paris, the threat of extreme violence hung over the course of the Revolution, and men of all shades of opinion were always aware of that threat.

It all seems to have begun with a girl beating a drum in the center of the wholesale food market at seven in the morning. She shouted to her co-workers that they should march to Versailles to remind the king that Paris was still short of bread. The women marched first to the Hôtel de Ville, not far away, where they encountered *another* demonstration—the workers employed in the demolition of the Bastille who were protesting the arrest of a mason on some charge or other. The two demonstrations merged; the market women convinced the workers to join them in their march. Then they fanned out to the surrounding neighborhoods, calling on all women to enlist in their crusade. Their persuasions were sometimes violent; there are reports of servants being dragged out of their kitchens by force.

The whole story sounds a bit like a fairy tale and it has become a patriotic legend, like Paul Revere's ride.* There are

* *In the Sacha Guitry film,* Si Versailles m'était conté, *Edith Piaf, leading the women of Paris, clings to the wrought-iron gate of the*

some reports of men in women's dress among the marchers, presumably the organizers of the whole affair. But that was not really necessary; the revolutionary press had been demanding that the king and the Assembly move to Paris for months, and Parisian women had already staged several demonstrations to protest the bread shortage, saying that "men know nothing about it."

By the time the actual march began, Lafayette had been alerted. He first tried to dissuade the marchers, then called up the National Guard and ordered them to go to Versailles to preserve order—although some detachments had already joined spontaneously, as participants. The bedraggled horde —it had rained all afternoon and Versailles is twelve miles from Paris—began to arrive at their destination early in the evening. They went first to the Assembly, which listened to their demands; a deputation of six women was chosen to speak to the king. The National Guard arrived last, at about midnight, and surrounded the palace. But toward dawn some of the Parisian demonstrators managed to get into the château. Marie-Antoinette fled by a hidden passageway to her husband's apartment. One of her guards fired out of a window and killed a seventeen-year-old marcher. In retaliation the crowd killed two of the palace guards and cut off their heads. Lafayette's troops restored order.

A short while later Louis, Marie-Antoinette, and Lafayette went out on a balcony to assure the Parisians of their good faith. They were greeted by shouts, "The King to Paris!" Louis agreed to go to Paris and the Assembly decided to go with him. They arrived that afternoon, again in the rain.

This was the episode that inspired some of Burke's most eloquent prose, which is really too delicious not to quote at length:

———
palace and, under a bright blue sky, sings Ça ira! *In fact the women got to Versailles in the evening, it was raining, and* Ça ira! *did not become a popular revolutionary song until the following July.*

History will record, that on the morning
of the 6th of October 1789, the king and
queen of France, after a day of confusion,
alarm, dismay, and slaughter, lay down,
under the pledged security of public faith,
to indulge nature in a few hours of respite,
and troubled melancholy repose. From this
sleep the queen was first startled by the voice
of the centinel at her door, who cried out to
her, to save herself by flight—that this
was the last proof of fidelity he could give
—that they were upon him, and he was
dead. Instantly he was cut down. A band of
cruel ruffians and assassins, reeking with
his blood, rushed into the chamber of the
queen, and pierced with an hundred strokes
of bayonets and poniards the bed, from
whence this persecuted woman had but
just time to fly almost naked, and through
ways unknown to the murderers had
escaped to seek refuge at the feet of a king
and husband, not secure of his own life for
a moment.

This king, to say no more of him, and
this queen, and their infant children (who
once would have been the pride and hope of
a great and generous people) were then
forced to abandon the sanctuary of the
most splendid palace in the world, which
they left swimming in blood, polluted by
massacre, and strewed with scattered
limbs and mutilated carcases. Thence
they were conducted to the capital of their
kingdom. Two had been selected from
the unprovoked, unresisted, promiscuous
slaughter, which was made of the gentlemen
of birth and family who composed the
king's body guard. These two gentlemen,
with all the parade of an execution of
justice, were cruelly and publickly dragged
to the block, and beheaded in the great
court of the palace. Their heads were stuck

upon spears, and led the procession; whilst
the royal captives who followed in the
train were slowly moved along, amidst the
horrid yells, and shrilling screams, and
frantic dances, and infamous contemelies,
and all the unutterable abominations of
the furies of hell, in the abused shape of the
vilest of women. After they had been made
to taste, drop by drop, more than the
bitterness of death, in the slow torture of
a journey of twelve miles, protracted to
six hours, they were, under a guard,
composed of those very soldiers who had
thus conducted them through this famous
triumph, lodged in one of the old palaces of
Paris, now converted into a Bastile for
kings.

But what really provoked Burke's fury when he
wrote his "Reflections" the following spring was that the violence and the threat of worse violence had paid off—the
march on Versailles had by then been accepted as a great victory of the Revolution. "Is this a triumph to be consecrated at
altars? To be commemorated with grateful thanksgiving? . . .
The actual murder of the king and the queen, and their child,
was wanting to the other auspicious circumstances of this
'beautiful day' . . . What hard pencil of a great master, from
the school of the rights of man, will finish it, is to be seen
here after."

And it was seen thereafter—three years later when Louis
and Marie-Antoinette were guillotined. But during those
three years there was a valiant attempt, by the very men
whom Burke was attacking in his "Reflections," to contain the
forces that led the Revolution within nonviolent channels,
an attempt that Burke's impassioned prose, if it had any influence in France, certainly contributed to undermining.
And Burke was not alone. He quotes a letter from a M. de
Lally Tollendal, which may be taken as an example of the

hysteria of the right at a time when the National Assembly was doing all it could to restrain passions, repress violence, and promote national unity.

Tollendal had been one of the deputies of the nobility to the Estates; he had resigned from the Assembly because of the events of October 5th and 6th. "It was more than I could do to support any longer the horror I felt at this blood—those heads—the queen almost butchered—the king, brought back a slave. . . . M. Bailly called that a *great day* . . . M. Mirabeau stating that the ship of state, far from being stranded, would move more rapidly than ever toward its regeneration. . . . That is why I could no longer set foot in that cavern of Anthropophages."

For the royalists the Assembly had become a nest of cannibals, while at the same time Marat was calling them a pack of cowards. Several months later Marat was accused of aiding the royalists by his violent attacks on the Assembly. The accusation could be reversed; the royalists certainly aided Marat by calling for a violent counterrevolution.

Aside from the shouting in the press, Paris was quite peaceful during 1790 and the first half of 1791. But other parts of France, especially the Rhone valley, were the scene of disorders of varying degrees, some of them very bloody. These disorders were the work of the *right* at a time when most of the left still regarded Marat as a freak and refused to take seriously his warnings that the Revolution could be completed only by violence. Eventually troops from other regions were sent in, and the attempt at a counterrevolution was put down.

The king had given no encouragement to the royalist insurrections in the south of France, much to the disgust of many of his supporters. For the moment he was following the advice of Mirabeau and Lafayette. When it came to the event that became known as the "Massacre of Nancy" the Assembly took the same tack, much to the disgust of many patriots.

In the American army today the men in command from sergeants up, the career men, the "lifers," tend to have a very different outlook from the draftees and volunteers in the ranks. In France after 1789 the situation was similar but much worse. Almost all the officers were drawn from the nobility, the troops from the common people. When the troops began to join revolutionary clubs the officers were outraged. They singled out the "patriotic" leaders for hard treatment and various punishments. The Assembly had voted a pay rise for the men in the ranks, but the officers held back their wages.

The leaders of the Assembly—Mirabeau and Lafayette—were aware of what was going on, but they were still hoping for a very limited revolution. When the troops mutinied, as they did in garrisons all over France, the Assembly took the side of the officers. The worst example of this occurred in Nancy in August 1790. The soldiers demanding their back pay were supported by the people of the city and the local National Guard. Lafayette deliberately misrepresented the facts of the situation to the Assembly, which passed a decree calling for immediate disciplinary measures. Troops were brought in from other places, many of them German mercenaries. A bloody pitched battle took place. The rebels who weren't killed in the fighting or executed afterward were sent to the galleys.

As the facts of what had actually happened became known, the episode aroused a great deal of emotion. Only the left, of course, called it a massacre, but the name stuck. It was the first step in discrediting Lafayette as a revolutionary leader in the eyes of many who had viewed him as a hero in 1789, an evolution of popular sentiment that would be completed by another "massacre" a year later, that of the Champ de Mars.

Before jumping ahead to massacres worthy of the name, let us tot up the score on the question of violence for the first three years of the Revolution; 1789 witnessed many profound changes which were certainly due, in part, to violent episodes—the storming of the Bastille, the *Grande Peur* in the countryside, the march on Versailles. After that the level of violent rhetoric in the press may have been equal on the far left and the far right, but the actual instances of violence were either provoked or committed by the *right*. Ultraconservatives may talk about law and order and warn of anarchy, but they are at least as prone to violent action as their counterparts on the left. Or so they were in France during 1790 and 1791.

But the role of violence during those years shouldn't be exaggerated. The massacre of Nancy and the massacre of the Champ de Mars left a profound impression in the minds of many Frenchmen, but they did not change the course of events. What destroyed the moderate compromise represented by the Constitution of 1791 was neither the violent rhetoric of the press nor any of the incidents discussed in the last couple of pages; it was rather the flight to Varennes and the miserable performance of the French army a year later when war had been declared. It was those major events that reactivated the earlier impressions. Bouillé, who mismanaged the king's attempted escape from France, had been the commander in Nancy at the time of that massacre. Lafayette was the general of the Army of the Rhine in the spring of 1792, and under his command his troops only moved backwards; the previous summer, at the time of the massacre of the Champ de Mars, he had been the general of the National Guard in Paris.

All in all, despite the rhetoric of Marat and his counterparts on the right, France as an organized society functioned as well during the first three years of the Revolution as it had during the first eighty-nine years of the century, if not better. *Anarchy* is an often-used word but a rarely observed reality, if it has ever existed. When people warn against the danger of anarchy they are usually warning about a lack of respect for the law—and, as Marat made clear, the people who do the warning are usually those best protected by the law. Lack of respect for the law will, it is true, raise the level of violence. But an organized society can, if it must, tolerate a very high level of violence. Innocent individuals will suffer but the society as a whole will take its losses, bury its dead, and go on functioning.

The upward escalation of "normal" violence can, as we Americans may yet learn, go much further than anyone might expect before a society collapses. That is the hidden weakness of terrorism as a political technique. No terrorist movement has ever won a war or achieved a successful revolution on its own; at most terrorist movements have provoked wars or revolutions that were won by organized forces. "Anarchy" is a bugaboo of the right and the chimerical ideal of a certain segment of the left. Man in a "state of nature," be it the pastoral vision of Rousseau or the dog-eat-dog vision of Hobbes, is a purely philosophical concept with no experimental base. All human societies that anyone has observed, including the most primitive, are highly organized. And all, except for the most primitive, are very resilient. The anthropologists and sociologists of our century have proved conclusively that cultural shock is far more destructive than the vain threat of anarchy.

By the summer of 1792, with France betrayed from within and invaded by the Prussians, Marat no longer seemed a freak; he had become a sage and a prophet. The monarchy was overthrown on August 10th in just the way Marat had always said it must be overthrown—by an insurrection. There were three hundred and ninety killed or wounded among the besiegers of the Tuileries palace, which was double the number of casualties suffered by the men who had stormed the Bastille three years earlier. But the casualties of August 10th were ascribed to treachery by the king and the troops guarding the palace. Four hundred men of the Marseilles regiment had begun the day by asking the Swiss Guards to lay down their arms and join the revolutionary cause; the response was a murderous volley that killed sixty of the Marseillais. This helps explain the bloody aftermath of the attack during which six hundred of the Swiss were slaughtered. In 1789 the men who stormed the fortress received the honorary title of "victors of the Bastille." The killed and wounded at the Tuileries in 1792 were called "the victims of August 10th." The shift from *victors* to *victims* is indicative of the evolution of popular psychology from the triumphant optimism of 1789 to the almost paranoid suspicion of 1792.

In 1789 the stabbing of the commander of the Bastille in the rue St.-Antoine, the lynchings at the famous *lanterne,* had been deplored by many liberals. No voice was raised to protest the slaughter of the Swiss Guards in 1792. An English observer, Dr. John Moore, noted the next day: "The naked bodies of the Swiss, for they were already stripped, lay exposed on the ground. . . . The garden and adjacent courts were crowded with spectators, among whom there was a considerable proportion of women." Two days later he notes: "The public walks are crowded with men, women, and children of all conditions with the most gay unconcerned countenances imaginable. A stranger just come to Paris, without having heard of the late transactions . . . would naturally imagine, from the frisky behaviour and cheerful faces of the company he meets, that this day was a continuation of a series of days appointed for dissipation, mirth and enjoyment."

Even making allowance for the tendency of an English observer to exaggerate the reputed frivolity of the French, it is apparent that the level of acceptable violence had been greatly escalated in three years.

Volunteers continued to arrive in Paris on their way to the front. But with the fall of Longwy, by treason, the desertion of Lafayette, it began to seem that Paris itself would be the front. On August 30th three thousand suspects were arrested after a house-to-house search, including many men and women whose papers were simply not in order. The royalists in Paris—they were not all imaginary—did not help matters by painting slogans on walls and defacing the statues of Law and Liberty that had been erected for a memorial service for the "victims of August 10th." No doubt they believed, as did many others, that the Prussian Army would soon be in Paris to put Louis XVI back on his throne. From the windows of the overcrowded prisons, royalist songs floated out to the streets.

This was the situation that produced yet another massacre, one whose magnitude so far surpassed its predecessors' that it is always referred to in the plural: the September Massacres.

The suspects in the prisons were regarded as a potential fifth column that would deliver Paris to the Prussians when they arrived. As early as August 11th the National Guard was warned of radical "projects" to break into the jails and exterminate the prisoners. Placards were posted up urging the volunteer troops to take care of their enemies in the capital before they marched off to fight the Prussians. One of these was signed Marat. As it happened it was dated September 3rd, a day after the massacres began. On September 2nd the unfounded rumor that Verdun had fallen, again by treason, had spread around Paris. (Verdun had fallen on that day, and by treason, but the hard news was a couple of days in arriving.) That afternoon a group of royalist priests being conducted to the Abbaye jail were seized by a mob at the prison gate and put to death.

That was the start. The killers entered the prison, set up a kangaroo court, and ordered the guards to bring out the prisoners to be judged. Most were found guilty after a short interrogation and hacked to death in the prison courtyard;

many of them were innocent of any kind of political activity.
A few were judged innocent and released with tears and
cheers, among them several royalists later sent to the guillotine.

The action (or whatever it should be called) spread to
other prisons and to monasteries that had been converted
into prisons. The procedures varied from place to place but
the results were the same. However, a certain shift of em-
phasis can be noted during the four days that the massacres
continued. What began as a political action (eliminating
potential traitors) became an exercise in revolutionary virtue (getting rid of the "scum"). Ordinary criminals and
prostitutes were put to death. Again we must suspend our
own ideologic categories. The summary execution of thieves
and whores, most of whom had grown up in the slums of
Paris, was a manifestation of revolutionary violence, even if
it seems fascist to us—and even if it contradicted all the
theories of Marat.

The number of those killed, according to estimates, was
between eleven hundred and fourteen hundred. Meanwhile
life in Paris went on apparently unaffected; there was no
"anarchy." The elections for the Convention proceeded according to plan. When it was all over every political leader
from the far left to the center (there was no right) dis-
claimed any responsibility. Even Marat protested his innocence. It wasn't until the following spring that some men
began to assert that the massacres had been a necessary and
salutary event. But the word *Septembrist* remained pejora-
tive, an accusation of bloodthirstiness.

Some of the reports of those four days show that the accusation was not unfounded. There are good arguments to
be made for the use of violence as a political tactic and
especially for its necessity in certain situations. Marat put
the case as well as anyone ever has. The same arguments,
of course, can be used to justify warfare. ("War is a con-

tinuation of politics by other means"—Clausewitz.) The apologists for violence usually acknowledge that there will be innocent victims; they justify this as a necessary evil, maintaining that there will be *more* innocent victims if the violence that is inevitable is postponed too long.* What they overlook is the intimate corruption of the men who have to commit the violent acts they recommend.

Very few men are so psychologically structured that they can perform acts of violence purely as a logical necessity. The military chain of command implicitly recognizes this fact. The men who have to make the logical decisions, the generals, do not participate in their execution. It is not that the generals want to save their skins—often they are eager to get into the "action"; what must be preserved is their sanity. From Homer to the novelists of the twentieth century every poet who has described warfare has pictured the men who actually do the killing as temporarily insane. Or if not insane in a condition akin to that produced by drugs—or perhaps actually produced by drugs, as in the case of the winner of the Medal of Honor who ascribed his bravery in Vietnam to marijuana. There are exceptions, of course—the men who are permanently insane. Sometimes the exceptions become generals and the results are terrifying.

The same psychology also applies to political violence, except that the chain of command is usually much weaker. One of the victims of the September Massacres was the Princesse de Lamballe, a close friend of Marie-Antoinette but otherwise unimportant. After she was hacked to death her butchers sliced off her genital area, hoisted this obscene trophy on the point of a pike, and paraded it around Paris,

---

* In 1790 Marat wrote: "When I think that to spare a few drops of blood we run the danger of pouring out a great flood, I become indignant despite myself at our false maxims of humanity." And, "Five or six hundred severed heads would have guaranteed tranquillity, liberty, and happiness; a false humanity has held back your arms and your blows; it will cost the lives of thousands of your brothers."

finally going to the Temple where the royal family was imprisoned and shouting to the queen to look out to see what
had become of her friend. Such actions would usually be
relegated to the realm of abnormal psychology, but in the
context of the moment they must be considered normal
psychology.

That is the aspect of violence its proponents never mention. Marat was called a "madman" many times while he was
alive and after. Well, no, he wasn't a madman. Perhaps, as
he claimed, he wasn't even cruel, couldn't hurt a fly. But
perhaps he underestimated the potential madness of the
world in which he lived.

When it was all over the massacres were condemned by
everyone. The norm of violence had again been raised, but
the consequences of that escalation were not apparent for
some time. The Prussians never got near the half-completed
fortifications on the heights of Montmartre; instead the
French army invaded Belgium. The Convention was busy
running the war, trying the king, and engaging in political
bickering. Within Paris the National Guard, which now included all able-bodied men who were in the army, drilled
and marched; the city remained quite orderly, aside from
the looting of a few grocery stores in February (provoked by
the high price of soap) and the assassination of the deputy
Lepelletier on the eve of the execution of the king.

But then in March the French army in Belgium was suddenly defeated and began a precipitate retreat. This time,
instead of calling for volunteers, the Convention passed a
conscription law. In Paris radical groups began calling for a
new insurrection, this time against the Girondins, and the
prisons again began filling up with arrested suspects of all
sorts.

What *nobody* wanted to see was a repetition of the September Massacres. The special Revolutionary Tribunal that
had been created the previous August (the one Robespierre

refused to head) had been dissolved in December after doing very little. Now a new Revolutionary Tribunal was created with extraordinary powers to move swiftly, disregard the usual rules of evidence, and carry out its sentence immediately. Any kind of court, no matter how Draconian its operation, seemed preferable to frenzied, indiscriminate slaughter by bands of thugs. In the heat of the moment the Convention went so far as to suspend its own inviolability, permitting delegates to be tried by the new court if a majority of the Assembly voted that they were suspect.

The new court was *the* Revolutionary Tribunal; it functioned without interruption until Thermidor, eighteen months later. It did succeed in its original purpose; there was no repetition of the September Massacres. But six months after its creation it had become the instrument of a new kind of revolutionary policy, a policy justified by fear of treason and fear of violence, the policy, of course, that became known as the Terror.

As for Marat, he was, oddly enough, the first member of the Convention to be judged by the new court. At the beginning of April the general of the French army in Belgium, Dumouriez, imitated Lafayette's example by deserting to the Austrians. This immediately intensified the power struggle within the Convention—Dumouriez had been Foreign Minister when war was first declared and his treason gave Robespierre the opportunity to claim that Girondin policies had *all along* been aimed at the defeat of the Revolution. The Gironde, which still commanded a numerical majority in the Convention, retaliated by an inept accusation that Marat was trying to undermine the assembly. Marat went into hiding for three weeks until he felt that the political climate was favorable enough for him to stand trial.

He was not, of course, found guilty. The day that he appeared at the Tribunal, the courtroom and the surrounding streets were packed with his supporters, all of them indig-

nant that the Friend of the People should be accused of anything. The judges were afraid of being lynched and hardly
bothered to ask any questions. Marat conducted his own
trial, recounting all his actions since the start of the Revolution, naturally in the most flattering light. The jury brought
in the expected verdict in one minute. Marat's followers then
carried him through the streets to the Convention, whose
work was interrupted for half an hour by cheers and songs.
When Marat was finally back in his seat he turned on his
accusers, the leaders of the Gironde. "The people will ap-
plaud you also," he shouted, "but at the guillotine!"

And they did, but not for another six months. By then
Marat was dead.

At the beginning of June the struggle between Gironde
and the Mountain was finally ended by yet another Paris insurrection, this one carefully organized by Robespierre and
without bloodshed. Troops of the National Guard, commanded by one of Robespierre's men, surrounded the
Tuileries palace (the Convention had moved from the
Manège in May) and held the delegates captive until they
voted the expulsion of twenty-two leaders of the Gironde.
The expelled delegates were placed under house arrest, but
most of them escaped to other parts of France, where they
tried to organize movements to overthrow the Montagnards
in Paris.

One of the centers of this Girondin activity was Caen in
Normandy, today known for its *tripes à la mode de Caen* and
its applejack. On July 7th, in the presence of three of the
expelled delegates, there was a parade of volunteers for a
march on Paris. The parade must have been short; only
thirty men turned up. One of the spectators at this nonevent
was a young woman, Charlotte Corday, a descendant of the
seventeenth-century playwright Corneille; her father was
a royalist nobleman. Was she also a royalist? Probably not.
At her trial she declared that she had been "a republican

long before the Revolution." But she was fascinated by politics and claimed to have read over five hundred political pamphlets since 1789, as well as the moderate newspapers to which she subscribed. She had been shocked by the execution of the king, indignant at the expulsion of the Girondins, and shamed by the indifference of her countrymen to what she considered the tyranny of the Mountain in Paris.

Two days later this young idealist took the coach to Paris, having decided to save her country by killing Marat. Why Marat? Perhaps as an avid reader she exaggerated the importance of journalism. Her initial scheme was absurd, to do the deed in the Convention itself. But once in Paris a certain practical good sense took over. She bought a knife, learned Marat's address, and managed to get herself admitted to his apartment by saying she was "an unfortunate woman" who needed the protection of the Friend of the People. He received her seated in the covered bathtub which was the only spot where he could find temporary relief from the torments of an incurable skin disease. The convent-educated young intellectual managed to kill him with the first stroke.

It would be neat poetic justice if Charlotte Corday had been a political activist, converted to violent action by the writings of Marat himself. But reality is rarely so neat and poetry is never so banal. At her trial, the judge of the Revolutionary Tribunal asked, "Hadn't you practiced in the past, before you stabbed Marat?" Mlle Corday answered, "Oh! the monster! he takes me for an assassin!"

When reminded that she got to see Marat by claiming that she was persecuted, she answered, "Why should I care that he was humane toward me, since he was a monster for others?"

She was sent to the guillotine in a red dress, the traditional costume for parricides—Marat, in July 1793, had become a Father of His Country.

The assassination of Marat seemed to justify, retroac-

tively, the expulsion of the Girondins. Two months later the
Convention decreed "the Terror is the order of the day."
Marat became a martyr of the left; in September 1794 his
remains were transferred to the Panthéon, a consecration
that Charlotte Corday had ironically said he deserved. But
Charlotte Corday, guillotined at twilight in her red dress,
her severed head blushing when slapped by the executioner,
became a martyr of the right.

Yet far more than his bizarre assassination it is the Sep-
tember Massacres that represent the realization of all that
Marat had preached, even before the *Plan de Législation
Criminelle* submitted to the jury in Bern in 1779. At the time
Marat was accused of full responsibility for the massacres.
In his excellent biography, Gerard Walter examines all the
accusations, one by one. He concludes, and the argument is
convincing, that Marat had no direct part in the event. As
for indirect responsibility, Walter points to statements by
Robespierre, Danton, and others that were at least as much
incitements to violence as anything published by Marat at
the time. But Walter does not try to absolve Marat of all
responsibility. He quotes Napoleon's judgment of Marat:
"The source of his popularity was that in 1790 he anticipated
what would happen in 1792."

That is the crux of the matter. Marat was an intellectual
—philosopher, pamphleteer, journalist—who became a political figure during the last years of his life. His actions as a
politician were often theatrical (putting a pistol to his
head), but they did not change very much. What did have a
profound effect was the exhortations of *l'Ami du Peuple*,
those calls for violent action that were eventually translated
into action. That he did not wholly approve of the action
when it came, that he did not directly participate in it, is
beside the point, as beside the point as the endless agonizing
over how they should vote in this or that election in which
many intellectuals currently indulge. (If they are in any

position to influence the opinions of others—if they are teachers, scholars, or writers—they have voted a long time ago.) Marat's immediate responsibility for the September Massacres and the other violent episodes of the French Revolution remains an open question for historians to investigate. But his justification of violence as a political necessity is not yet only an academic subject.

‖The Terror

God, protector of innocence and truth, since
you have led me into the company of perverted
men it is no doubt so that I should denounce
them. . . .
Circumstances seem difficult only for those
who fear the tomb. I demand it, my tomb, as
a gift of Providence, so I will no longer witness
unpunished crimes against my country and
against humanity. . . .
It is certainly a slight thing to take leave of an
unhappy life in which one is condemned to
vegetate as the powerless witness or accomplice
of crime. . . .
I despise the dust of which I am composed
and which is speaking to you; this dust may
be tortured or killed but I defy anyone to
take from me the independent life I
have created for myself in the centuries
to come and in eternity!

THE words, of course, are St.-Just's, even if certain
phrases suggest either an Old Testament prophet, a seventeenth-century English Puritan, or a twentieth-century idealist, any of whom might also be a young man who was put to
death at the age of twenty-six. But even this small sampling
of St.-Just's personal notebooks is enough to indicate that
their author was a Romantic, or rather a pre-Romantic, who
could have lived only at the end of the eighteenth century.

[140]

They are taken from the slim volume published posthumously under the dull title *Republican Institutions*. (Posthumous works appealed to the Romantic sensibility; Chateaubriand's autobiography was entitled *Memoirs from the Tomb* —and published posthumously.)

Robespierre also frequently referred to his imminent death, even before the politics of the Revolution became a gladiatorial combat. "Heaven which has given me a soul impassioned for liberty may call me to mark with my blood the path that will lead my country to happiness and liberty; I accept with joy this sweet and glorious destiny" (April 1792). The day that he was finally outvoted he was more direct: "I demand death; deliver me from the spectacle of crime!" (July 1794). It was not necessary to be Charlotte Corday, a descendant of Corneille, to believe that a noble death was the crowning achievement of an heroic life; almost everyone of the revolutionary generation shared the same ideal, nourished not only by seventeenth-century drama but also by Greek and Roman history, which they had all studied in school. That is why the Terror was the occasion for so many memorable last words (Mme Roland: "Oh Liberty! what crimes are done in thy name!"), so many theatrical gestures (the twenty-two Girondins singing the Marseillaise in a diminuendo chorus as they were guillotined one by one), so many last letters that read as if taken from an historical novel (Camille Desmoulins to his wife*). Even Danton, whose remarks after his arrest had a characteristic earthy quality: "Robespierre doesn't know how to boil an

---

* *"A blessed sleep suspended my misery. One is free when one sleeps.* . . . *But at one moment I saw you in my dreams.* . . . *I awoke and found myself in my cell. The dawn was breaking. Not able to see you and talk to you, for in my dreams you and your mother were with me, I got up to speak to you by writing. But, opening the shutters, the thought of my solitude, the hideous bars and locks that keep me from you, overcame all the resolve of my soul. I melted into tears, or rather I sobbed in my tomb, crying, Lucile! Lucile! oh my dear Lucile, where are you?"*

egg. I wish I could leave him my balls," had a noble order for the executioner: "Show my head to the people, it is good to look at." Two days before, at the Revolutionary Tribunal, Danton had responded to the judge in the tone of St.-Just: "My name is Danton, age thirty-five. My residence tomorrow will be nothingness, but I shall live forever in the Pantheon of History."

Among all the prominent victims of the Terror—the less prominent usually died unnoticed, as they had lived—the only one who refused to die heroically was Mme Dubarry. Dubarry had been the mistress of Louis XV, the grandfather of Louis XVI, some twenty years before the Revolution. She had been quite young at the time and when her royal lover died she had retired to a comfortable private life, out of the public eye although still of interest to visiting tourists like Benjamin Franklin. Her position was that of a movie star whose vogue has passed and who remains in Beverly Hills, paradoxically younger than most people would guess. Dubarry had no dreams of making a comeback, although she did not lack lovers of high rank who did not disdain to re-plow a field that had been consecrated by a king. During the Revolution some of these friends of her middle age used her house for some amateurish espionage, transmitting messages to royalists abroad. It was ostensibly for that that she went to the guillotine, but the real reason was to remind the public of the corruption of the monarchy and its supporters. (There were no mistresses of Louis XVI available to fill the bill; he hadn't had any.) Dubarry, age fifty, declined to rise to the occasion. She belonged to an earlier generation that preferred old age to an heroic death; she had to be dragged up onto the scaffold; she trembled and struggled until the blade fell, shouting that she wanted to *live*. Her performance made a greater impression on the crowd that turned out for executions than the stoic courage of Mme Roland, whose husband was always called "the virtuous."

I do not mean to suggest that the ideal of a noble death was the cause of the Terror, but it certainly oiled the works once the machine began to operate. By dying heroically the victims at once protested and sanctioned their sentence. They affirmed their innocence, or at least their high motives, but at the same time they cooperated by playing the game according to unwritten rules. Charlotte Corday, in a letter to her father from prison, quoted a line by the lesser Corneille:

> Le crime fait la honte, et non pas l'échafaud.
> (Crime is shameful, not the scaffold.)

By denying that it was shameful to be guillotined they became martyrs, but at the same time their conduct added to the prestige of that device whose virtues were novelty, efficiency, reliability, and speed. "With my machine I cut off your head before you can blink and you don't feel anything."

There is a partial parallel in the confessions of the brainwashed accused men at the Stalin trials, the Rajk trials, the Prague trials, etc. Twentieth-century totalitarianism, aware of the precedent, does not permit its victims to affirm their innocence, but it does demand that they participate in their own condemnation, that they sanction their own deaths. Terror, as a political instrument, requires this participation; that is one of the things that distinguishes it from a simple settling of political scores by violent means. The men of the French Revolution created this process, like so many others, without knowing what they were doing.

Before we go any further we should note the scale of the phenomenon. There is something repugnant about playing numbers games with death, but sometimes it is instructive. In modern terms we can say that the number of victims of the Terror was minimal. In all of France, a nation of twenty-five million, about eighteen thousand men and women were guillotined, plus about twenty-five thousand who were shot or killed by other means. But most of the latter figure is accounted for by the reprisals that followed the suppression of counterrevolutionary movements in the Vendée, Lyons, and the south, rebellions that had been cruel and bloody, claiming at least an equal number of victims among the men and women who supported the Republic, not counting casualties on the field of battle. War is always bloody; civil wars are particularly bloody—the Terror occurred in the context of both an international and a civil war. During our own Civil War, six hundred thousand Americans were killed by other Americans, out of a population of thirty-one million. In South Vietnam, that half of a nation with a population of seventeen million, there have been an estimated three hundred and twenty-five thousand deaths since 1965. Compared with either of those episodes in our own history the Terror is a minor affair, numerically. Compared with Hitler's "final solution" or Stalin's purges, it becomes insignificant, even making adjustments for the differences in population.

The ultimate criterion for the effect of violence is its reflection in population statistics. Statistics for the seventeenth century are scanty, but it seems that the population of Germany was reduced by a third in the course of the Thirty Years' War. France suffered a major hemorrhage of its male blood during the insane hecatomb of World War I. The Soviet Union has not yet recovered from its twenty million dead of World War II (plus a few millions starved or killed earlier by Stalinism). The Jewish communities of Eastern Europe were virtually wiped out by Nazism. There were three million Jews in Poland before World War II; there are thirty thousand now—so that even the Poles find it hard to keep anti-Semitism alive. The final statistics for Vietnam are not yet available.

Nothing of the sort during the French Revolution. Even its wars and those that followed under Napoleon had no appreciable effect on the statistician's graphs. After the battle of Austerlitz Napoleon was informed that there were seven thousand French dead, about twice as many as were guillotined in Paris during the Terror. *"Bah!"* he exclaimed, *"c'est une nuit de Paris."* He was quite right; one night of making love in Paris could easily replace seven thousand dead soldiers. The Terror, and even the wars it engendered, had no demographic impact.

If the Terror remains of interest today—and it is certainly more interesting than the battle of Austerlitz—it is not because of the numbers killed, nor even the number of innocent victims. There were innocent victims; there always are even under the best judicial systems; that is one of the usual arguments for the abolition of capital punishment. The Terror pretended to be orderly, methodical, rational, and just. In practice it was often disorganized, arbitrary, whimsical, and prejudiced. No, what is interesting about the Terror is not that it functioned badly but that it functioned at all, that it functioned well enough to have served as a model for so many more efficient totalitarian systems since. And especially that among its victims were almost all the leaders of the Revolution, until the Terror swallowed the Revolution itself.

We return to the moment when the Revolutionary Tribunal was created. It is March 8, 1793. Louis XVI has been dead for forty-six days, during which England and Spain have joined Austria and Prussia as belligerent enemies of France. Danton arrives from Belgium with news of the disastrous turn of military affairs; at his suggestion the Convention sends envoys to the forty-eight Paris *sections* to call for volunteers. The next day the black flag declaring that "the nation is in peril" is flown at the Hôtel de Ville and volunteers are signing up—it seems like the summer of 1792 all over again. During the afternoon the print shops of two Girondin newspapers are sacked by gangs of hired thugs; there are rumors of an "insurrectional committee." Some of the *sections* demand that the Convention deal with traitors before their men leave for the front; one of these petitioners is the painter David (appropriately from the *section du Louvre*).

A deputy named Carrier, still unknown, translates the petitions into a motion. "I demand the establishment of a revolutionary tribunal!" The Convention sends Carrier's motion to its legislative committee, which draws up a preliminary plan that night. Two innovations: a special office will be opened to receive denunciations and all persons who had held any government position before the Revolution, or whose words or conduct seem aristocratic, will be subject to the new jurisdiction.

This plan is submitted to the Convention the next day. One of the Girondins, Vergniaud, protests, "If it is proposed to establish an Inquisition a thousand times more powerful than that of Venice, we must die rather than consent!"

Danton responds by invoking "the supreme tribunal of popular vengeance." An accusing voice cries, "September!"— but that is precisely what Danton means. "The security of the people demands strong measures and drastic actions. There is no middle ground between normal forms and a revolutionary tribunal. Since someone in this assembly has dared recall the bloody days whose memory makes all good citizens tremble, I will say that if there had been a revolutionary tribunal then the people who have so often and cruelly been reproached for those days would not have stained them."

Conclusion—the Convention must create a "sword of liberty" so that the people will not again have to act on its own.

In the circumstances the argument was unanswerable. If any doubts still remained they were removed when Dumouriez deserted to the Austrians; obviously there were traitors everywhere, as Robespierre and Marat had been saying all along.

The new Revolutionary Tribunal went into operation in April and it began slowly. In its first six weeks it tried two hundred and eighty-six cases. Of this total there were sixty-nine guillotined as opposed to one hundred and ninety-two acquitted. The remaining twenty-five were either deported, returned to prison, or remanded to lesser courts. One of the accused would certainly have been condemned by any court —Charlotte Corday. Two were generals whose crimes were that they were noblemen and that they had been defeated. There was also a royalist who had made some suspicious remarks in a café, a fifty-year-old cook who had sung some old army songs in the police station after she had been arrested for public drunkenness, and a twenty-year-old *émigré* who had made the mistake of returning to France and who had shouted "*Vive Louis XVII!*" before he died. And yet, for this period at least, only a fourth of those accused of treason were sentenced to death. It was the relative moderation of the new Revolutionary Tribunal that made it an accepted institution of the revolutionary government, despite the fact that some of those whom it condemned to death were guilty of little more than imprudent behavior.

But by the end of the summer of 1793 the whole context in which the Revolutionary Tribunal operated had changed, both politically and militarily. The leaders of the Gironde had been expelled from the Convention; Marat had been assassinated. The war, begun so thoughtlessly eighteen months before—the way most wars begin—had become a permanent affair, without any glimmer of a light at the end of the tunnel. And France itself had been torn by civil war. The royalists of the Vendée had taken many towns at the mouth of the Loire. Supporters of the expelled Girondin deputies had provoked troubles in sixty of the eighty-three *départements* that had replaced the provinces of the Old Regime. Troops had to be withdrawn from the frontiers to prevent the rebels from joining forces. In short, during the summer of 1793 France seemed to be falling apart. Even if the immediate *internal* threat had lessened by the autumn, with the surrender of the rebels in Marseilles, Bordeaux, and Lyons, the moment was not forgotten.

After the expulsion of the twenty-two leaders of the Gironde, the Convention became dominated by the Mountain, the men who had been considered radicals only nine months earlier. The year that followed is sometimes called the dictatorship of Robespierre, but it was hardly a dictatorship in the modern sense of the word since the Mountain immediately split into various groups and factions that fought one another as bitterly as any of the earlier groups and factions in the various assemblies since the start of the Revolution. And yet Robespierre was preeminent during that year and his peculiar blend of caution and daring determined the course of political events. Also his profound sense of political realities—earlier displayed in his attitude toward the Church—which seems to have deserted him only in the six weeks that preceded his downfall.

Robespierre was aware that his "minority of virtue" had become in fact a minority in the nation as a whole, even if he was able to command majorities in the Convention on all important votes. Since the heady days of the storming of the Bastille, one group after another that had initially supported the Revolution had come to feel that it had gone too far. For some, the most conservative, this had occurred in October 1789 with the march on Versailles. For others it was the nationalization of the Church in the spring of 1790. For others the insurrection of August 1792 and the proclamation of the Republic. For others the execution of the king in January 1793. For others the expulsion of the Girondins in June 1793. Those who remained enthusiastic about the Revolution were clearly in the minority, even if many of the doubtful continued to support the government in Paris because there was, after all, a war going on.

At the same time Robespierre had to deal with the increasingly urgent demands of those who felt that the Revolution had not yet gone far enough, the demands expressed by the leaders of the Paris Commune whose power base was the *sans-culottes*. The alliance between the middle class who had led the Revolution since 1789 and the urban poor who had supported them at every decisive juncture had broken down. As Chaumette, the leader of the Commune, put it, "It has come to open war between the rich and the poor. They want to grind us down. Well then! we must prevent that, we must crush them first, we have the force of numbers!" It was in response to a mass demonstration of the *sans-culottes* that the Convention decreed (September 5, 1793): "The Terror is the order of the day." But the chief demands of the demonstrators had been economic, not political, and these— price controls and rationing—the Convention did not grant until later. The Terror was in part a manifestation of this class struggle and in part a means of preventing it from destroying the Revolution; it showed the *sans-culottes* that their enemies were being punished and at the same time it intimidated them into obedience. Robespierre was aware of the constant threat of yet another Paris insurrection led by the Commune, this time directed not at the king or the Gironde but at *him*.

During the year of his "dictatorship" Robespierre attempted to retain his popularity with the *sans-culottes* while at the same time following a middle-of-the-road policy that would win back the loyalty of that part of the middle class that had been alienated from the Revolution—an attempt he could make only by terrorizing all opposition into impotence. It was a grand bluff but it failed, like most bluffs anywhere but around a poker table. It would have been an improbable *tour de force* in any circumstances—and the rules of the game, by the fall of 1793, made all bets irretrievable since any player who lost a hand went to the guillotine. If Robespierre had really been a dictator in the modern sense he could have spared more of his opponents on the right or the left, held them in reserve in some prison until the right moment to invite them back into the game. But the peculiar mentality of that peculiar year compelled him to send most of them to the scaffold, until he held the only ace left in the pack. And one ace is nothing against a full house of low cards, which is what happened in Thermidor.

Robespierre's *tour de force* might just have worked if everyone involved in the Terror had been as supremely rational as he, as capable of using the Terror as a "sword of Liberty" and using it with restraint. But most human beings are often irrational, and the emotion-charged appellation, the Terror, should alert us to leave a large place for irrational actions if we are to get to any true understanding. At the very least much of what occurred during this period must be described as an overreaction. The circumstances explain why the Terror occurred; Robespierre's policies explain the directions it took; but neither explains the proportions it assumed.

For example, the repression that followed the defeat of the *fédéraliste* middle-class revolt in Lyons. The final assault on that city was led by Robespierre's associate Couthon. On October 8th he received the rebels' surrender. Seeking to avoid further bloodshed, he permitted two thousand armed men to escape before occupying the town. Once there he set up a Revolutionary Tribunal but proceeded slowly, beginning by razing some houses that belonged to the Girondin leaders of the revolt. (The Convention, inspired by the Roman destruction of Carthage, had declared: "Lyons made war on liberty, Lyons no longer exists." The name of the town had been changed to *Ville Affranchie*—Liberated City.) A few rebels were guillotined, many more fled.

But this moderation seemed cowardly to the men of the far left in Paris, who at that moment were at the height of their power. Couthon was recalled; he might well have been guillotined had it not been for Robespierre's protection. In November two new envoys of the Convention arrived in the Liberated City, Collot d'Herbois and Fouché. Before the Revolution Collot d'Herbois had been an actor, director, and playwright; since then he had turned his dramatic talents to revolutionary oratory; now he was to prove himself as a man of action. Fouché, his assistant, was to become Napoleon's chief of espionage and later chief of police; he is often considered the founder of the modern police state.

A great "expiatory fête" was celebrated and the reprisals began. The guillotine, it was decided, worked too slowly. On December 4th sixty men, tied two by two, were exposed to artillery fire after having dug their own graves. Only a third were killed; the rest had to be finished off by rifle shots. After that botched essay the firing squad became the standard means of execution. By February, when the killing was finally stopped, sixteen hundred and sixty-seven men had been shot.

This butchery cannot be ascribed to the heat of combat, since the siege had been over for two months when it began. But Collot, who later was to denounce Robespierre as a "tyrant," was not satisfied; he proposed that sixty thousand workers in Lyons, who he said would never be republicans, be dispersed to other parts of France. Robespierre vetoed the proposal.*

* *Collot's subsequent career remained theatrical. In June 1794 a drunken assassin, Lamiral, took a shot at him as he was going home at 1:00 A.M. (Lamiral's original target had been Robespierre, but the Incorruptible was too well guarded.) Collot survived to become one of the principal actors in the plot against Robespierre a month later. When the political climate changed he was arrested as a terrorist, but instead of being guillotined he was sent to French Guiana in South America. Still a revolutionary, he attempted to organize a revolt of the blacks of the colony. Arrested again, he was imprisoned in the fort of Sinnamary, where he succumbed to yellow fever. As he was being transferred to the hospital in Cayenne he asked for water. He was given a bottle of rum which he gulped down; he expired in acute pain before he reached the hospital.*

Carrier, the delegate who had proposed the establishment of the Revolutionary Tribunal, was sent to Nantes as the envoy of the Convention after the defeat of the royalist peasant revolt in the Vendée. He was responsible for the same sort of excessive vengeance there as Collot's in Lyons, with more imagination as to the means. It should be mentioned that the royalists, when they were winning, committed assorted atrocities and ordered mass executions that claimed hundreds of lives. Carrier seems to have been terrified by the reports of the ferocity of the rebels; he had a personal bodyguard of fifty men. On his orders the prisons of Nantes were crowded with suspects; an epidemic of typhus and cholera broke out that threatened to spread to the town. Carrier sent the rebel leaders to Paris to be judged by the Revolutionary Tribunal there. To get rid of the others, he improvised a novel means of execution, the *noyades*. Rafts were constructed, designed to fall apart when a few ropes were cut. The prisoners were herded aboard, their hands tied to prevent them from swimming; the rafts were towed to the center of the Loire, then sunk. Three or four thousand men and women perished in this fashion, many of them priests and nuns. Carrier wrote, "What a revolutionary torrent is the Loire!" Another four thousand were shot outside the town, their bodies dumped in a quarry and covered with a thin layer of earth so that the odor of a charnel-house hung over the area. It was only then that there was any protest by the inhabitants of the region.

Neither Collot nor Carrier was Robespierre's man; both were political allies of the radicals of the Commune. The point needs to be made because the equation "Robespierre equals the Terror" is still with us. That is of course a myth invented by the men who engineered Robespierre's downfall, the Thermidorians, to absolve themselves of responsibility when the tide of public opinion finally turned. They need a lot of absolving since many of them had been far more bloodthirsty than Robespierre at his worst; Collot and Carrier were both Thermidorians.

But we should hardly go to the other extreme and absolve Robespierre of all responsibility for the excesses of the Terror. From September 1793 to July 1794 the Revolutionary Tribunals in Paris and elsewhere were staffed by men he had appointed; if Robespierre intended the Terror to be a political scalpel, they often used it as a broadsword, so that many perished who were innocent even by Robespierre's standards.

For the moment, however, let us forget about the excesses of the Terror—which are dwarfed, at least numerically, by similar butcheries in our own century—and zoom in to focus on the political Terror in Paris, for which Robespierre is certainly responsible. Let us examine that peculiar phenomenon of "the Revolution, like Saturn, devouring its own children" (to quote Vergniaud, the Girondin leader). Of course Paris is not France, as the French Tourist Office continually reminds us in its ads, and the fascination exerted by the events in Paris during this period has often been blamed for misinterpretations of the overall picture. But it is only by neglecting the rest of France as well as the international context that we have a frame in which the politics of September 1793 through July 1794 makes any sense.

That, in itself, is significant. The leaders of the Paris Commune—Chaumette and Hébert, to mention only two of them—exerted far more influence in Paris than they did in France as a whole. It is true that Hébert's journal *Le Père Duchesne* had replaced Marat's *l'Ami du Peuple* as the voice of the radical left, and that it was distributed with government subsidies to the troops in editions that numbered six hundred thousand, an unprecedented circulation for any newspaper at that time. But it was only because the Convention and its executive committees were in Paris, subject to the threat of an insurrection organized by the Commune, that those leaders could not be ignored. Eventually, of course, the undue influence of the *sans-culottes* of Paris ceased to determine national policy, but only after the fall of Robespierre.

We can view the events of that year as a classic tragedy, with Robespierre as a tragic hero. He has all the qualifications for the role—his incorruptibility, his stature and eminence, his vision of a society ruled by virtuous men. And of course the tragic flaws that are the inverse of all his qualities—his lack of compassion for the corruptibility of others, his increasing vulnerability as he becomes more and more isolated, his blind spot as to the limitations that the war imposed on his projected transformation of France. That blind spot is particularly interesting, since no other leader of the Revolution displayed such an acute awareness of political realities—on all other issues.

But that tragedy still awaits its dramatist; we have yet to attend the première of a great play entitled "Thermidor." Part of the explanation for the neglect of his tempting subject is Robespierre's bad press; for a century after his death he was regarded as a villain, not a flawed hero. The greater obstacle is the amount of exposition required for the drama to make sense. During the final year of Robespierre's life all the threads of the Revolution are tied up in one tight knot; to unravel that knot requires a knowledge of the entire fabric. Büchner chose to ignore that problem in writing *Danton's Death*, which may be why the play has never been as popular as it deserves. The form of the novel is really more appropriate—if Dostoevski had been interested he would have found in Robespierre, Danton, Desmoulins, *et al.* an ideal set of characters. Lacking Dostoevski we have Michelet, who uses many of the techniques of the novel with consummate skill; no one who has read the final third of his *Histoire de la Révolution Française* can ever forget it. Historians since Michelet have added new facts and interpretations, but they make their readers do the work of re-creating the human reality.

In the fall of 1793 the Place de la Révolution was the set for a series of spectacular executions that took the lives of many of the leading players of the earlier stages of the revolution. Marie-Antoinette was guillotined. Also the duc d'Orléans, her brother-in-law, who had sat on the "Mountain" alongside Robespierre and Marat just a year before and voted for the death of the king. Also Bailly, former mayor of Paris (for him the guillotine was moved to the Champ de Mars to dramatize his guilt for the "massacre" of 1791). Also Mme Dubarry, thrown in for effect. And, most important, the twenty-two leaders of the Gironde who had been formally under arrest since the previous June.

Putting aside the question of the guilt or innocence of particular individuals—Marie-Antoinette was even *more* guilty than her accusers knew; her trial was an inconclusive, shabby affair—these executions can be regarded as circuses to make the people of Paris forget they had no bread. The victims, in a sense, were so many morsels thrown by Robespierre to the lions of the Commune to keep them happy until he was ready to deal with *them*.

The radicals of the Commune wanted to use the Terror as an instrument for the redistribution of wealth—a position that Robespierre would adopt, if only tentatively, the following spring. They wanted social equality, not merely equality before the law; they wanted the revolutionary government to curb the growing power of the businessmen who were making fortunes by selling supplies to the armies, to assure that every worker in Paris, and his family, had at least enough to eat. But Robespierre knew that Paris was not France, that the demands of the radicals of the Commune could not become working realities by decree. To *over*simplify, France in 1793, having just eliminated the vestiges of feudalism, was not ready to jump forward into socialism. Nor did Robespierre, the middle-class lawyer from Arras, want to make that jump.

But the radicals of the Commune made the mistake of adding a doctrinaire antireligious attitude to their social and economic revindications. In November 1793 they organized a *"Fête de la Raison"* at the cathedral of Notre-Dame to demonstrate the triumph of Reason over the forces of religion. Many detachments of the National Guard were required to be present at this rather dull ceremony in which an actress played the role of Liberty, wearing a white robe. Robespierre was aware, as the radicals of the Commune were not, of the deep attachment of French peasants to religion as the sole consolation in their miserable lives. Aside from his personal beliefs, Robespierre felt that the Revolution had enough difficulties to contend with as it was; there was no sense in arousing the hostility of the huge mass of simple believing people whom it was supposed to benefit. It did not take long for Robespierre to denounce the *Fête de la Raison* as a "counterrevolutionary" maneuver.

Robespierre was not bloodthirsty, otherwise he would no longer be of interest. There are too many bloodthirsty actors in that often superficial pageant we call history for that characteristic to arouse our curiosity. It is Robespierre's cold-blooded attempt to use the Terror as a political scalpel that remains fascinating. We must return for a moment to the grisly arithmetic of death to keep our sense of proportion. Paris, where the Revolutionary Tribunal was under the thumb of Robespierre, never saw anything approaching the large-scale exterminations of Lyons or Nantes. From October 1793 through the end of Germinal in the spring of 1794— the era of all the great political trials—there were five hundred and fifty-five executions in the capital. During the same period the Revolutionary Tribunal acquitted five hundred and three suspects and sent fifty-eight back to prison.

The political intrigues of the winter of 1793–1794 are

confusing if fascinating. All the actors were drawn from what had been the far left, only a year before. A series of accusations and counteraccusations revealed that many of these men had associated with bankers of foreign origin (Austrian, Swiss, Belgian). By that fact alone they became "suspect" of being agents for the Coalition. It was generally believed and it may have been true that the English were pouring money into France to buy agents and wreck the economy. And the economy of France was in a terrible state. The paper money issued by a succession of revolutionary governments had depreciated disastrously on all international markets, and the resulting inflation was bringing commerce to a halt. The food supply of Paris was in a precarious state and was rendered still more precarious by riots during which shops were looted and by holdups on the outskirts of the city that prevented farmers from bringing their produce to the markets.

(Notice, by the way, that two of the problems that had sparked the Revolution five years earlier had reappeared—a financial crisis with rising prices and food shortages. Add to these the coincidence of a hard winter. You can see why some people felt the Revolution had accomplished nothing.)

There were, as always, two factions vying for power in the Convention, this time both stemming from the Mountain of a year before. On the left the radicals (*ultras*), whose most prominent member was Hébert, the journalist. On the right the moderates (*citras*), sometimes called the Indulgents, although they could be as ferocious as their opponents on occasion; their most prominent leader was Danton. Both factions knew that they could win, ultimately, only by gaining the approval of Robespierre. The leaders of both factions, by mutual accusation and counteraccusation, were tarred with the brush of corruption and the suspicion of treason because of their association with foreign bankers. Many of the accusations seem to have been well-founded. Never had

Robespierre's reputation for being Incorruptible stood him in better stead. And it was not only a reputation—of all the leaders of the Revolution he seems to have been the only one who could resist an invitation to a good dinner.

Robespierre was quite clever in playing these two factions against each other, first seeming to favor one, then the other. In the course of these maneuvers he got everyone to vote for the policies he believed in. The radicals abandoned their campaign against religion. Hébert denied that he had ever been an atheist and used his journal to advise the soldiers to read the gospels for true revolutionary doctrine. The moderates permitted Robespierre to staff government posts with men he picked. Both factions voted for the arrest of some associates when Robespierre wanted them removed.

At times Robespierre could be severe. He asserted that "moderatism has the same relation to moderation as impotence to chastity" (one of the few faintly witty remarks to be found in his speeches); he denounced "ultrarevolutionaries," claiming that their policies served the counterrevolution (and implying that the men themselves were counterrevolutionaries "under a mask of patriotism"). At times he could be humane. He let it be known that he did not approve of the excesses committed in Nantes and Lyons. There were seventy-three delegates who had been imprisoned for having signed a petition protesting the expulsion of the Girondins; Robespierre refused to bring them to trial, saying that many had merely been misled. He encouraged new accusations and revelations by accepting them as proof of patriotism. Men who thought they might be compromised by some of their associations were eager to be the first to denounce their friends, in the hope that this conduct would put them in the good graces of the Incorruptible. All the while Robespierre maintained a noble stance above the battle, deploring factionalism, speaking often of the necessity of restoring the unity of the Revolution.

The true audience for this performance, much of it played in the setting of the Jacobin Club, was the mass of uncommitted delegates in the Convention, the Plain (or the Swamp). The web of accusations became so extensive that there was hardly a delegate who did not fear he might be next on the list. It was Robespierre's relative clemency, as testified to by his protection of the seventy-three who had signed the Girondin petition, that led these men to hope that Robespierre would spare them if they presented a low but correct profile. They attended sessions of the Convention as rarely as possible, and when they did attend they approved everything that Robespierre proposed.

This is certainly politics at its dirtiest but not, in its broad outlines, so very different from what has been seen in various state legislatures in the United States when scandals and crooked deals came to light. (There was more than a bit of Robespierre in Huey Long.) With one important difference, of course—what awaited the accused men was not loss of power, disgrace, or impeachment but rather death. There is a certain finality to death, an irreversibility that completely alters the nature of politics, even dirty politics.

The hidden weakness of Robespierre's position was that his power had come to depend, in large measure, on the continuation of the Terror, or, more precisely, the political terror. It was, of course, Robespierre's own attitudes, his high and rigid standards of personal conduct, his belief that there were conspiracies everywhere, his assumption that anyone whose actions had ever harmed the Revolution must have intended to harm the Revolution, that anyone who made a mistake must be a counterrevolutionary, that anyone who accepted a bribe must be a traitor, that was largely responsible for raising the political stakes to the point where death was the usual punishment for any error. Now Robespierre was caught in his own trap. The one thing he could not do was stop the Terror or even slow it down. This had been demonstrated in October when his friend Couthon had been so lenient toward the rebels in Lyons. On that occasion the Indulgents and the Hébertists had united *against* Robespierre in calling for more blood. It took all Robespierre could do to prevent Couthon from being arrested.

So the political terror was hardly a one-man show; it was the product of a collective mentality that can at least partially be explained by revolutionary zeal. Except perhaps for Danton, none of the important actors was cynical enough to accept dirty politics as a part of the Revolution. They were all inebriated by their own rhetoric, inspired by the heroes of ancient Greece and Rome. The slogan of the time added "OU LA MORT!" ("or death") to *liberté, égalité, fraternité*. Even Camille Desmoulins inscribed "Live free or die!" on the first page of his *Vieux Cordelier*. With ordinary soldiers dying on the frontiers or fighting the remaining rebels within France they thought it unworthy that Paris should not be on the front line.

And yet another sort of rhetoric blossomed in the shadows cast by the heroic postures, one that has unfortunately proved more durable. The guillotine in Paris may have claimed only five hundred and fifty-five victims in seven months, but by April 1794 the prisons of the capital were choked with seven thousand "suspects" who never knew when they might be brought to trial. The category of *suspect* had been created by the law of September 17, 1793, and it included not only former noblemen, *émigrés*, and priests but also anyone who by word or deed had shown himself to be an "enemy of liberty," anyone who had been refused a "certificate of civism" by his *section*. Every local assembly, every town and village, had its political intrigues, its accusations and counteraccusations that mirrored those at the Jacobins, its crop of informers who found that denouncing their enemies was an easy path to personal advancement. The press was no longer free; it was more severely censored than it had been before the Revolution. In Paris a well-organized secret police kept tabs on public opinion. In high circles certain statements might be said to *frise la guillotine*—"be within a hair's breadth of death," an accusation not to be considered lightly. The people had invented a number of slang terms for the guillotine: the little window, the national razor, the cat trap, the money press; the executioner was dubbed, affectionately, Charlot; the basket in which the heads fell was *sans farine*—without flour. In the streets children made a game of mock executions.

In short the whole mentality of the modern totalitarian state had been created overnight. Because it was all improvised it did not hide in the abstruse jargon of twentieth-century bureaucracies (although Robespierre's phrase, "the despotism of liberty," came close). There was no need for an Orwell to write an *Animal Farm* since the words *suspect, certificat de civisme, friser la guillotine, rasoir national* spoke for themselves. Instead of an Orwell there was Camille Desmoulins and his *Le Vieux Cordelier.*

Now, Desmoulins' credentials as a humanitarian were highly "suspect." He had been the Attorney General of the Lamppost, he was a close associate of Robespierre, his attacks on the Girondins had been vicious, unprincipled, and unfair (which he regretted; at their trial he exclaimed, "Poor men! my book has killed them!"). In *Le Vieux Cordelier* itself, a series of seven pamphlets written between December 1793 and April 1794, he attacked Hébert and his followers in terms that could only contribute to sending *them* to the guillotine. He goes along with the conspiratorial obsession of the times that attributed all the ills of France to the evil genius of the prime minister of England, "the enemy of the human race," by beginning his first number (perhaps ironically), "Oh Pitt! I pay homage to your genius!" And yet despite all that there are passages where he speaks

in the voice of a sane man who has been clapped in a mad-
house and still insists that he is sane:

> Oh my dear fellow citizens! Have we
> become so vile that we must bow to such
> idols? No, Liberty, the liberty of heaven,
> is not a chorus girl from the Opéra, is not
> a red stocking cap, a dirty shirt or rags.
> Liberty is happiness, reason, equality,
> justice; liberty is the Declaration of the
> Rights of Man, your sublime constitution!
> Shall I fall at her feet, shed my blood for
> her? open the prisons that contain those
> two hundred thousand citizens you call
> suspect; in the Declaration of Rights there
> is no mention of a prison for suspects, only
> prisons for the guilty. Suspicion is a cause
> for investigation, not prison; there is no
> such thing as a *suspect*, only an indicted
> criminal. Don't think that this measure will
> harm the Republic; it will be the most
> revolutionary ever taken. You think to
> exterminate all your enemies by the
> guillotine? what madness! For every man
> who dies on the scaffold you make ten
> enemies among his friends and family. Do
> you really believe that these women, these
> old men, these cripples, these egoists, these
> camp-followers whom you imprison, are
> dangerous? Of your enemies only the
> cowardly and the sick remain in your midst.
> Those who are strong and courageous have
> emigrated. They have died in Lyons or in
> the Vendée; the remnant is unworthy of
> your anger.

He calls for freedom of the press, indignant that the
opposition in England can publish its views while that is for-
bidden in France:

> See how boldly the *Morning Chronicle*
> attacks Pitt and the war effort. What

> journalist in France would dare reveal the
> mistakes of our committees, our generals,
> the Jacobins, the ministers, the Commune,
> as the opposition reveals the errors of the
> British prime minister. And I, a Frenchman,
> I, Camille Desmoulins, must be less free
> than an English journalist! The idea is
> revolting. Don't tell me that we are in the
> middle of a revolution and that the liberty
> of the press must be suspended during a
> revolution. Is not England as well as the
> rest of Europe also affected by the
> Revolution? Should the principle of the
> liberty of the press be less sacred in Paris
> than in London? . . . What is the difference
> between a republic and a monarchy? Only
> one thing: the freedom to speak and write.
> Establish liberty of the press in Moscow
> and tomorrow Moscow will be a republic.

Desmoulins had shown the first two numbers of the *Vieux Cordelier* to Robespierre before publication; he approved them. If they criticized certain excesses of the Terror it was within the context of an attack on the Hébertists; Robespierre also had attacked the *ultras* for their "exaggerations." Number 3 was something else again and Camille did not show it to Robespierre before publication. Using the transparent disguise of an attack on *monarchy* (which was a dead issue in December 1793)—long citations from Tacitus, some of them fabricated, condemning the reigns of the first Roman emperors—Desmoulins attacked the very principle of the Terror:

> Accused of counterrevolution, Cremutius
> Cordus, for having called Brutus and
> Cassius the last true Romans. Accused of
> counterrevolution, one of the descendants
> of Cassius for possessing a portrait of his
> great-grandfather. Accused of counter-
> revolution, Mamercus Scaurus, for having

written a tragedy with some ambiguous
verses. . . .
    You had to show joy at the death of a
friend or relative if you didn't wish to
expose yourself to peril. . . . Men were
afraid that fear itself might mark them as
guilty. . . .
    Was a citizen popular? He might start
a civil war. Suspect.
    Were you rich? Suspect.
    Were you poor? You must be hiding
something. Suspect.
    Every day a new informer made his
triumphal entry into the palace of death.
. . . Accusation was the only way to get
ahead. . . . The courts, protectors of life
and liberty, had become slaughterhouses
where the terms "punishment" and
"confiscation" hid what was only theft and
assassination.

In a footnote Desmoulins quotes his old rival, Marat,
"whose authority is almost sacred, judging from the honors
given his memory" (Camille could not resist that jealous remark): "Any accusation before a tribunal for an opinion is an
injustice." He goes on to state that the rule of despotism is "It
is better that many innocent men perish than a single guilty
man escape" while that of republican justice is "It is better
that many guilty men go free than that a single innocent be
punished"—and leaves it to his readers to draw their own
conclusions.

They drew them. Number 3 of the *Vieux Cordelier* became
the Bible of all counterrevolutionaries (and they did exist).
In the climate of the Terror, such a reception was not a good
omen.

But Camille persisted. Number 4 begins:

There are those who condemn Number 3
where, according to them, I drew parallels
that tend to show the Republic and true

> patriots in a bad light. . . .They think the
> pamphlet refuted and the present state
> of affairs justified by saying, "We know that
> the present reign is not that of liberty, but
> be patient, some day you will be free."
> Apparently they think that liberty, like a
> child, must outgrow its shouts and tears
> before it is mature. But it is rather the
> nature of liberty that, to enjoy it, one has
> but to desire it. A people is free when it
> wants to be free. . . . Liberty has neither
> old age nor childhood. It has only one age,
> that of strength and vigor.

In the meanwhile—which is to say the four weeks that
saw the publication of Numbers 1–4 of the *Vieux Cordelier*
—the political tide had changed. The *ultras*, who seemed
ready to take power in November, had been called to order
by Robespierre; some of them had been arrested. Robespierre, continuing his juggling act, now turned on the Indulgents. Camille, having proposed a "Committee of Clemency,"
was an obvious target. He hastened to publish Number 5,
which is a long self-defense combined with an attack on the
corruption of those who said that he risked the guillotine for
Numbers 3 and 4. "And so I am treated as an aristocrat
within a hair's breadth of the guillotine, while Nicolas is a
sans-culotte, within a hair's breadth of a fortune." The defense was weak; on January 7th Camille was put on the
carpet at the Jacobins. The offending pamphlets were read
aloud and condemned by the membership.

Robespierre was disposed to be kind. He defended his
friend's good faith even as he attacked his "heresies" (the
word is Robespierre's). He tried to save Camille by minimiz-
ing his importance. "We must make a distinction between
the individual and his publications. He is a child who has
been led astray by bad companions. . . . I ask only that as an
example his pamphlets be burned by the Society."

To which Camille, perhaps out of injured pride, responded, "Burning is not a refutation, Robespierre!"

I notice that I have been led to use the kind of language that belongs more properly to fiction: "Robespierre was disposed to be kind"—"Camille, perhaps out of injured pride, responded. . . ." The subject seems to demand it. And yet, if it were only a matter of an ordinary political quarrel, even a dirty political quarrel (which may be the same thing), such language could easily be avoided. It is the guillotine waiting in the wings, the fundamental irrationality of the Terror, that excites our curiosity about the motives behind every word and action.

For what an historian with *no* reticence about using the language of the novel can do with the subject, this passage from Michelet.

> [Robespierre] could not dream of arguing
> with Desmoulins. A god who argues is lost.
> Besides, Robespierre's lyre had but one string,
> which sounded always the same note, serious
> and mournful. He had no defense against
> irony. . . . He was incapable of making fun
> of Desmoulins, but he could kill him.
>
> We have no doubts that he was terrified
> the first time the idea occurred to him. That
> amiable, kind, good comrade who had done
> so much for Robespierre's renown! Were
> these memories nothing? Was there still a
> human being in Robespierre? Even if he had
> crossed the Styx and returned on the tide of
> the dead, did there not remain in some
> hidden corner of his being a drop of woman's
> blood? I maintain and will swear that his
> heart was torn.
>
> Besides, to kill Desmoulins implied much
> more; there was no stopping after that. What
> was poor Camille? Only an attractive blossom
> on a branch of Danton. There was no up-
> rooting one without the other. That knotty

> tree, tall and powerful, had strewn its leaves
> to the winds, but even as it remained what
> hand could be sure of chopping it down?*

Camille persisted. In Number 6 of the *Vieux Cordelier,* suppressed before it could be published but undoubtedly read by Robespierre, he attacked the essential principle of the political terror:

> I believe that a representative is no more
> infallible than inviolable. Even if, at some
> moment during a revolution, public safety
> commands restraints on the liberty of the
> press, I believe that a deputy should never
> lose the right to express his opinion; I believe
> that he should be permitted to make a
> mistake; that it is to allow for error that the
> French people has so many representatives,
> so that the few can be corrected by the many.
> I believe that without this unlimited liberty
> there is no such thing as a National
> Assembly.

Common sense, perhaps, but in the irrational atmosphere of the Terror an *extreme* position. So extreme as to merit the guillotine.

Number 7, published posthumously, ends with the words of the Spanish priests to Montezuma before he was killed: "The gods are thirsty."

This long discussion of the *Vieux Cordelier* tends to exaggerate Desmoulins' importance. Camille was only a supporting player, an "attractive flower," a journalist, opinion-

---

* *My translation is a bit free, as becomes the subject. I do not mean to imply that Michelet was "only a novelist," as our skeptical and naive age would put it. Michelet was an historian who was not ashamed to write as a novelist when the techniques of fiction were the most direct and accurate way of saying what he meant. Our contemporaries indulge in the same speculations about the hidden thoughts and motivations of individuals—as indeed they must—but without the courage to admit it. The result is often confusion and bad writing.*

molder, but not a principal. And yet he did speak out when so many others remained silent.

The last act of the drama of the *ultras* and the *citras* took only one month—March 13 to April 13, 1794. (Act IV had ended with a threatened insurrection by the radicals that got nowhere.) Like an incompetent playwright who doesn't know what else to do with his characters, Robespierre sent everyone to the guillotine. First the Hébertists were arrested, tried, and executed. Then Danton and Desmoulins took the same road. The Revolutionary Tribunal served as the *deus ex machina* and it was indeed a machine by this time; the actors barely had a moment to gasp their memorable last words. There were a few exciting scenes, if hurried, but in the end the stage was littered with corpses. No one noticed, for the moment, that among the dead was the Revolution itself. The final mopping up operation saw the widows of Hébert and Desmoulins along with Chaumette and the former archbishop of Paris all sharing the same tumbril tumbling down the rue St.-Honoré to the Place de la Révolution. By then the shops on the rue St.-Honoré had begun to put up their shutters when the *charettes* went by.

The Terror was not over—its bloodiest weeks in Paris were still to come. But what remained was an epilogue: Thermidor. Robespierre proved not only a bad dramatist but also a strangely inept politician, since he killed so many of his best friends and left alive the men who three months later sent him to his death. I am sure that Camille Desmoulins, at least, would have protested against declaring Robespierre an "outlaw."

Thermidor has become a recipe for cooking lobsters— appropriately enough, because they turn such a fiery red and of course die. But before we go on to that we must pull back from the tight Parisian cockpit for a larger view if we are not to be left with nothing more than a bungled play.

The Pursuit of Happiness

Le but de la société est le bonheur commun.
—"Constitution of 1793," Article I

Happiness is a new idea in Europe.
—*St.-Just*

. . . life, liberty and the pursuit of happiness. —*Jefferson*

Anyone who was not alive during the years around 1780 has not known happiness. —*Talleyrand*

OBVIOUSLY there is happiness and happiness. Actually Talleyrand said "*le plaisir de vivre*—the joy of being alive," and his "anyone" was clearly neither a peasant nor a worker. As for St.-Just, how can "happiness" be a new idea? Jefferson's "pursuit of happiness" was a last-minute substitution for Locke's original "property" as a fundamental right, along with life and liberty; and yet for two hundred years the pursuit of happiness in the United States has been, for the most part, the pursuit of wealth. I have not dared translate *le bonheur commun* since its force resides in its ambiguity, but we can at least say what it is *not*—it is not

[169]

salvation, in Christian terms; it is not the triumph of any one group or class; it is not that pessimistic formula, "the greatest good for the greatest number." Perhaps the article means, "The purpose of society is to make *everyone* happy." That "happiness" would certainly have been a new idea in Europe, and everywhere else.

I introduce all these perplexities as a reminder that the French Revolution was much more than merely a political event. It was inspired by the Enlightenment, which attempted, on paper, to transform all aspects of human life. The men of the Revolution tried to do the same thing, no longer exclusively on paper. We could call this attempt a cultural revolution, had not the recent Chinese experience modified the meaning of those words. Semantics aside, beginning in 1789 France experienced a profound cultural and social revolution, some of it trivial, some of it accidental, some of it still only words and hopes, but in its net result a real change in the way French men and women related to one another and even to themselves. And much of that change persisted even when the net political results of the Revolution had been reversed.

It is much harder to describe cultural and social change than political change; there are no constitutions of 1791 and 1793 to serve as mileposts. But it is clear that when Talleyrand, long after Napoleon, spoke of *le plaisir de vivre* in *les années voisines de 1780,* he had reverted to the vocabulary of his youth, that of the Old Regime. It is said that Talleyrand was once stopped by a beggar to whom he refused even a penny. "But sir," said the beggar, "I have to live!" Talleyrand answered, "I don't see why that is necessary." That again is the language of the Old Regime; a man born after the Revolution would have responded with some hypocritical platitude.

The society of the Old Regime (in both senses of the word "society") was a society rotten to the core that knew it and

enjoyed it. That constitutes its charm today when both
Talleyrand and the beggar are safely dead. Today Louis
Quinze and Louis Seize pieces of furniture and bric-à-brac
fetch top prices when they are auctioned at Sotheby's or
Parke-Bernet because Texas millionaires like to furnish their
air-conditioned showplaces in the style of eighteenth-century
French aristocrats. The paintings of Watteau, Fragonard,
and Boucher, as well as thousands of engravings depicting
plump gentlemen calling on ladies in their ravishing morning *deshabillés,* still seem the ultimate image of *le plaisir
de vivre* for the square majority of today's superrich—challenged only by Renoir's Paris workers in their undershirts
enjoying a Sunday outing. But the reality was not all that
charming.

The Old Regime was a society with a parasitic class at its
apex: the nobility (one and a half percent of the population) who lived on inherited wealth as well as government
and church pensions and sinecures that they did nothing to
earn. There were colonels who never saw their troops, abbots
who lived in a grand house in Paris and never went near the
monastery and whose revenues paid for their gilded coaches
and liveried servants. Within that class, which was also a
caste, there was a miniature social pyramid, with poor country noblemen at the bottom and the Court at the top. But life
at Court, that endless house party in the barracklike palace
at Versailles, had grown so boring that even the royal family
tried to escape whenever possible, which is why Marie-
Antoinette built the Petit Trianon as well as the rustic
Hameau, where she and her ladies-in-waiting played at being
milkmaids and shepherdesses.

The two moral pillars of the Old Regime were religion
and the monarchy, the Church and the king. By 1789 both
were in wide disrepute. The Church owned ten percent of
the land and treated its peasants no better than the nobility
did theirs, which was not surprising since the upper echelons

of the hierarchy were reserved for noblemen (like Charles-Maurice de Talleyrand-Périgord, named bishop of Autun in 1788 despite his reputation for impiety). Many convents were only fancy finishing schools and some were luxurious boarding houses where unmarried or widowed noblewomen lived a comfortable and worldly life. The vows of chastity taken by noblemen in the Church were as blithely ignored as the vows of matrimony taken by those out of it. As for the monarchy, its "image" had been ruined by Louis XV, who kept a personal brothel at Versailles known as *le parc aux cerfs* and took the already notorious Dubarry as his mistress when the more respectable Mme de Pompadour grew too old. Stolid and serious Louis XVI was an improvement, but his virtues were more than balanced by the extravagance of Marie-Antoinette, her reputed lovers, her patronage of the sorcerer Cagliostro, and the Affair of the Diamond Necklace.

None of this was confined to France, of course. Casanova's most interesting amour was with a Venetian nun who was already the mistress of the French ambassador, the Cardinal de Bernis (the diplomat who arranged the "reversal of alliances"—according to Casanova, Bernis watched through a peephole while the great lover and "*M*" demonstrated their sexual prowess). Nowhere in Europe were monarchs still taken seriously as God's regents on earth. George III of England had spells of total madness; Catherine the Great had a succession of official lovers; Frederick the Great's father was a petty tyrant who amused himself by drilling a regiment of seven-foot giants; Frederick himself, probably the most interesting despot of the century, tore up treaties as scraps of paper and lived fairly openly as a homosexual when he was not leading his troops into battle (he also played the flute, entertained Voltaire, and commissioned concerti by Johann Sebastian Bach). But in France the decadence of official values seemed more acute than elsewhere, partly because there was a large, articulate, educated class of men of letters to write about it, and partly because in France, with its great natural wealth, the contrast between the grinding misery of the peasants and workers and the luxurious life of the nobility was particularly flagrant.

The decadence was not only institutional, it was also personal. With plenty of money (never *enough*, of course) and too much free time the nobility of the Old Regime spent their lives as most people in that situation spend theirs: busy with fashion, social climbing, and sex (in French *"la vie sentimentale,"* which sounds better). In this last category they often displayed great ingenuity and persistence, which led to the myth that the French somehow know more about sex than other people and are more highly sexed (they don't and aren't). There were, of course, noblemen who devoted their lives to science, philosophy, philanthropy, to schemes for improving agriculture or political reform; the noblemen (like Talleyrand) who would be among the liberals of 1789. But if we are to understand the Puritanical phase of the Revolution, the phase dominated by Robespierre, the Incorruptible, we must remember that fashionable life and sexual license were equated with each other in the minds of most Frenchmen, and also equated with the nobility.

The *bourgeoisie*—the bankers, merchants, factory-owners, government officials who really kept the country functioning —had a different moral and cultural outlook, long before the Revolution. There were, to be sure, a few who aped the clothes, carriages, manners, and amours of the nobility; but in general other values prevailed in middle-class circles: family, hard work, thrift, education.* Most of the *philosophes* had come from this class and of course it was the class

* *In 1671 Molière had satirized the rich middle class who put on airs in* Le Bourgeois gentilhomme. *It is interesting that the values in the play are all middle-class, not aristocratic. (Molière was the son of a merchant who was commissioned upholsterer to the king.) We do not laugh at M. Jourdain because he is bourgeois, but because he makes himself ridiculous trying to be a "gentleman."*

most receptive to the ideas and ideals of the Enlightenment, which were, after all, a modern restatement of the values by which they already lived. It was the bourgeoisie that presided over the first years of the Revolution and that was, in the end, its chief beneficiary—even if, in the interim, the Revolution went a little too far (for *them*), partially because of the influence of that renegade, Robespierre.

But Robespierre, personally, always remained completely bourgeois, even to his dress. In February 1794, during the most radical phase of the Revolution, he summed up the opposition of middle-class values and aristocratic vices in his "Report on the principles of political morality that should guide the Convention in the domestic affairs of the republic":

> In our country we wish to substitute:
>> morality for egotism
>> probity for honor
>> principles for customs
>> duties for etiquette
>> the empire of reason for the tyranny
>>> of fashion
>> scorn of vice for scorn of misfortune
>> self-respect for insolence
>> greatness of soul for pride
>> love of glory for love of money
>> honest men for high society
>> merit for intrigue
>> genius for wit
>> truth for brilliance
>> the joy of life for the boredom of sensuality
>> the greatness of man for the pettiness
>>> of the high-born.

Aside from one phrase—"love of glory for love of money" —occasioned by the circumstances of the moment (the war) —that is an adequate statement of the moral precepts of the Enlightenment. But it is also a statement of those middle-class, capitalistic virtues that Max Weber called the Protestant ethic, whose origins the founder of sociology discerned as far back as the fifteenth century. The values are the same as those that guided the men of the American Revolution. And yet the passage could not have been written by an American, because the thirteen colonies had no native aristocracy to be overthrown. (That, even more than the fact that George III was across the ocean in England, is why the American Revolution was so much less a social revolution than its French counterpart.)*

And yet by the time Robespierre articulated those anti-aristocratic ideas, they were already being challenged by the spokesmen for a class that had never had ideals, much less spokesmen, before—the *sans-culottes*. To see how that happened, we must take a look at the revolutionary press.

The censorship of the Old Regime authorized only two newspapers to be published in Paris, the *Gazette de France* and the *Journal de Paris*. These continued in their established fashion throughout much of the Revolution. For the last half of 1789, most of the *Journal de Paris* consists of summaries of the proceedings of the National Assembly, although there is some more adventurous reporting, such as a delayed account of the fall of the Bastille. Each issue begins with a weather report, evidence that the Paris Observatory continued to function without interruption; there are announcements of plays, operas, and concerts at ten different theaters (again, almost without interruption); there are obituaries, book reviews, stock-market quotations, letters to the editor, notices of houses for sale and apartments for rent —all reminders of how much of Parisian life went on unchanged. Yet at times the Revolution makes its presence felt

---

* *The so-called Southern Aristocrats were capitalistic farmers growing a cash crop (first tobacco, later cotton) in the plantation system based on black slavery. Black slavery, as opposed to the feudal serfdom of Europe, was an invention of capitalistic colonialism; it had begun on sugar plantations in the Canary Islands in the fifteenth century.*

even in these minor notices. In December the editors announce that their annual supplement, *l'Année Littéraire*, will henceforth be called *l'Année Littéraire et Politique* because, "Intelligence has assumed a new direction. . . . Republican ideas have taken the place of the desire for pleasure and frivolous amusements." The editors obviously regret the change. "We are not turning away from literature; it is literature that turns away from us." But they assure their readers that "the true principles of religion and morality are fixed and invariable . . . on this essential point *l'Année Littéraire,* superior to any sort of revolution, has not changed and will not change."

Brave words of a sort, even if they proved to be blowing in the wind. Once the censorship was abolished, or rather simply forgotten, the *Journal de Paris* had dozens of competitors. An engraving of the period shows a street vendor surrounded by all her wares on a Paris sidewalk; papers were also available for those who did not want to buy in cafés and taverns. These sheets, many of them purely opinion and entirely written by one man, the equivalent of today's columnists, covered the whole spectrum of opinion, ranging from l'Abbé Royou's *l'Ami du Roi* to Marat's *l'Ami du Peuple.* Everyone, whatever his point of view, could find something to read that he would find agreeable and that would keep him ex cited about political affairs; no literate person could possibly relapse into an exclusive preoccupation with his private affairs, as he could have done so easily, and was encouraged to do, before the Revolution. In that sense the medium was the message, and it is a sign of a fairly high level of literacy that so many of the poorest workers and artisans of Paris— the *sans-culottes*—got the message. The power of the press was one of the prime movers of the early years of the Revolution. This makes all the more poignant the protests of Danton ("Freedom of the press or death!") and Desmoulins ("Establish freedom of the press in Moscow and tomorrow

Moscow will be a republic") during the later era when the
Terror had imposed its own censorship, far more thorough
than that of the Old Regime, since the men of the Terror
knew from experience just what a free press could do.

After January 1791 Marat had a competitor for the attention and affections of the *sans-culottes,* Hébert's *Le Père
Duchesne.* Hébert's sheet was something new in journalism,
more like today's underground press than anything else.
(Although eventually *Le Père Duchesne* became the first
mass-circulation periodical in history.) If Marat was always
radical in his ideas and often violent in his rhetoric, his
language, at least, remained correct. But Hébert, instead of
speaking directly as himself, took as his mouthpiece a figure
from folklore, an old soldier who used the language of the
people, the language of taverns and army barracks, with
every sentence peppered with obscenities. The full title of his
journal was "The Great Anger of Father Duchesne"; its mast-
head was a crude woodcut showing the hearty veteran smoking a pipe, an ax in his hand and two pistols stuck in his
sash; under this the legend read, "I am the true Père
Duchesne, fuckit!"

Of course Hébert's mouthpiece did not really speak as an
uneducated veteran; that would have been too limiting. Le
Père Duchesne could quote Molière and Rousseau on occasion and showed a surprising familiarity with Greek and
Roman history. But the popular audience that Hébert addressed was no doubt flattered to be told, by implication, that
they were just as clever as any of the lawyers in the Assembly. As for the slang and the obscenities, they were not only
amusing but had the additional advantage (which may seem
like a disadvantage) of alienating the middle-class liberals
who presided over the first phases of the Revolution; they
were *not in good taste,* which, for the men of the Enlightenment, was a far worse sin than blasphemy. (Even when the
philosophes amused themselves by writing hard-core pornog-

raphy, and some of them did, the language was always polished.) Hébert wanted to be loved by the poor and hated by the rich and he was. Herewith an example, whose subject is as significant as its mode of expression:

> *LA GRANDE COLÈRE DU PÈRE DUCHESNE*
>
> Against the merchants who say fuckit to the *maximum* (price controls), who hoard, willy-nilly, all the grain; against the grocers who steal day after day from the poor *sans-culottes;* against the wine sellers who poison them with their buggering mixtures . . . against the shoemakers who can't find leather for the poor *sans-culottes* but have plenty of cardboard to put under the soles of our brave armies. His great delight to see that little by little the virtue of the holy guillotine will deliver us from all these munchers of human flesh. . . . You have to eat to live, as the learned Molière says, and so the aristocrats who know you have to eat to be free find the best short cut to the counter-revolution is cutting off our supplies. . . . First of all we need bread, fuckit; when you have it you don't starve, but it's not enough, god damn it, to stay alive; the hard-working *sans-culottes* should be happy; along with their bread they need some cash, a touch of patriotic booze to pep them up when they're down, they need clothes, shirts, and shoes or at least sabots; and fuckit, if things don't look up soon no *sans-culottes* will be able to make a stew, we'll drink water like ducks which, believe me, is a punishment that should be reserved for moderates, aristocrats, and royalists. . . . The farmers who owe every-thing to the Revolution are as ferocious as the wild animals who used to eat their crops. They forget all the *sans-culottes* of the cities have done for them . . . they forget that the

> country owes all its wealth to the cities
> because, fuckit, what would they do with
> their crops, those dumb peasants, if the cities
> didn't buy them? . . . Yes, fuckit, I wish that
> at the first sign of shortages a law would
> condemn all the rich, the merchants, the big
> farmers, and others who starve the people
> to fast; soon abundance would return, fuckit!

The passage loses a lot in translation, for which I apologize, but it states very clearly the attitudes of the *sans-culottes* during the Terror, that brief period when they assumed an importance all out of proportion to their numbers. No one has ever found a better name for the *sans-culottes* than the original; to call them an "urban proletariat" or even the precursors of the nineteenth-century urban proletariat is to falsify history. Sometimes the most valuable lesson to be learned from history is its specific character: the fact that certain social and cultural configurations are unique to a certain time and place. The emergence of the *sans-culottes* as a distinct social, political, and cultural class was not foreseen by any of the theories of the Enlightenment, and to attempt to interpret its brief period of importance in Marxist terms is only to put it in a straitjacket that will not fit.

Paris at the end of the eighteenth century was not an industrial city. Réveillon's wallpaper factory, employing three hundred and fifty men, was one of the largest enterprises, but many of those men were highly skilled craftsmen. Most manufacturing was done in small shops where the owner was almost as poor as his employees. Certain industries, printing for example (an industry that prospered during the Revolution, for obvious reasons), were still regulated by rules inherited from the guilds of the Middle Ages. There were many small shops and small businesses of all kinds. The men and women who owned or worked in these establishments, some of them artisans, some salespeople, some delivery boys, some part-time workers—plus the street vendors, the unemployed, the beggars—plus the families of all these people, were the *sans-culottes,* a class that could acquire an identity only because they all lived on top of one another in the teeming tenements of the poor districts of Paris.

The word itself is instructive, because it is based on an article of clothing, rather than an occupation or a level of income. The *culotte* was the bottom half of the suit of an eighteenth-century gentleman, those knickers that surmounted stockings that clung to the calf of the leg and shoes with buckles. The *culotte* could be plain or fancy; it could be worn by anyone, a nobleman or a banker, a man of letters or a merchant; all it denoted was a certain degree of respectability, like wearing a jacket and tie today. The *sans-culottes* were all those men whose relative poverty or physically demanding occupations led them to wear that much more practical garment: pants. (We are all *sans-culottes* today, even the women.)

During the first three years of the Revolution the *sans-culottes* lent their support to the middle-class leaders who were trying to reform the monarchy and get rid of the nobility. They manned the barricades; they stormed the Bastille; their wives and sisters marched on Versailles; they volunteered to construct the amphitheater at the Champ de Mars. During those years the class distinction between the bourgeoisie and the *sans-culottes* was effectively blurred by references to the *people,* which included everyone who was neither nobility nor clergy. The middle-class revolutionaries of those years referred to themselves as "patriots," a somewhat blatant way of appealing to the "people" for support.

But the class distinction was always latent. It had been seen in action in the Réveillon riot of April 1789. When the "patriots" of July 1789 created a militia to assure order in

Paris it was first called the *milice bourgeoise*. Even when the name was changed to *Gardes Nationales* it remained a thoroughly middle-class institution, one of whose functions was to keep the lower classes in their place. The abolition of the nobility (June 1790), the ban on liveries and coats of arms, the fact that silver buckles on the shoes of the well-to-do were replaced by tricolor rosettes, could amuse the *sans-culottes* for only so long. When the king tried to leave the country, when the National Guard fired on the people at the Champ de Mars, when merchants began to get rich selling supplies to the volunteer armies, the *sans-culottes* were no longer amused. They could no longer be flattered by references to the "people" or appeals to their patriotism. As *le Père Duchesne* put it, "*La patrie, foutre, les négociants n'en ont point*—A country, fuckit, the moneymakers don't have one."

Strange how things persist, even to the words. Our National Guard, which is called to duty whenever our *sans-culottes* get threatening (be they blacks, chicanos, or students) is also a "bourgeois militia." The dress of American youth today, and some Americans who are not so young, recalls the vestmental root of the word *sans-culottes* even if, today, it is often a costume adopted by middle-class individuals trying to deny their origins. The *tie,* that useless symbol of respectability, is universally eschewed. If there is any one garment that is universally adopted, any one garment that, like the pants worn by the *sans-culottes,* could serve as a symbol for a social and cultural attitude not to be defined by theoretical categories of class, it would be blue jeans, dungarees. But blue jeans were originally the practical, durable, and washable pants worn by American workers. If our antique Constitution manages to survive into the twenty-first century, we shall no doubt one day see a President take the oath on the steps of the Capitol (in a heated, bulletproof plastic box—the date is January), *sans cravate* and wearing dungarees—which by then will be as respectable as striped pants. (And maybe she will be black, to paraphrase the old racist, male-chauvinist joke.)

By the summer of 1792 the *sans-culottes*, like everyone else in France, felt betrayed, but perhaps they felt more betrayed than others. As Marat put it, "For three years we have been fighting to recover our liberty and yet we are further from it than at the beginning; never were we more enslaved."

The first phase of the Revolution had abolished feudal taxes and duties, had given some peasants a clear title to their land, but it had done little for the workers in the cities. If the various revolutionary governments managed to keep bread in ample supply, they did nothing about the rising prices of other articles that the *sans-culottes* regarded as necessities, such as sugar, meat, wine, soap, firewood. Once the war began the government was forced to issue increased quantities of paper money, the *assignats*. This caused a rapid inflation, and, as is usual during an inflation, rising wages could not keep up with the rising cost of living.

But the cumulative effect of the writings of Marat and Hébert, plus the insurrection of August 10th, directed by the Paris Commune, had finally given the *sans-culottes* a sense of identity and a taste of power. They were no longer content to follow middle-class leaders or to accept continued privation because of the war and the Revolution. As le Père Duchesne put it in our earlier citation: "First of all we need bread, fuckit; when you have it you don't starve; but it's not enough, god damn it, to stay alive; the hard-working *sans-culottes* should be happy." *Happy*—that "new idea in Europe." The "people" had always been crying for bread, but in their brief period of importance the *sans-culottes* also demanded a bit of cake.

The economic doctrine that the men of 1789 had inherited from the Enlightenment was that of *laissez-faire*—the theory that the best way to make a nation wealthy was to abolish all government controls on the economy, the theory of Adam Smith's *The Wealth of Nations*. This was a "liberal" theory in contrast to the traditional economic policies of Old Regime monarchies, which tried to put as much gold as possible into the national treasury by an elaborate system of tariffs and customs duties, both internal and external, as well as government monopolies of certain luxury products designed for export.* One of the first things the liberals of 1789 did was to destroy the customs barriers on the roads leading into Paris. The Le Chapelier law of 1791 forbidding workers to organize or strike was an expression of *laissez-faire* doctrine and, as such, it remained in force long after the Revolution.

The *sans-culottes* didn't know anything about economic theories but they knew what they wanted. The law forbidding labor unions never became a major issue because very few of the *sans-culottes* were employed in shops or factories where a union would have been in a powerful bargaining position. But they did want price controls to combat the growing inflation. They did want rent control since landlords were taking advantage of the fact that Paris was over-crowded with migrants from the more backward regions of France. If necessary they wanted rationing to assure that everyone could buy meat and shoes, not just the rich. They were not impressed when they were told that in the long run, according to the theories, price controls and rationing would

---

* *The older theory was known as "mercantilism." One of the government monopolies was the Gobelins tapestry factory, established by Colbert in 1667 and still making money for the French government today. The tobacco industry in France was and remains a government monopoly, which may be why there has never been a French Surgeon General's Report on the danger of cigarette smoking. Air France and most other international airlines are twentieth-century mercantilist operations; Colbert would understand why they keep their fares so high and Louis XIV, like President Pompidou, would have taken a ride in the prototype of the Concorde and loved it.*

hurt the economy and make everyone poorer. They were interested in the short run and they were poor already.

They were poor but not abject, not ground down to the level of total misery where thought, imagination, and action are impossible. For the poor to become a revolutionary force they must be able to read Marat and Hébert, or watch the six o'clock news.

There was no six o'clock news in Paris in 1793, but there were the frequent meetings of the Paris *sections,* where the *sans-culottes* could not only learn about politics but take part in it. The *sans-culottes* instinctively believed in what we call "participatory democracy"—the idea that all citizens, meeting in local councils on the community level, should take a continuous part in making political decisions, rather than leaving that to their elected representatives. This idea can be traced back to the town and village assemblies of the Middle Ages; it reappeared in the New England town meetings, the Commune of 1871, the Soviets of 1917, the Chinese Cultural Revolution, and of course our current demands for decentralized, community control of schools, housing, welfare, etc. But the historical tradition should not be over-emphasized; in most of these cases the notion reappeared spontaneously among people who were ignorant of the precedents. It is, after all, a very simple and attractive idea, far easier to understand than the various complicated systems of representative democracy, with their elections, political parties, vetoes, Supreme Court rulings, etc. What is difficult is to make it work.

It is significant that, except for the New England town meetings, all the examples mentioned above were short-lived phenomena. It is one thing to make local democracy work in a New England town where the rich are not terribly rich and the poor not terribly poor and another to make it work in a complex modern society. The *sans-culottes* and their leaders wanted to do more than manage their local affairs in a democratic fashion; they wanted to change the whole course of the Revolution. They could try to do this—and actually do it, for a while—only because the seven hundred and forty-nine delegates of the Convention, who represented all of France, were in Paris, subject to the threat of the same kind of insurrection that had deposed the king. The ultimate form of the political power of the *sans-culottes* during the short while that they had any was not participatory democracy, but the threat of violence. That was why their leaders during that period insisted that all men not in the army be armed, admitted to the National Guard, and drilled daily.

(While talking about "participatory democracy" we can note that the Commune, to ensure that the well-to-do would not dominate the meetings of the *sections*, had instituted a payment of forty sous to indemnify all *sans-culottes* who attended for their loss of time. It does seem an anomaly to pay people to exercise their rights and powers as citizens but perhaps we should try it. So much for attending a PTA meeting, so much for voting in a primary, so much for voting in a regular election. After all people are paid for jury duty.)

To clarify the political situation in 1793 we could draw the following diagram: The Commune of Paris, which was the city government, elected by the forty-eight *sections*, represented the *sans-culottes*, their demands for social and economic justice, and the principle of local democracy. The Convention, the seven hundred and forty-nine delegates from all over France, represented the continuation of the middle-class, patriotic revolution of 1789, purged now of all royalist and aristocratic elements, dedicated to a centralized government, now made imperative by the war, with all power residing in the "representatives of the people." In short, democracy versus the Republic; the *sans-culottes* versus the middle class.

The only thing wrong with that diagram is that it is inaccurate. The moment of the Commune's greatest power was the interregnum between the insurrection of August 10th and the first meeting of the Convention, September 21, 1792. During those hectic days, which included the September Massacres, the leaders of the Commune were the "triumvirate," Robespierre, Danton, and Marat. Robespierre and Danton, at least in their origins, were middle-class (Marat was *sui generis*). Once the Convention met, Hébert and Chaumette became the leaders of the Commune. But Robespierre, Danton, and Marat, all delegates of the Convention, continued to draw support from the *sans-culottes;* it was indeed an insurrection of the *sans-culottes,* stage-managed this time by Robespierre, that expelled the Girondins from the Convention in June 1793. But after that, Robespierre, as the leader of the Convention, had to clamp down on the Commune, even if he continued to make certain concessions to its demands. France, at war with all of Europe, could not be ruled by the *sans-culottes* of Paris, even if Robespierre sympathized with many of their aspirations.

Robespierre again, always Robespierre. The one short year of his ascendance encompasses both the best and the worst of the Revolution—the Constitution of 1793 and the Terror. During that year the Revolution overreached itself, wallowed in metaphysics, proclaimed happiness a new idea in Europe, had a Festival of Reason and a Festival of the Supreme Being, made Dr. Guillotin's humanitarian device into the Holy Guillotine, and meanwhile organized the most powerful armies Europe had seen since the fall of Rome. That year created the Revolution as an ideal for which men are still willing to die, for better or for worse.

The device that the Republic painted on all public buildings was, of course, *Liberté, Égalité, Fraternité.* Liberty can be taken to summarize the ideals of the first, middle-class phase of the Revolution—personal liberty (what we would call "civil rights") and the absolute liberty to use and accumulate property, according to the theory of *laissez-faire.* Equality is something else again. It is the key word in all demands of the *sans-culottes*, where it means far more than "equality before the law," that law which, as Anatole France once remarked, forbids the rich as well as the poor to beg and sleep under bridges.

The *sans-culottes* wanted *l'égalité des jouissances*—a fair share of all the necessities of life as well as some of its pleasures. They wanted the rich to be taxed to assist the poor; they wanted everyone to have a job with decent wages; they wanted free education and medical care. (These demands anticipate American Populism and the modern welfare state.) The more extreme spokesmen for the *sans-culottes* demanded a limitation on the size of all personal fortunes, whatever their source. *Égalité* was taken to mean not only that no one should be poor, but also that no one should be rich. Only in this way could there be a truly democratic society that would ensure that *bonheur commun* that the Constitution of 1793 had called the aim of society.

The logical conclusion of this demand for social equality might seem to be the abolition of property altogether, the sharing of all wealth—in short, communism in the pre-Marxist sense of the word. During the period of their greatest political influence (1792–1794), none of the spokesmen of the *sans-culottes* went that far, perhaps because many of the *sans-culottes* were small businessmen, attached to the idea of property, so long as it was small. But in 1795, Babeuf, in his short-lived journal *le Tribune du Peuple*, did draw this ultimate conclusion, and Babeuf's friend Sylvain Maréchal expressed it in a hortatory form in the "Manifesto of the Equals" of 1796. Both Babeuf and Maréchal used the by then familiar rhetoric of Marat and Hébert and spoke to the *sans-culottes*, whom they hoped to rouse to yet another insurrection—"*Peuple! réveille-toi à l'espérance!*—People! awake to hope!" But by then, two years after the fall of Robespierre, the moment had long since passed, and their "conspiracy of equals" was quickly suppressed.

As for *fraternité*, in 1793 it was followed by the words,

"*OU LA MORT*" ("or death"). (Chamfort later said, "The fraternity of these men is that of Cain and Abel.") Death is, of course, always a part of any definition of the human condition, but the Frenchmen of 1793 had more reasons than most to be reminded of this unpleasant fact. Perhaps for this reason, all of them, *sans-culottes* and bourgeois revolutionaries alike, felt a great urgency to complete that transformation of society *a priori* that had begun in 1789. Since it is much easier to change the names of things than to change the things themselves, they changed a lot of names. First of all those of the streets of Paris. Rue Richelieu became rue de la Loi. The Place Royale became Place de la Fédération, the rue d'Orléans, rue de l'Égalité, etc. There is a report of a Parisian coming home after a year's absence and finding that he didn't know where any of the addresses he was given were located.

Then there was a new calendar, to mark the start of a new era. The Convention had proclaimed France a republic on September 21, the autumnal equinox, a handy astronomical date, certainly more scientific than January 1. So September 21 became the new New Year's Day. There were twelve months of thirty days, each divided into ten-day weeks called *decades*. The months all had pretty names relating to the seasons, such as *Brumaire* (month of fog), *Germinal* (month of seeds), and *Thermidor* (month of heat). The five days (six in leap years) left over at the end of the year were called *Sans-Cullotides,* which is rather a mouthful. Since this new calendar was decreed in November 1793 but dated from the founding of the republic in 1792, it began with the Year II. Napoleon ordered a return to the old style in 1806 but, as Carlyle remarks, "a New Era that lasts some twelve years and odd is not to be despised."

The language itself was altered, if only in a few details. *Citizen* replaced *Monsieur* as the term of address, just as in Russia after 1917 *Comrade* took the place of *Gospadine*.

The familiar *tu* replaced the more formal *vous* as the second person singular, to show that all Frenchmen were now brothers. Woe to anyone who, out of habit, forgot the new mode, especially if he were being interrogated by one of the local Revolutionary Committees, a situation that demanded a great deal of self-possession; the use of *Monsieur* or *vous* might mark the man as a *suspect*.

In the course of the Revolution the *sans-culottes* completed the costume from which their name was derived. In addition to pants and a shirt, the costume included a short vest known as a *carmagnole* (which was also the name of a dance) and a red stocking cap, sometimes called a "liberty bonnet," another imitation of ancient Rome where a similar hat had been worn by freed slaves. The perfect *sans-culottes* also carried a pike to show his militancy and often sported a large mustache. In 1793 a certain amount of "radical chic" was in evidence; men who had never been *sans-culottes* adopted the costume and aped the manners. Hébert denounced the hypocrites who wore "floppy pants, a tight vest, a black wig and a red bonnet to hide their blond curls, a fake mustache, a pipe in their mouths instead of a toothpick," who peppered their speech with oaths, "neither more nor less than le Père Duchesne," whereas formerly they had lisped and mumbled.

In the area of personal morality the *sans-culottes* by and large agreed with the idea of "republican virtue." In the early years of the Revolution prostitution and gambling had flourished. Once Robespierre was in charge there was a crackdown on both these activities in the usual form of police raids and roundups and with the usual result: prostitution and gambling went underground and continued. It is curious that conservatives always believe that would-be revolutionaries are immoral and dissolute while when revolutions succeed they are usually far more puritanical than the regimes they replace; Cuba is a good example. The *sans-culottes,* however, demanded that the state recognize common-law marriages and give illegitimate children the same rights as those born in legal wedlock; Robespierre would have none of it.

In the realm of art and literature the balance sheet of the Revolution is clearly negative. The theaters of Paris produced many new plays expressing revolutionary sentiments; they are all, quite justly, forgotten today. David, who later became court painter for Napoleon, designed several revolutionary celebrations whose visual focus was often immense and vulgar statues that fortunately deteriorated quickly. These meager accomplishments are overshadowed by a great deal of "trashing." Furniture, paintings, and decorations that had belonged to the royal family or to noblemen were piled up and set on fire. Stained-glass windows were smashed; the statues adorning the portals of many of the churches and cathedrals of France were "guillotined" by peasants and *sans-culottes* because they represented kings and queens. The fine arts had, after all, been patronized by the monarchy, the nobility, and the Church, and could therefore be considered counterrevolutionary.

But even in the fervid atmosphere of the Terror the leaders of the Revolution did not think this vandalism necessary or desirable. The Convention declared that works of art that had belonged to the royal family were the property of the nation; they decreed that the former royal palace, the Louvre, should be a museum, open to the people, to house these treasures.* When St.-Just went to Strasbourg as the envoy of the Committee of Public Safety, he ordered that the portals of the cathedral be boarded up and covered with revolutionary posters. This measure delighted the *sans-*

---

* *The Louvre became a great museum only later when Napoleon gave it the spoils of his Italian and Egyptian campaigns. Napoleon was a successful Goering, much of whose booty remained in France even after he had been defeated.*

culottes of the town; it also—intentionally—kept the sculptures hidden by the boards from being mutilated.

All this—changes in dress and language; the new puritanism, the new calendar; even the demolition of churches and monasteries, the decapitation of statues—was only froth on the wave. The fundamental issues remained wages and prices, shortages of food and other necessities, treason, and of course the war. The winter of 1793–1794 was one of the saddest Paris has ever experienced, even if certain *sans-culottes* managed to dance the *carmagnole*. The Terror was the least of it, those score or more "enemies of the people" executed every day at the Place de la Révolution. The politicians enacted their Dostoevskian drama at the Jacobins and in the Convention; the meetings of the *sections* were dominated by militants who denounced one another for this and for that reason. Meanwhile the housewives of Paris got used to waiting in queues at bakeries and butcher shops, beginning at four in the morning in the hope of coming home with something when the shops opened at seven, assuming that the bread had been baked or the meat delivered. The weather was terrible; the streets were even more filthy than usual; a new class of prostitutes appeared at the Palais Égalité—abandoned children.

The Convention, still dominated by middle-class lawyers, would never even consider rent control. It did institute a *maximum* on the price of bread, then limited rationing; then a *maximum* on the price of other necessities. But, aside from a growing black market, these regulations were often evaded by the merchants. For example, the butchers took to roasting all the pork they received because raw meat was subject to price control but not cooked. When the Convention, very late in the day (July 1794) tried to reform the whole system of controls, it added a *maximum* on wages—sound economic policy perhaps, but one that left the *sans-culottes* even more disenchanted than before.

Yet if the fundamental demands of the *sans-culottes* were never satisfied, even during the most radical phase of the Revolution, there were a great many distractions and entertainments—*fêtes,* large and small, marches, demonstrations, and a series of theatrical funerals and entombments, the funerals of Mirabeau, Lepelletier and Marat, the ceremonies on the anniversary of the fall of the Bastille or the execution of the king, the transferrals of the remains of Voltaire and Rousseau to the Panthéon. And then the guillotine, while it remained at the Place de la Révolution, was a daily entertainment of a sort. There were spectators who never missed an execution and on certain days the crowd could be enormous. The attendance record was set by Hébert, whose journal had set the circulation record. The day le Père Duchesne was guillotined the Place de la Révolution was a solid mass of humanity (if that is the right word), ringed by carriages whose tops were rented to affluent spectators eager to see the idol of the *sans-culottes* "put his head in the window" and "spit in the basket."

.Even Robespierre, whose talents were not theatrical, had the *Fête de l'Être Suprême* as the culmination of his short career. (His execution, six weeks later, was one of the most dramatic, but the attendance did not equal that at Hébert's.) No event of the whole Revolution seems more ludicrous than this Festival of the Supreme Being, partly because its intended significance was systematically distorted by Robespierre's detractors after his death. For example, Carlyle says that Robespierre "made the Convention *decree*" the existence of the Supreme Being. In fact the text approved by the Convention and plastered up all over Paris was, "The people of France *recognizes* the Supreme Being and the immortality of the soul." Not a very stirring formula, perhaps, but not, as Mercier (one of Carlyle's sources) later wrote, "inept, ridiculous, and meaningless." (Mercier, who was one of the seventy-three deputies whom Robespierre spared, wrote about the event from hearsay, since he was in prison at the time. In *Le Nouveau Tableau de Paris* he accuses Robespierre of wanting to be a new Muhammad, then berates him for not being enough of a "pontiff." He also suggests—seriously—that Robespierre should have appeared Bible in hand to proclaim France a *Protestant* country.)

But, even undistorted, Robespierre's festival was certainly a turkey, both as theater and as politics. It was intended as a sign of the reconciliation of all Frenchmen who had ever supported the Revolution, excluding only die-hard royalists, papists, and atheists. It was planned as an immense "be-in," with the entire city of Paris participating. The date chosen was the twentieth of Prairial, Year II of the Republic (June 8, 1794). This just happened to be Pentecost, the celebration of the descent of the Holy Spirit on the Apostles. The formula "The people of France recognizes the Supreme Being" was deliberately vague, and yet it expressed not only Robespierre's convictions but also the Deism of most of the *philosophes* of the Enlightenment. Two months had passed since the leaders of the *ultras* (Hébert and Chaumette) and the *citras* (Danton and Desmoulins) had been sent to the guillotine. During those two months the news from all the fronts where French armies were fighting had been good. A lovely spring had followed the terrible winter, alleviating, if only temporarily, the misery of the *sans-culottes*. On the day itself the weather was glorious, a sign that perhaps the Supreme Being favored the enterprise. Paris was a "sea of flowers," distributed gratis for the occasion. People were told to wear their best clothes, instead of displaying a "republican" austerity.

And yet everything went wrong. Robespierre had breakfast with some of the jurors of the Revolutionary Tribunal who kept him too long so that when he finally appeared in his sky-blue silk suit everyone was annoyed at the delay. The guillotine had been covered with red draperies for the occasion and many people hoped this was a sign that Robespierre was about to announce the end of the Terror. Instead he made a long speech, praising the Supreme Being, but also reiterating the familiar theme that the Revolution was threatened by treason. Then came the great theatrical moment. David, the Albert Speer and Claes Oldenburg of the Revolution, had created four giant cardboard statues of Atheism, Egotism, Discord, and Ambition that Robespierre was to set on fire. When they had been reduced to ashes, a hidden statue of Wisdom was to be revealed. Robespierre, whose long speech had been largely unheard since David had placed him too far from his audience (and there were no microphones or loudspeakers), did his bit. He descended from the podium, walked all alone across a large empty space, and lit the cardboard statues with a torch. They went up in flames as planned, but Wisdom, unfortunately, emerged covered with soot. After that there was more. Robespierre led the Convention from the Tuileries garden to the Champ de Mars, which is a good hike. He walked faster than everyone else and found himself out in front, again alone. Then there was yet another ceremony at the Mountain of the Fatherland. The details are available, if you are interested.

All in all a rather tepid and mismanaged apotheosis of the hopes and dreams that had created the French Revolution. And yet in our own century we have seen revolutionary leaders who had much less to offer than Robespierre stay in power for decades—of course they do have microphones and loudspeakers. Perhaps, as Michelet suggests in *his* Monday-morning quarterbacking, Robespierre might have made it if he had used his *Fête* to announce the end of the Terror. Perhaps. In any event what actually followed was the six most murderous weeks of the operation of the Revolutionary Tribunal in Paris, then Thermidor, then the reaction, and eventually Napoleon. And always, of course, the war.

St.-Just had seen the writing on the wall as early as April: "*La révolution est glacée*—The revolution has become frozen." The Festival of the Supreme Being did not, as Robespierre perhaps hoped, thaw the Revolution; if anything it accelerated its demise. Happiness for everyone—*"le bonheur commun,"* the purpose of society—was again postponed for some vague future epoch, just as the application of the Constitution of 1793 was postponed until the end of the war, which never ended. Meanwhile the unhappy men and women of France were forced to live with history.

‖Thermidor

Our liberty shall have gone by like
a summer storm, and its moment of
triumph like a thunderclap.
>   —*St.-Just*

The great days of the republic were
now at an end. Personal rivalries
took the place of ideas. Politicians
took the place of policy. All the
statesmen were dead.
>   —*Albert Mathiez, "La Réaction
>   Thermidorienne"*

THE day after the *Fête de l'Être Suprême* the draperies that had hidden the guillotine were removed. The day
after that the Committee of Public Safety submitted to the
Convention a law reorganizing the Revolutionary Tribunal
and its procedures; it was, of course, approved. According to
the new law there were to be four courts instead of one; the
jury could cut short a trial at any moment by declaring that
they had heard sufficient evidence to make up their minds;
there were to be no defense attorneys—the innocent would
have to rely on the patriotism of the jurors.

This law of 22 Prairial is another reminder of the old
cliché that in politics, as elsewhere, the extremes meet. (The
annoying thing about clichés is that so many of them are
true.) The far left and the far right both deny the validity of
that precious middle ground where men and women who do

not agree can nonetheless talk to one another, that middle ground that is necessary for politics, even corrupt politics, even dirty politics—which are better than no politics at all. Robespierre was the Incorruptible and the law of 22 Prairial was made in his image; for it to function with any semblance of justice the judges, juries, police, informers, and perhaps even the defendants would also have to be incorruptible. The kindest thing that can be said about this law is that it was Robespierre's last attempt to make virtue at last a majority. If that was indeed its aim it implied exterminating a substantial portion of the population of France, and on paper the law created an efficient machine to accomplish that end. In fact it operated for only two months, which is evidence of the corruptibility of the men who were running France in 1794 and the good sense of the French people.

As always, when discussing anything concerning Robespierre, we are forced to confront fundamental issues. The law of 22 Prairial was a hideous, vague, formless piece of legislation that makes the procedures of the Spanish Inquisition look good by comparison. In our own century we would call it fascist, which wouldn't add anything to the description. And yet the men who had Robespierre guillotined two months later were all vicious, mean, petty, and unprincipled. Not even the most conservative historians ever tried to depict them as heroes. (France managed to survive without another hero for five years; then succumbed to Napoleon.)

Legend has it that the Athenians of the fifth century B.C. sent Aristides into exile because they were tired of hearing him called "the Just." The legend may leave out a few details. Robespierre was guillotined not because his compatriots had grown weary of hearing him called "The Incorruptible" (no doubt many of them had), but because too many of them would have been "shortened by the national razor" if Maximilien hadn't gone first.

By June 1794 a majority of the delegates of the Convention feared and hated Robespierre, if only because they were worried about their necks. And yet getting rid of the Incorruptible seemed to be impossible, partly because the usual charges—treason, taking bribes, etc.—could not be made to stick. The situation recalls the fable of the mice who decided to bell the cat, but could not find volunteers to do the deed.

And yet this cat was belled either cleverly or accidentally. Before we get to that, notice that there was no ideologic issue in the situation, as there had been a year earlier when the Girondins were expelled or even as there had been in Robespierre's quarrels with the *ultras* and the *citras* during the winter. In so far as they had any ideologic position, the Thermidorians—the men who did bell the cat—were very close to Robespierre, which is why they were still around. Two of them, Carnot and Cambon, spent most of their time running the war and financing the war; they tended therefore to oppose Robespierre's concessions to the *sans-culottes* because they put brakes on the war effort. And yet Robespierre's concessions were nothing more than that, and by July 1794, when the *maximum* was applied to wages, the *sans-culottes* knew it. On July 7, incredibly enough, the printing workers employed by the Committee of Public Safety went on strike; three of them were arrested but it was a straw in the wind. The *sans-culottes* did nothing to aid Robespierre three weeks later.

Five years earlier, when the Estates General first met, it had seemed that everything was possible. Even in 1792, with France threatened by the Prussians, it still seemed that everything was possible. Ditto 1793, with France torn by civil strife. But by the summer of 1794, even though internal dissension had been effectively repressed and the French armies were victorious on all fronts, the pressures of history, the circumstances of the moment, had closed in on the Revolution, destroying that optimism that had been its essential ingredient from the start. The newspapers that were still published were all dull sheets, all blindly following the party line laid down by Robespierre. There were no orators on café tables; there were few customers in the cafés. Despite the forty sous paid to *sans-culottes*—and the number of those eligible to receive the indemnity had been reduced— attendance at most meetings of the *sections* was down, and all questions of local affairs were decided by the Commune, now completely staffed by Robespierre's men. Participatory democracy, what there had been of it, was being abandoned.

Robespierre's apologists in this century, led by Mathiez, assert that Robespierre was about to give the Revolution a new dimension by implementing the decrees of 8 Ventôse that ordered the confiscation of the property of all suspects and its distribution to the poor. We have recently seen a revolutionary dictator attempt to shake up a system that had grown rigid, *glacée,* and give it a new spark—Mao's Cultural Revolution. For Robespierre to have attempted anything comparable—if that indeed was what was on his mind—he would have had to accept and use all the power he had as virtual dictator of France. What he did instead, in the crucial eight weeks between the *Fête de l'Être Suprême* and the 9th of Thermidor, was to retire from the scene, speaking at the Convention only rarely and missing many of the meetings of the Committee of Public Safety, leaving to St.-Just the task of stating his point of view.

Robespierre had pulled this disappearing act several times before; the cause may have been ill health. The details of those eight weeks still remain obscure—just as the details of just what happened in the Kremlin during Stalin's final illness may still be obscure a century from now. The Tuileries palace, former residence of Louis XVI, now housing the Convention and the powerful Committees of Public Safety and General Security, had become the Kremlin of the French Republic, in whose corridors the mice were planning to bell the cat.

Just one week after the *Fête de l'Être Suprême*, Vadier, of the Committee of General Security, read to the Convention a report on a new conspiracy that his committee had uncovered, a conspiracy that was given the curious name, "The Mysteries of the Mother of God." The details were equally curious.

There was an old woman named Catherine Théot who lived in a tenement on the rue Contrescarpe behind the Panthéon. For years she had been the head of a secret religious cult based on her assertion that she had been granted personal revelations direct from the mouths of the Archangel Gabriel and the Virgin Mary; her adepts were mostly young girls of the neighborhood who washed their oracle's feet every morning. One of her recent converts was an ex-monk and ex-deputy named Christopher Gerle, who was a Jacobin and had been given a certificate of civism signed by Robespierre himself. The sect had also attracted a number of royalists in hiding, even though the "Mother of God," who was also inspired by the prophecies of Nostradamus and a book of black magic entitled "The Clavicles of Rabbi Salomon," had proclaimed that Robespierre himself was the Messiah, the Prophet of the Supreme Being, the redeemer of humanity who was due to appear after the death of all kings.

It was hard to imagine how this "conspiracy" was a threat to the safety of the Republic, worthy of the attention of the Convention. The chief, and intended, effect of Vadier's report—with the memory of the Festival of the Supreme Being fresh in everyone's mind—was to make Robespierre ridiculous. Even though the Incorruptible himself was the presiding officer the day the report was presented, many of the deputies could not help giggling; afterwards they voted that a hundred thousand copies of the report be printed and sent all over France—it was also hawked in the streets as a pamphlet. Robespierre, behind the scenes, had the whole affair quashed, but not without violent arguments in the

Committee of Public Safety, where the shouting got so loud that it was overheard on the street outside. (The Committee then moved to a room on a higher floor, to preserve its secrecy.) The "Mother of God" was brought to trial only after Thermidor, and she was acquitted.

Two days later the Revolutionary Tribunal judged the affair that became known as "The Conspiracy of the Red Shirts." On May 22 an ex-lottery clerk named Ladmiral had decided to assassinate Robespierre. Not able to get near him, he decided to settle for Collot d'Herbois, the butcher of Lyons. (Collot was an enemy of Robespierre's, but politics in 1794 was confusing for assassins.) He took a shot at Collot as he was returning home at 1:00 A.M. and missed. The next day, May 23, a simple-minded girl named Cécile Renault tried to imitate Charlotte Corday by assassinating Robespierre. She was so simple-minded that she never got near her intended victim and moreover left her knife behind in a basket in a shop on the rue St.-Honoré. Beginning with these two bungled attempts, the Revolutionary Tribunal found evidence of a huge conspiracy to do in the Incorruptible.

On the 29th of Prairial, the Revolutionary Tribunal took one day to hear evidence and pass sentence on this conspiracy. Fifty-four men and women were condemned to immediate death, including some who had been called as witnesses but whose testimony was judged suspect. The "red shirts" were an invention of the court, a fine theatrical touch, prepared in advance, as were the *charettes* waiting outside. As in the case of Charlotte Corday, they denoted that the conspirators were parricides and therefore that Robespierre was a Father of his Country. (But Charlotte Corday had already become a kind of saint in the eyes of many Frenchmen.)

Just five days earlier the guillotine had been transferred from the Place de la Révolution at the fashionable, western edge of Paris to the Barrière du Trône, out past the unfashionable, eastern edge of Paris. This meant that the *charettes,* carrying the fifty-four victims, had to traverse the whole length of the narrow rue St.-Antoine through the most crowded slum in the city. The *sans-culottes* of the district that had spawned the Réveillon riot five years earlier were now exposed to the human reality of the Terror on their doorsteps. They were also exposed, in the weeks that followed, to the miasmal odors that drifted over their neighborhood from the hastily improvised Picpus cemetery whenever the wind blew from the east. They did not appreciate the favor.

Street vendors appeared selling pamphlets entitled, "The Holy Guillotine—the Fifty-Four Red Shirts—Robespierre's Assassins." If the entire episode wasn't designed to put Robespierre in a bad light it certainly had that effect. Louis XVI, when he was king, had never taken such spectacular vengeance on his enemies. The Revolutionary Tribunal was staffed by men appointed by Robespierre, but perhaps they were not incorruptible nor immune to influence by men on the Committees who had not yet revealed that they were Robespierre's enemies.

Certain newspapers, while singing the praises of the Incorruptible, let their readers know that in England Robespierre was regarded as the absolute ruler of France and that French troops were called "Robespierre's armies." This procedure anticipated those of modern totalitarian states where dissent, if it is expressed, can be discerned only by those who know how to read between the lines.

The Revolutionary Tribunal then discovered a new way of reducing the number of suspects detained in the prisons. Instead of investigating the suspicions that had put the prisoners behind bars in the first place, they now revealed a series of counterrevolutionary conspiracies within the prison walls. This made it possible to send *fournées*—"batches"—

of prisoners to the guillotine with very little evidence. The victims of these last weeks of the Terror—the Tribunal did not, of course, know they would be the last weeks—seem to have been chosen by class (which is why Picpus became such an aristocratic cemetery). In the eight weeks between the Law of 22 Prairial and the 8th of Thermidor the Paris guillotine claimed twelve hundred eighty-five victims, as many as the sum total of the preceding fourteen months.

There were many signs that this acceleration of the Terror aroused the conscience of the people of Paris. The shops along the rue St.-Antoine put up their shutters when the *charettes* went by. There were few spectators at the executions. One of the *sections* collected two thousand signatures on a petition calling for the immediate application of the Constitution of 1793, which implied an end to the Terror. To celebrate French victories in Belgium, "fraternal dinners" were organized; tables were set up in the streets and the rich and poor alike shared what food they had. These dinners were denounced by the Commune as an "aristocratic" ploy to pave the way for a "premature amnesty"; but they had been popular.

And yet when Robespierre came out of his semireclusion to speak at the Jacobins he adopted the menacing tone that everyone knew preceded the denunciation of a new conspiracy. He talked of "the faction of the Indulgents . . . allied with others . . . who slander the Revolutionary Tribunal"; he noted that the English papers were calling him a dictator. From that to accusing his enemies of being the "agents of Pitt" would be only a step. The only "indulgent" he named, for the moment, was Fouché, who had been Collot's assistant in Lyons.

At the Commune there was talk of the necessity of another 31st of May, that is of a new purge of the Convention. That was enough to make every deputy uneasy, especially since Robespierre had not yet named his enemies and since those deputies who were, in fact, his enemies kept that fact hidden. The situation was made still more obscure because the most important political maneuvering took place during the sessions of the two executive committees, that is, in secret. Some of the members of these committees seem to have swung this way and that, hoping only to find themselves on the winning side when the chips were down. The great majority of the delegates kept silent.

If there is any explanation of Robespierre's hesitant conduct during that crucial July, it is that the two key men he wanted to replace (and send to the guillotine) were in a strong position because the war was going so well. They were Carnot, of the Committee of Public Safety, who had assumed control of the armies, and Cambon, of the Committee of General Security, who had assumed control of financial matters. It would have been hard to denounce them as "agents of Pitt" when the French had just won the Battle of Fleurus and occupied the key port of Antwerp.

What is clear is that if Robespierre had been willing to be a Hitler or a Stalin he could have disposed of both Carnot and Cambon whatever the consequences. (Both Hitler and Stalin "liquidated" many of the best military talents of their countries in the years before World War II.) He had the means at his disposal. It may be true, as Michelet asserts, that France was not yet ready for an "18th Brumaire"—the *coup d'état* that five years later made Napoleon the undisputed ruler of France—but Robespierre never tried it. He did not even attempt a repeat of the insurrection of the 31st of May (when the Girondins were purged), perhaps because he was aware of the disaffection of the *sans-culottes*. Instead he chose to rely on the political means that had served him so well since 1791 to assure his ascendancy.

On the 8th of Thermidor (July 26), Robespierre finally reappeared at the Convention and made a long speech that he had been preparing for weeks, again refuting the accusations that he wanted to be a tyrant, again hinting darkly that there was a conspiracy against the Republic, and again not naming the conspirators. Historians agree that this last omission was Robespierre's big mistake. If he had denounced a dozen deputies, the Convention would have voted their arrest with relief. As it was every delegate still felt threatened. But the time had come when the mice had to bell the cat.

Robespierre's speech was applauded and it was voted that it should be printed. But then Cambon (the financial expert) took the floor to protest. "Before I am dishonored I must speak. . . . There is one man who is paralyzing the Convention; that man is Robespierre!"

There was a second vote and this time the Convention decided not to print Robespierre's speech.

That evening the Jacobins, as always loyal to Robespierre, excluded from their Society every deputy who had voted against their leader. Part of the power of the Jacobins had always been derived from the fact that they were a second assembly. Now they had excluded a majority of the Convention.

The Committee of Public Safety remained in session until five in the morning, a session marked by violent arguments between Robespierre's supporters and the members who finally admitted that they were his enemies.

St.-Just, at the Committee of Public Safety, spent the night rewriting a long defense of Robespierre that he intended to read to the Convention. But in the morning, before he could begin, he was interrupted by delegates who feared the effect of St.-Just's oratorical talent. "Last night the Jacobins declared that they wanted to slit the throat of the Convention! etc."

In an atmosphere of confusion and fear the Convention, now dominated by Robespierre's enemies, acted quickly. Legend has it that Robespierre, demanding to be recognized by Collot d'Herbois, shouted, "I ask for the floor, *président* of the assassins!" He was shouted down. In short order Robespierre, St.-Just, Robespierre's brother, and several of his close associates were declared under arrest. More than that, they were declared "outlaws" so they could be executed without being tried by the Revolutionary Tribunal, controlled, of course, by Robespierre.

The mice had belled the cat. Or had they? Robespierre was taken to the Luxembourg palace, now serving as a jail. Instead of being locked in a cell he was received in the office of the warden, one of his supporters. A few hours later he was taken in a carriage to the Police Headquarters on the Il de la Cité. From there, after a few more crucial hours wasted in discussions, he went to the Hôtel de Ville, where he met with the leaders of the Commune, who had already made plans for an insurrection. But Robespierre was hesitant, and the discussions continued far into the night.

By then the moment had perhaps already passed. The Convention, which would have been defenseless earlier in the day, was now surrounded by battalions of the National Guard, drawn from the more fashionable districts. And many of the troops that the Commune had assembled earlier at the Hôtel de Ville had gone home, dispersed by a violent July thunderstorm.

Robespierre's hesitation to assume the leadership of an insurrection is perhaps attributable to the fact that he had unexpectedly been declared an "outlaw," and so could find it hard to devise any *legal* justification for such an action—he remained the middle-class lawyer from Arras to the end, even when his life was at stake. But there were signs that an insurrection might not have been successful, whatever Robespierre had decided. At the Hôtel de Ville the day had begun with a demonstration by *sans-culottes* against the recent *maximum* on wages. The *sans-culottes* might have rallied round once they learned that Robespierre had been

arrested, but some of the *sections* that might have been expected to respond did not ring the tocsin when that call of
distress had been ordered by the Commune. The bells of
Notre-Dame were missing in the chorus that they had led
five years earlier when Paris was threatened by the mercenary armies of the king.

The leaders of the Commune and Robespierre were still
meeting in the Hôtel de Ville at two in the morning. Robespierre had finally been persuaded to sign his name to a proclamation addressed to the armies. He had written the first
three letters of his signature—"Rob_____"—when his legal
scruples got the better of him. "In whose name?" he asked.

At that moment a handful of troops loyal to the Convention burst into the room. There are conflicting reports as to
what happened. Robespierre's younger brother jumped out
of a window and broke a leg. The deputy Lebas, one of the
"outlaws," killed himself with a pistol shot. Robespierre
either tried to do the same thing (the official version) or,
more likely, was shot by a policeman with the unfortunate
name of Merda. In any case his lower jaw was shattered by
a bullet.

Robespierre was carried to the Tuileries palace, the scene
of his greatest triumphs. He lay there for hours on a table in
an antechamber, nursing his hastily bandaged jaw, surrounded by a milling crowd that shouted insults. That afternoon (10 Thermidor), he and the other "outlaws" were
transported to the Palais de Justice, where the Revolutionary
Tribunal had only to recognize their identities to condemn
them to death.

The guillotine, meanwhile, had been moved back to the
Place de la Révolution so that the people could more easily
witness the execution of the "tyrant." The streets were
crowded as the *charettes* went down the rue St.-Honoré;
places at the windows above the fashionable shops had been
hastily rented to eager spectators at high prices. After Robes-

pierre had been carried up to the guillotine, one of the assistant executioners ripped off the bandage that held his shattered jaw together. A hideous animal cry escaped from the lungs of the Incorruptible. The blade fell.

The 11th of Thermidor saw a record number of victims; seventy-one members of the Commune, condemned as accomplices of Robespierre. As the *charettes* went by a worker shouted, "There goes the fucking *maximum!*" But there went, also, the fucking Revolution. Twelve more followed the day after that, the 12th of Thermidor.

The rest, as they say, is history. Perhaps it was *only* history, but there was a lot of it.

The day of Robespierre's execution, Barère (who had switched sides at the last possible moment) declared that the events of the 9th of Thermidor were only "a partial commotion that leaves the government intact." He also denounced "a few aristocrats in disguise who speak of indulgence." In short, the Terror was to continue as before.

But, as it happened, once the immediate "accomplices of Robespierre" had been guillotined, the Terror stopped short. Robespierre's influence, the power of his political machine, had been so all-pervasive that the Committees, the Revolutionary Tribunal, the *sections,* and almost every government bureau had to be completely reorganized if they were to be purged of the men who were now called "Robespierrists." The initial phase of this reorganization took less than a month, but during that month many of the *suspects* in the prisons had been released—over five hundred during the first week of August—including friends, associates, and mistresses of the men who were now in power. The released prisoners were cheered by crowds at the prison gates—it would have been difficult for the Thermidorians to set the machinery of the Terror in motion again, even if they had wanted to. But none of them really wanted to; they were all too compromised, one way or another. By the time the government had been reorganized the Terror itself was being denounced as "Robespierrist."

Meanwhile the infamous law of 22 Prairial had been repealed. More significantly, as a sign of what was to come, the National Guard had been put under the command of the army so that it could never again serve as the spearhead of an insurrection. The forty-eight Parisian *sections* were reduced to twelve *arrondissements*, which soon became mere administrative districts. The municipal government of Paris became a part of the national bureaucracy, severed from its democratic base.

The restaffed Revolutionary Tribunal, however, continued to operate until the end of May 1795. There were more trials and executions, but for the most part they were trials and executions of the men who were now called "terrorists," such as Carrier, who had ordered the *noyades* at Nantes, and Fouquier-Tinville, who had been the chief judge of the Tribunal under Robespierre.

Robespierre's "republic of virtue" vanished even more quickly than the Terror. The secret police reports inform us that the prostitutes came out in the open ten days after the fall of the Incorruptible. A short time later it was no longer chic to be *sans-culottes* and even the true *sans-culottes* no longer dared wear the red liberty bonnet. *Monsieur* replaced *Citizen* and *vous* replaced *tu.* Robespierre had known that "virtue has always been in the minority," but the class that set the tone of the years known as the Thermidorian Reaction was also a minority—those men of wealth who had managed to hold on to their fortunes by lying low during the Terror and also, more important, those businessmen who had made new fortunes by financial manipulations, speculating in foodstuffs, and especially selling munitions to the war machine: the *nouveaux riches.*

This class was finally able to enjoy its new wealth instead of having to wear drab clothes and profess to love the *sans-*

culottes. They made the most of the opportunity. Now that a display of luxury was no longer politically dangerous or subject to confiscation, the houses, furniture, carriages, paintings, jewelry, and *objets d'art* that had once belonged to the *emigrés* or the victims of the Terror were put up for sale at auction; anyone who had money could set himself up on the grand scale that under the Old Regime had been reserved for the nobility. Outrageous new styles of dress became the fashion, as one would expect in a society of *nouveaux riches;* gauzy Grecian dresses that often revealed the breasts of the ladies who wore them; vests with eighteen buttons, huge cravats, jackets with wide lapels and trailing skirts for the men. Those who wore the extreme versions of these styles were called *merveilleuses* and *incroyables*—literally "marvels" and "unbelievables." The Palais-Royal, noted in 1789 for its bookstores and revolutionary cafés (and its prostitutes) was now notorious for its wildly expensive restaurants (and its prostitutes). During the winter of 1794–1795, when many of the poor literally died of cold and hunger, eighteen new dance halls opened in France where the new clothes could be seen to their best advantage.* Ten years later the most clever men and women of the *nouveaux riches,* those who kept making the right political bets, would even acquire Napoleonic titles—like the *Madame Sans-Gêne* of Sardou's play, the "Duchess of Leipzig" who had once been a laundress.

All of this did not happen overnight, but it happened very fast. The new calendar remained in force and revolutionary ideals continued to mold the rhetoric, if not the content, of the speeches at the Convention. In September 1794, as a sign that the Revolution was to continue, Marat's remains

---

* *That winter also saw the* bals à la victime, *where admittance was limited to close relatives of the victims of the Terror. At these balls the costume was completed by a red ribbon about her neck—in memory of the guillotine—and the dance was the* carmagnole *of the* sansculottes.

were transferred to the Panthéon. But at the same time a new species of thugs began to infest the streets of Paris—the *jeunesse dorée,* remote ancestors of London's Teddy Boys of the 1950s. These "gilded youth" were gangs of middle-class young men who wore the new clothes plus heavy locks of hair that hung down on either side of their faces. They also carried thick wooden canes that made very effective clubs when they provoked fights in the streets or cafés with anyone still wearing the patriotic styles of the previous year or anyone reputed to be a Jacobin. The police did little to stop them, as the *jeunesse dorée* had the active support of several members of the Convention. In November 1794, with emotions running high because of the trial of Carrier, the gilded youths attacked the Jacobin Club itself as it was in session, having been incited by the deputy Fréron to "surprise the ferocious beast in its lair." This time the police did intervene—and closed the *club* in the name of law and order. The Convention confirmed the decision of the police the next day.

Marat's remains did not enjoy the consecration of the Panthéon for long. They were tossed out in February 1795. But for months before that the *jeunesse dorée* had been seizing busts of Marat and tossing them into the sewers.

The *jeunesse dorée* were only the most blatant manifestation of the reaction of the men of money against the egalitarian aspirations of the *sans-culottes.* The *nouveaux riches* had bought the houses, furniture, and jewelry of the exiled aristocrats of the Old Regime; along with the trappings they acquired a callousness toward the sufferings of the poor that surpassed that of the former nobility. The attempt to control the economy so that the poor would be assured the necessities of life was quickly abandoned. By October 1794 most grain was sold on the black market at high prices; in December the Convention confirmed what had become an economic fact by abolishing the *maximum.* It also continued to issue paper money to pay for the war; the resulting inflation attained proportions that were not seen again until the early years of the Weimar Republic. In April 1795 prices in Paris were nine times what they had been in 1790. By the following November prices had again multiplied by seven. In March 1796 the government tried the remedy of replacing the *assignats* with a new currency called *mandats territoriaux,* to no avail; even beggars refused to accept the new paper money.

As always wages lagged far behind prices. The *sans-culottes* were desperate but not yet resigned to accepting the new regime that condemned them to misery. In March 1795 a delegation from the *faubourgs* told the Convention, "We are about to regret all the sacrifices we have made for the revolution." In April there was an attempt to organize an insurrection, but it amounted to nothing more than a demonstration, since all the radical leaders were gone. The next month (May 1795—Prairial) the *sans-culottes* again marched on the Convention, this time assisted by some of the Guards who aimed their cannon at the palace. But an appeal to revolutionary fraternity calmed the insurgents. The Convention listened to the demands of the *sans-culottes,* applauded their orators, and everyone went home.

This time the Convention reacted by doing what Louis XVI had never dared to do once the Revolution had begun—it brought in troops from outside Paris to occupy the faubourg St.-Antoine. There were twelve hundred arrests and thirty-six executions. And so, six years after the Réveillon riot of 1789, the faubourg St.-Antoine was again hungry and patrolled by cavalry. The only visible change wrought by the Revolution was purely symbolic—the Bastille was now a ruin.

Outside of Paris that spring saw a new *terror*—called the White Terror—chiefly in those regions of France that had been torn by civil war during the spring and summer of

1793 and that had suffered the most from the original Terror. Unlike its predecessor, the White Terror did not assume
an institutional form. Its executioners were masked assassins, many of whom came from good families and belonged
to religious fraternities; they attacked the men (and their
families) who were labeled "Robespierre's tail" because they
had supported the government of the Year II. The prisons of
Lyons, Aix, Nîmes, Marseilles, and Tarascon saw a repetition of the scenes of the September Massacres in Paris.
There were also many isolated assassinations. In some ways
the White Terror was a classic *vendetta* action, and it was
most widespread in the Mediterranean regions of France
where the medieval tradition of private wars was still alive.
It also anticipates the Ku-Klux Klan with its masks, mumbo-
jumbo, and membership of respectable citizens. A society
whose norm of violence has been escalated as was that of
revolutionary France does not become peaceful again overnight just because Robespierre has been executed.

With the Convention moving so far to the right, the Jacobin Club closed, republicans being tossed into the Rhone,
the royalists outside of France thought that their moment
had come at last—exiles are always overly optimistic about
the chances of overthrowing a regime from which they have
fled. In June 1795, a small army of *émigrés,* armed and uni-
formed by the English, transported by ships of the British
navy, landed at Quiberon in Brittany. This attempted invasion proved a Bay of Pigs. The *émigrés* never captured more
than a small peninsula. After a month's siege they were
forced to surrender. Seven hundred and forty-eight were executed as traitors in their British uniforms. Not only did the
expedition fail, it also served to unite France behind the new
regime, whatever its faults.

That same spring the coalition against France dissolved;
Prussia, Spain, and Holland signed peace treaties recognizing the Republic, which left only England and Austria still

belligerents. The Convention decided it was time to end its labors. But no one thought of calling elections on the basis of the Constitution of 1793, now considered far too radical. Instead a new constitution was hastily drafted—with the help of Sieyès, that perennial expert in basic documents—a constitution even more conservative than that of 1791, even if France remained a republic.

In May 1792 Robespierre had said, "I would prefer to see a democratic representative assembly with a king than an enslaved people under the whip of an aristocratic senate and a dictator. I do not prefer Cromwell to Charles I." Louis XVI had been executed, like Charles I. Robespierre, despite himself, had been Cromwell. Now the Constitution of 1795 was to provide the aristocratic senate—or rather an oligarchic senate—in the form of the Directory.

The social and economic basis of the new constitution was defined with brutal clarity by one of the delegates, Boissy d'Anglas. His words read like a speech by the villain in a Marxist propaganda play:

> You must now guarantee the property of the
> rich. . . . Civil liberties are all a reasonable
> man can ask for. . . . We must be governed by
> the best element, those with education who
> want to maintain the rule of law. . . . If you
> give political power to men without property
> and if they are found on the legislative
> benches, they will provoke or permit agitation
> without caring about the results.

Just before the Convention that had met with such high hopes in September 1792 was dissolved, it added a last-minute clause to the new constitution, requiring that two-thirds of the delegates to the new assemblies must be former Conventionals. The press dubbed the outgoing deputies "*les perpetuelles.*" (Contrast Robespierre's last-minute addition to the Constitution of 1791 that *none* of the new delegates could be ex-Constituants.)

A few days before the elections under this conservative new constitution there was yet another—and the last, for this period—Paris insurrection, that of Vendémiaire (October 1795). The insurgents were a strange mixture, *sans-culottes* and royalists, united only in their opposition to the "perpetuals." Barras, responsible for maintaining order, put the troops loyal to the Convention under the command of a young general who had acquired a certain reputation during the siege of Toulon in 1793, Napoleon Bonaparte. In June 1792, Bonaparte had watched the people invade the Tuileries palace to protest Louis XVI's dismissal of the Girondin ministers. He told a friend, "If four or five hundred of them were mowed down by cannon, the rest would still be running." He took his own advice in Vendémiaire, Year III of the Republic. The troops under his command fired into the crowd and the insurrection was over. Carlyle later enriched the English language by describing Napoleon's order as "a whiff of grapeshot." Again the Thermidorians had done what Louis XVI had never dared to do.

Could Louis XVI have averted the whole complex and bloody series of events we call the French Revolution by a "whiff of grapeshot" in 1789? We will never know because poor, fat, bumbling Louis was certainly no Napoleon. Putting aside such fruitless speculations we are left with the fact that in 1795, just six years after the start of the Revolution, the men of property controlled the destiny of France with a total power that had been beyond their wildest dreams in 1789, when the most any of them wanted was to eliminate the privileges of the nobility and limit the powers of the monarchy.

And yet the Revolution, in the course of those six crowded years, had called all social values into question, including that of property itself. Despite the assertion that France was to be "a nation governed by men of wealth" the men of 1795 remained uneasy. Property was no longer an undisputed "natural right" like life and liberty; it had been accused of being only another form of privilege, like the *taille*, the *corvée*, and the *dîme* of the Old Regime. Forty-five years later Proudhon would echo Marat by declaring, "Property is theft."

Babeuf tried to set the Revolution agoing again in 1796 by the same accusation; he was guillotined for his initiative. The "Conspiration of the Equals" did not even amount to an insurrection; it was nipped in the bud by the police before it got near that stage. But Babeuf, in his journal *Le Tribun du Peuple*, did manage to write a number of letters to posterity before he died, letters that questioned the whole idea of property as a *right*, indeed denied it, messages in bottles cast into the great sea of history whose ultimate destinatories may still be waiting on some lonely beach.

After the Revolution

Now, however, the time is come for it, and the man; and behold, you have it; and the thing we specifically call French Revolution is blown into space by it, and become a thing that was!   —*Thomas Carlyle*

THUS the author of what remains the most popular history of the French Revolution in the English language on the quick, brutal suppression of the last Paris insurrection. But is such a phenomenon to be blown into space by "a whiff of grapeshot," even metaphorically? Carlyle, who for all his hyperbole could sometimes be cautious, avoids the question with that word *specifically*—"the thing we specifically call *French Revolution.*" With that qualification the statement is plausible; one can argue only that the revolutionary process had, to all intents and purposes, ground to a halt over a year before, with the death of Robespierre.

Napoleon was the dominant figure of the next twenty years of French and European history, first as general, then as First Consul, then as Emperor. At first liberals outside France regarded him as the ultimate embodiment of the Revolution; later, to many, he seemed its negation. (In 1803, when Beethoven learned that Napoleon was to assume

[217]

the title of emperor, he changed the title of his just completed third symphony from *Napoleonic* to *Eroica*.) But even after Waterloo, when a younger brother of Louis XVI was "restored" to the French throne, it was obvious that the quarter of a century since 1789 could not simply be ignored. Louis XVIII did not even attempt to return to the Versailles of his childhood; instead he moved his court into the Tuileries palace in Paris, the scene of his brother's captivity and ultimate defeat. Taking the advice of Talleyrand, he granted the French people a charter, acknowledging that if France were again to be a monarchy it must be a constitutional monarchy. The Code Napoléon, which had summarized many of the decrees of the succession of revolutionary assemblies, remained the basic law of France (it remains so today); no one could even consider returning to that confused body of ancient customs and usages that had been the basic law of the Old Regime, just as no one thought of reviving the minuet.

But the Charter of 1814 was to prove only the first of a long series of constitutional acts that would determine the structure of the government of France—the most recent of which is the Constitution of the Fifth Republic. By 1814 the Revolution had already become a tradition, an event to be recalled with nostalgia by some and to serve as the model for future revolutions for others. In the sixty years that followed the restoration of the Bourbons, France again went through the whole cycle that had begun in 1789—a monarchy, a constitutional monarchy, a republic, and a Bonapartist empire. When that empire met *its* Waterloo at Sedan during the Prussian invasion of 1870, it seemed likely that the cycle would begin all over again. In the National Assembly that met in 1871 to decide on a new form of government for France, a majority of the delegates were monarchists. The end result was the Third Republic only because the two pretenders to the throne, the comte de Chambord and the comte

de Paris, couldn't agree on which one was to be king and
how. By this time, however, the tradition of the Revolution
as an historical event was already overshadowed by a new
revolutionary tradition, looking forward to the Revolution as
a *future* event. Even while the Assembly was meeting in Versailles, trying to decide between the comte de Chambord and
the comte de Paris, the workers of Paris seized control of the
city and hoisted, in place of the tricolor, the red flag.

This revolt, which lasted only three months, took its name
from that of the insurrectionary government of Paris in
1792—the Commune. Its final days were more bloody and
violent than any Paris had seen during the Terror or since.
The die-hard Communards set fire to the Tuileries palace,
the Palais de Justice, and the Hôtel de Ville. The repression,
when the troops of the Versailles Assembly finally gained
control of the city, was swift and terrible; seventeen thousand men, women, and children were shot.

The Communard anthem was not the *Marseillaise*, but a
new song that was to have a long history, *L'Internationale*.
The Commune, in its turn, became a hallowed event for a
continuing international revolutionary tradition. In 1964,
when the Russians launched a space ship that for the first
time was capable of carrying more than one man into orbit,
their sputnik Voskhod, along with its three cosmonauts, carried a portrait of Marx, a portrait of Lenin, and a ribbon
from a Communard flag.

The path from "the thing we specifically call *French Revolution*" to that scrap of cloth in orbit leads us on a detour
from the history of France in the nineteenth century—the
revolution of 1830, the revolution of 1848, the Second Republic, the Third Empire, etc.—into the realm of ideas: a
detour from history to theories of history. Yet it is not, after
all, a byway, but rather the *camino real,* since the most important effect of the French Revolution was not its influence
on the subsequent history of France, but rather its influence

on subsequent revolutions everywhere. And that influence was due to the way certain intellectuals interpreted the events of what came to be regarded as the original, archetypical revolution.

Of course that original Revolution had itself been begotten by certain *ideas*. Before jumping ahead to the age of orbital voyages, let us consider that fact. Back in 1789, when the Revolution was just beginning, it was generally agreed that one of its causes was the Enlightenment, the concepts and attitudes to be found in the works of the *philosophes*, Voltaire, Rousseau, Diderot, etc. Now, none of the *philosophes* had been revolutionaries—they couldn't be, because the revolution had not yet occurred. Most of them hoped that society would be changed by education; some put their faith in "enlightened despotism." None of them were exclusively political writers. Many modern critics have gone to great lengths to demonstrate that they would have approved of none of the things that were later done in their names.

Why then did everyone at the time, on both the left and the right, hold them responsible, at least in part, for the revolution? The answer is simple, almost simple-minded: it was because men like Robespierre and Danton, and even Mirabeau and Lafayette, claimed that their actions were directed by the principles of the Enlightenment. The *philosophes*, in short, were revolutionary because their works had created a generation of revolutionaries. Today, alerted by the precedent, conservatives blame the generation gap on progressive education and psychoanalysis, although it is certain that neither John Dewey nor Sigmund Freud would have approved of the SDS.

Among the leaders of the Revolution were two men of letters who continued the earlier tradition, Condorcet and Sieyès. Condorcet, at the height of the Terror, committed suicide in prison after having finished his optimistic *Tableau of the Progress of the Spirit of Man*. Sieyès, who helped draft

several constitutions, when asked later what he had done
during that period, responded, "I survived." Many of the
other revolutionaries might also be called intellectuals; their
collected works fill volumes that contain many purely
theoretical pages. But the origins of the intellectual impact of
the Revolution are not to be found in those books. As intellectuals, the revolutionaries were not very original. Mirabeau
tried to apply the doctrines of Montesquieu to the reform of
the government of France (and failed). Robespierre con-
stantly referred back to his mentor, Rousseau. The poetic
aura of St.-Just's pronouncements often conceals a paucity
of content. Marat may be considered an exception, but it was
The Chains of Slavery written ten years before the Revolution that Marx annotated, not *l'Ami du Peuple*.

All in all the intellectual legacy of the revolutionary generation is rather thin; what is remembered is not its words
but its actions. The French Revolution was something not
dreamed of by the philosophers of the Enlightenment. Because it had happened, and happened in France, and caused
twenty years of turmoil throughout Europe, there was a crying need for new concepts of history and politics. In a sense
Voltaire and Rousseau had gone to the guillotine along with
Robespierre—although their remains, unlike those of the
Incorruptible, were transferred to the Panthéon. The Enlightenment, like a parent baffled by his own children, could
not explain the revolution it had sired.

The search for new concepts of history and politics began,
quite naturally, with histories and analyses of the Revolution itself. First came the memoirs and documents, then the
multivolume narratives by Thiers, Carlyle, Michelet, and
Louis Blanc. Every political thinker had to offer an interpretation of the Revolution, its causes and effects. De Maistre,
a contemporary who spent most of his life in exile, laid the
foundations of the conservative interpretation. Tocqueville,
in *The Old Regime and the Revolution,* offered what we

would call a sociologic study of the causes of the obsessive event. Marx, of course, explained it all in terms of the class struggle. Meanwhile the Revolution continued as an historical force; many of the historians and interpreters of the first revolution were themselves participants in its sequels —for example Blanc and Marx. The Revolution was never a dead issue, of interest only to scholars.

This interaction of ideas and events—the Enlightenment engendering the Revolution, the Revolution in turn stimulating new political theories—recalls the *dialectic,* that logical process that organizes what is certainly the most influential of the various interpretations of history provoked by the French Revolution: that of Marx. Marx, of course, took the idea of a dialectical interpretation of history from his teacher Hegel, who had been one of the first men to create a theory of *world history,* indeed the first to create one flexible enough to include the French Revolution. But Hegel believed that Ideas (with a capital *I*) were the driving force of History (with a capital *H*); he said that "the philosophy of history is actually the history of philosophy"—a statement that, on first hearing, sounds lucid and even witty, but which grows more murky and more confusing the longer you think about it (like most of Hegel's statements). Marx turned Hegel's theory of history upside-down. He said he was "standing Hegel on his head," but he meant that he was trying to put his feet on the ground, no mean trick with Hegel. Marx insisted that the driving force of the dialectic of history was the way wealth was created, "the means of production," that its underlying process was the interaction of different groups of men with opposing economic interests; that interaction he called the "class struggle." The evolution of ideas—"the history of philosophy"—was only a pale reflection of the progress of the class struggle.*

* *For example—and this is an oversimplification—according to Hegel, a* thesis *(such as the Divine Right of Kings as embodied in the*

And yet Marx exempted his *own* theory from the pale-reflection category because of its revolutionary intentions. "Until now," he said, "philosophers have made theories about history, but the important thing is to *change it.*" Quite a head-swelling notion for intellectuals—changing the course of history—a notion that no one could have taken seriously before the French Revolution when intellectuals (like Marat) really did change history.

And they have continued to do so. It is a sign of the ideologic character of modern times that, for the past century, nearly all the great leaders have been theoreticians of one stripe or another (or at least writers), rather than generals or monarchs as in the past—Lenin, Trotsky, Stalin, Hitler, Mussolini, Churchill, de Gaulle, Mao. Franklin D. Roosevelt would appear to be an exception, although the New Deal was given a quasi-ideologic content by his Brain Trust. In this long-term perspective, Napoleon would seem a transitional figure. He inherited an ideology from the Revolution, but his personal stature, like that of Caesar and Alexander, was based on his military feats.

Before the Revolution history had been a minor area of human knowledge, certainly considered less important than theology. After the Revolution, and because of the Revolution, it became a major subject; in fact, along with science, *the* major subject. Especially for the intellectuals who wanted to change it. In the nineteenth century history still

---

Old Regime) *stimulates its own negation, an* antithesis (*the Enlightenment as embodied in the Revolution*). *These two are then fused in a* synthesis (*Nationalism as embodied in the modern state*). *For Marx, feudalism, based on agriculture and represented by the* class *of the nobility, had been replaced by its* antithesis, *capitalism, based on trade and represented by the bourgeoisie; that was the essential story of the French Revolution. Now that capitalism was triumphant it had created a new "means of production," modern industry, and with that a new class, the industrial proletariat. The proletariat, by another revolution, would eventually replace capitalism with its antithesis, socialism.*

included much of what today are called "social studies" (although the grim science of economics had already established its own territory); there was no sociology, anthropology, let alone social psychology, to dispute its preeminence. That is why theories of history were taken so seriously; they seemed to explain almost everything about humanity.

Now let us not exaggerate and try to prove too much. This broad change in the intellectual climate would certainly have occurred even if Louis XVI and the moderates of 1789 had been successful in reforming French society by peaceful means. But because the French Revolution and the wars it engendered had, in fact, marked the change—had, in fact, molded much of the theories of Hegel and Marx—the French Revolution became the model for all historical events, past and present. The American Revolution and the English revolutions of the seventeenth century were reexamined and their histories rewritten to fit the pattern, in ways that often made Americans and Englishmen gasp with astonishment. But the first gasp was often the last—could Americans and Englishmen claim not to be a part of *world history*? The Reformation, the histories of ancient Greece and Rome, as well as those of China and India, were somehow or another shoved into the new theoretical mold, like a medieval heretic fitted into the Iron Maiden. If the result was often an unrecognizable cadaver, such as would emerge from an Iron Maiden, the attempt, at least, was heroic. No one—except perhaps St. Augustine—had ever tried to write a history of the human race before.

Does it not—the attempt to write the history of the human race according to a theory—recall the attempt "to renovate a commonwealth *a priori*," to write a Declaration of the Rights of Man, rather than being content to define the rights of twenty-five million Frenchmen? The universalist aspirations of the men of the French Revolution were echoed by the universalist theories of Hegel and Marx. One can imagine

the ghost of Burke, Burke who was so wrong and yet so
prophetic in his appreciation of the events of 1789, shriek-
ing with horror at theories of the history of *humanity* and
shuddering at the thought of what their consequences might
be.

We have, by now, seen some of those consequences. They
are due less to distortions of past history than to the fact
that, according to the theories, the Revolution also became
the model for *future* events in the grand drama of world
history. The Revolution—without an adjective; the grand,
metaphysical Revolution; the Revolution as St.-Just used the
word—took the place of the millennium in what was really
a new theology, replacing that begun by St. Augustine. Once
the ultimate Revolution occurred the class struggle would be
over, in fact History would be over—the state would "wither
away," property would be abolished, economics would cease
to be the basis of all human relationships, mankind would
finally have achieved that state of nature that the *philosophes* of the Enlightenment had postulated as the beginning,
rather than the end, of human history.

The essential idea of the new theology had been expressed
as early as 1796 by Babeuf's associate, Sylvain Maréchal, in
le Manifeste des Égaux: "The French Revolution is only the
forerunner of another Revolution, which will be much
greater, much more profound, and which will be the last."

That *last* Revolution has obviously not yet occurred. Even
in the self-proclaimed "revolutionary" societies class dis-
tinctions persist and nowhere does the state show any signs
of withering away. But the idea of the revolutionary millennium has become all-pervasive; even President Nixon, God
save the mark, calls for "a new American Revolution."

The word "revolution" has never had a wider circulation
than it does in this eighth decade of the twentieth century—
which may mean that it has become debased currency indeed, so devalued that it will soon become of only antiquar-

ian interest, like *assignats* or Confederate dollars. Its usage is no longer exclusively political. Beginning with the Industrial Revolution, it filtered into the history of technology, where it continues with the Electrical Revolution, the Electronic Revolution, the Computer Revolution, etc. Afterwards, by osmosis, it infected the popularization of the history of science, so that we now speak of the Copernican Revolution, the Einsteinian Revolution, etc. The arts have not been immune; Impressionism, Cubism, Abstract Expressionism, Pop Art, Op Art and the works of aspiring young painters whose canvases (when they are still canvases) manage to capture the attention of the Saturday-afternoon strollers on Madison Avenue, are all described as "revolutionary" in (as the case may have it) histories of painting, the daily press, or the gallery's publicity releases. Heaven forbid that any new book, painting, sculpture, or rock disc should be called "classic"; that would be the kiss of death. Seed catalogues offer "revolutionary" new grasses to enable suburbanites to have better lawns, and every new detergent marketed by Procter and Gamble is, of course, "revolutionary."

But nowhere has the word "revolution" been more debased than in its original precinct, that of politics. We all speak of the Hungarian Revolution of 1956, the Czech Revolution of 1969, as if both of those heroic episodes had not been brutally cut short by the intervention of Russian troops. Perhaps we need a twentieth-century duc de Liancourt to recall us to reality, inverting the apocryphal anecdote of his reply to Louis XVI the night of the fall of the Bastille: "But that's a revolution!"—"No, sire, it was only a revolt; the army is in command."

The aspiration is taken for an accomplishment. In the United States we have the Black Revolution, whose concrete results to this date—slogans aside—are largely Acts of Congress unjustly deprecated by those "revolutionaries" (white and black) who automatically assume that any Act of Congress is *per se* negligible. These amount to certain reforms, reforms that have been of benefit chiefly to those black Americans who were already in the middle class before they were passed, but whose effects have yet to filter down to the "underprivileged" black mass. As for that subclass—to use yet another contemporary euphemism for the wretched of the earth—they are probably worse off under the "benign neglect" of the seventies than they were in the fifties. They continue to be driven from the rural South by the introduction of agricultural machinery, and when they go north they are trapped in urban ghettos where drugs, crime, filth, and lack of housing make a normal human existence, even on the poverty level, almost impossible. Some revolution.

There is also the Sexual Revolution, whose accomplishments consist largely of talking aloud about behavior that used to be mentioned only in whispers—adultery, homosexuality, masturbation, etc.—plus showing blue movies in public theaters instead of at stag parties. But the Kinsey Reports, garnered at the height of the McCarthy Era (the bad McCarthy) are there on the library shelves to remind us that even the most kinky forms of sex antedate Neil Armstrong's setting foot on the bosom of chaste Diana. There is also all of literature since Homer to remind us of the same thing. One of the real benefits of this so-called revolution is that all of this literature is available for everyone to read instead of being the exclusive property of wealthy collectors of banned books. But Clio, that tiresome, nagging Muse of History with her long memory, reminds us that there have been other periods of what was later called sexual license that were followed by eras of intense sexual repression. The Victorians of nineteenth-century England were delighted that Byron, that product of the dissolute Regency, had perished while fighting for Greek independence. A surviving, celebrated, revolutionary poet whose personal history included both homosexuality and incest, not to mention more conventional scandals, would have been an encumbrance in the succeeding era of middle-class Puritan virtue.

With so many revolutions taking place at the same time, it is hard to know what is *not* revolutionary. We can, if we wish, lump together all the current modifications of our institutions, manners, ethical standards, and social structures and call them "the New American Revolution"—as President Nixon has done. There is nothing semantically wrong with that use of the word; its original meaning was, after all, an orderly progression or change, as in the earth's revolution about the sun. But in the political sense bequeathed to us by the French and, oh yes, the American revolution, one essential quality is that the change be not only profound and far-reaching, but that it be *disorderly*. (Some revolutions have been more disorderly, i.e., violent, than profound.) The income tax was a "revolutionary" measure when it was first proposed—but because it was first enacted by an Act of Congress, then confirmed by a constitutional amendment (after the Supreme Court had struck it down), its adoption was not "revolutionary," in the more narrow sense of the word—although the John Birch Society still wants it repealed.

But the Declaration of Independence was the start of our revolution because it denied the authority of King George III in the thirteen colonies. The Tennis Court Oath was revolutionary because it was taken in defiance of Louis XVI's order that the Estates General be dissolved. It remained the first decisive action of the French Revolution even after Louis recognized the National Assembly. The interruption of the normal, legal forms of change could not be expunged from the record.

And yet every interruption of the normal, legal means of political change is not necessarily a revolution. When the German princess Sophie von Anhalt-Zerbst had her lover Orlov assassinate her husband Tsar Peter III and thus became the Empress Catherine II, it was only a palace revolt.

When Napoleon returned to France from Egypt in 1799 and overthrew the Constitution of 1795, becoming First Consul under a new basic law, it was only a *coup d'état*. In a revolution the power of the government is seized by the governed, not by men or women who are already a part of the ruling elite. Today, because of the prestige of the word "revolution," this distinction is often ignored, especially when the men who take over the government proclaim their leftist ideals. The *coup d'état* of 1952, when a group of colonels kicked King Farouk out of Egypt, is called the Egyptian Revolution. (In 1967 a group of colonels took over the government of Greece, but no one calls it the Greek Revolution.) But a *coup d'état*, even if it is celebrated by millions of people in the streets, remains a *coup d'état*.

So much for current use and misuse of the word "revolution." There really are two meanings, both ultimately derived from the French Revolution—a certain kind of violent political change and also the hope of making a reality of the slogan "*liberté, égalité, fraternité*." Part of the purpose of this book has been to question the various stereotypes the word evokes today, by examining the circumstances and events that led to its current usage. But what if—this is only a suggestion—instead of trying to be more rigorous and perceptive in our use of the word, we were to drop it altogether? Or at least give it a rest for a while? For all that this and that aspect of the French Revolution remain relevant today, perhaps it is time that we traded it in for a new model. No, that has already been done; there are the Russian, Chinese, Cuban, etc., revolutions—all model A's that have replaced the old reliable Model T, *circa* 1789. Perhaps it is time for something really *revolutionary* (the word is unavoidable), that will have some other name. Perhaps it is time that we liberate ourselves from the tyranny that those six years in Paris at the end of the eighteenth century still exercise over our vocabulary and our way of looking at the world.

No, I am not about to make any modest proposal for a

substitute word or concept, even if I had one to propose, which I don't. Instead we shall take the advice of Voltaire and cultivate our garden, which for the moment consists in asking what lessons are still to be learned from the revolutionary tradition that began in 1789. One of these, as Hannah Arendt points out, is that revolutions are not the result of a conspiracy by self-proclaimed revolutionaries, but instead the result of a breakdown of the power structure, a disintegration of "the system."* It was not a plot engineered by Robespierre and Marat but rather the threatened bankruptcy of the government that forced Louis XVI to call the Estates General of 1789. In 1848, according to Tocqueville, the monarchy of Louis-Philippe fell "before rather than beneath the blows of the victors who were as astonished at their triumph as were the vanquished at their defeat." The revolution was already going in Russia in 1917 when the Germans brought Lenin from Switzerland in a sealed railway carriage to aggravate it; the tsarist government that had successfully rendered all revolutionists impotent for decades was disintegrating because of the defeats suffered by the Russian armies.

There are signs, not yet definitive, of a similar disintegration of the power structure in the United States today. Certain areas of our cities look like "Dresden after the bombing," to quote the mayor of Seattle after he toured Brownsville in Brooklyn. The public schools no longer educate, the courts are inadequate, drug addiction is spreading, etc. The whole litany is too familiar to bear repeating. We should

---

* On Revolution, *Chapter 6, "The Revolutionary Tradition." Miss Arendt also reminds us that, before a revolution occurs, all that can be attributed to conspiracies is "a few spectacular crimes, usually with the help of the secret police. . . . It seems, for example, that there was not a single antigovernment action under Louis Napoleon which had not been inspired by the police, and the more important terroristic attacks in Russia prior to war and revolution seem all to have been police jobs." Compare with the history of the Black Panthers, passim.*

remember that revolutions can begin on the right as well as the left—the French Revolution began with *la révolte nobiliaire*. "Law and order" can become a revolutionary demand when enough people feel that they are insecure; indeed, it can be translated as the right to "life, liberty, and the pursuit of happiness." Meanwhile, as American society crumbles, the Defense Department eats up an excessive slice of each year's budget and the interlocking boards of directors of the five hundred top corporations listed by *Fortune* Magazine remind us of the virtues of free enterprise and say "Let them eat cake!" If the FBI is serious about keeping tabs on the men who may be causing a new American revolution—in the narrow, political sense of the word—it should perhaps have its agents infiltrate the Penn-Central Railway, General Motors, the Chase Manhattan Bank, and the Pentagon, instead of worrying about the Black Panthers and the Sierra Club.

The war, which is why the Pentagon has such a huge slice of the budget—as usual we have forgotten the war. But if a second American Revolution, however we define it, is something we can speculate about, the era of ideologic warfare that began in 1792 remains an all-too-present reality. Of all the leaders of the French Revolution, Carnot has been the most prolific in his posterity. Nationalism, that other major legacy of the events that began in Paris in 1789, has at least kept pace with its sometime rival, Revolution.

The extent to which nationalism, as we understand it, is a fairly recent phenomenon has been obscured by the rewriting of history that took place during the nineteenth century. If Michelet, for example, could find only dim foreshadowings of the Revolution in the history of medieval France, he could find plenty of evidence of the growth of the nation-state. So he depicted Joan of Arc as a patriotic heroine —almost a revolutionary heroine, like *la Pasionaria* of the Spanish Civil War—which was stretching things a bit.

Churchill, in his biography of Marlborough, rewrote English history in the same perspective. But while it is true that the fact that they were English or French did have a certain influence on the actions of men and women born in either England or France in the fifteenth, sixteenth, seventeenth or early eighteenth centuries, the meaning of the words "England" or "France" had been very different then from what it became in the nineteenth century—after the Revolution.

In western Europe, the nationalism that was a product of the revolutionary era is seen in its most unadulterated form in the subsequent history of the two linguistic regions that were not politically unified at the end of the eighteenth century—Italy and Germany. In Italy modern nationalism engendered Garibaldi, Mazzini, and Mussolini. In Germany, Bismarck, the Kaiser of World War I fame, and Hitler. Not a negligible record, and one that always had an ideologic content.

Postrevolutionary nationalism also gave eighteenth-century colonialism a new lease on life in the form of nineteenth-century imperialism. The English, having caught the Napoleonic fever after they had beaten the little Corsican, painted this and that region of the globe pink until the sun never set on the British Empire and Victoria was proclaimed Empress of India. The French made up for the loss of Canada ("a few acres of snow," according to Voltaire) by conquering a French Empire in Africa. The tsars extended the Russian Empire to the Pacific, until the territory ruled by their scepter was one-sixth of the world's dry land (the only nineteenth-century imperialist empire that is still intact). This development was important enough to prompt Lenin to a major revision of Marxist theory.

In our own century, most of these formerly colonial territories have become independent nations. Because the political elites of these territories have been educated in European schools, their struggle for independence was formulated in

the European revolutionary tradition, which proved serviceable enough for that purpose—in a colonial situation, nationalism and revolution can seem synonymous. *"Uhuru!*—
Freedom!"* was the African revolutionary slogan. But independence, once achieved, has often proved lacking; setting
up the political structure of a new nation within the confines
of boundaries that had been drawn in London, Paris,
Geneva, or Berlin at the turn of the century was not, after
all, a revolution.

Meanwhile, back at the ranch, Europe, things had hardly
been peaceful. The leaders of that complicated and peculiar
peninsula were not content simply to plunder the rest of the
world; they also led their peoples into two abominable conflicts that killed a hundred million Europeans, both justified by ideology and nationalism. When that half-century
of carnage was over the two nations that emerged as the
superpowers of the planet were both non-European in
eighteenth-century terms: the United States and the Soviet
Union.

One might think that, after the massive fratricide (or
perhaps suicide) of Europe in World Wars I and II, the
family line of the French Revolution would finally be ex-
tinct. But no; both the United States and the Soviet Union
are, each in its own way, heirs to the revolutionary tradition.
The era of ideologic conflict, begun in 1792, continues almost two centuries later, even if Europe is at peace, washing
its monuments and choking its roads with Volkswagens,
Fiats, and Renaults.

And yet the uneasy peace that prevails in Europe may be
a sign that the era that began in 1792 is drawing to a close.
The provisional settlements made at Yalta and Potsdam in
1945 have outlasted the Treaty of Versailles of 1919, perhaps because they were only provisional, and based on
realities instead of principles. In 1956 and 1968 the western
powers stood by while the Hungarian and Czech rebellions

were crushed by Russian tanks. In May 1968 the French Communist Party did not attempt to seize power, although it was the one occasion since World War II when it had a serious possibility of doing so; instead the French Communists cooperated in shoring up the tottering Fifth Republic in return for certain concessions to their hard-core union membership. This uneasy peace has assured neither social justice nor freedom; it satisfies neither the exiled democrats of East Europe nor the revolution-minded students of western Europe (who are now mostly Maoist because of their disillusionment with the Soviet Union). But it does seem preferable to the alternative.

The European example may mean only that Europe (or at least western Europe) is becoming a super-Sweden or Switzerland, prosperous and neutral. But it may also foreshadow an eventual global settlement that will finally close the era of ideologic conflict that began with the Revolutionary Wars. Such a settlement seems hard to imagine with the Third World racked by revolutionary ferment, with "Maoists" and sometimes Mao calling for "a hundred Vietnams." The eventual settlement may go no further than a continuation of the present nuclear stalemate, with local revolutions continuing to provoke "limited" wars like the Vietnam War—limited only by being nonnuclear and fought outside the territory of the major powers. But Nixon's visit to the Land of the Little Red Book shows that it is at least possible.

Lacking a reliable crystal ball, we have only history to provide a clue to understanding events as they occur. The French Revolution created many of the patterns of revolution, nationalism, revolutionary and counterrevolutionary wars that still apply today. For a glimpse of how the ideologic era might end, we have to go back still further to a dry-as-dust document called the Peace of Westphalia, signed in 1648.

Europe in 1648 had lived through a century and a half of

genocidal wars in which religious passions and power politics were inextricably linked—just as revolutionary passions
and power politics have been linked in all major conflicts
since 1792. The Peace of Westphalia finally resolved the
religious issue by an agreement that the religion of a territory was to be that of its ruler. This of course was nonsense
in terms of religious passions, but the settlement stuck because both Catholics and Protestants had learned that they
would never win a total victory by warfare. Eventually the
religious issue was resolved in a more fundamental way by
the idea of toleration, the separation of church and state,
with the choice of religion becoming a matter of individual
conscience—an idea that was anathema to *all* the powers
that signed the peace treaty of 1648 (except for Holland,
which already practiced it). But that *eventually* took several
centuries.

It may be objected that no such solution is possible in the
case of revolutionary ideologies—a "system" obviously cannot be made a matter of individual conscience. But if we
stand the question on its head, as Marx did to Hegel, and
ask what areas of human activities and concerns are non-
ideological, we suddenly have a wealth of answers. The
post office, the weather bureau, and the department of roads
and bridges functioned almost without interruption throughout the French Revolution, even though the personnel did
change. Nuclear weapons are not ideological, nor is the
space program, despite that Communard ribbon in orbit or
those tin American flags on the moon. The population ex-
plosion is not ideological; even China has instituted a birth-
control campaign. There already exists an international network of postal, telegraph, and telephone communications;
also an international air transport network. The gaps in
these networks can be knit up with remarkable rapidity
when international politics permits it. Buckminster Fuller
predicts that a worldwide grid of high-voltage electric power

transmission will become an economic necessity for rich and poor nations alike. What is significant about these areas where a tacit international settlement already exists is not only that they cross ideologic boundaries, but that their operation is the same everywhere. Whether it is called the Bell System or the Ministry of Communications, there is only one way to run (or misrun) a telephone system, and that is determined by technology, not ideology. (Marx may have been right about the importance of the "means of production" after all.)

Which is not to say that technology alone can provide the solution to all human problems—although it can provide a "final solution." The world will not be run by engineers, at least not tomorrow. If the statesmen do come up with an international ideologic settlement it will be as crude, cynical, and unjust as the religious settlement of 1648. Nor will history grind to a halt just because the major powers agree not to disagree and to restrain, rather than aid, troublemakers in their own camps who try to upset the applecart. The flagrant contrast between the condition of the two-thirds of the human race who live in "underdeveloped" (poor) countries and the one-third who live in "developed" (rich) countries—with its racial overtones—will supply plenty of motive power for the awful machine of history, even if there is an ideologic settlement. (European history did not stop in 1648.) But we can note that neither technology nor race is dealt with in the revolutionary tradition. These are two more reasons for suspecting that its day may be over.

If we are indeed, in fact, living "after the revolution," we should remember that the aspirations that created the revolution in the first place—"liberté, égalité, fraternité"—"life, liberty and the pursuit of happiness"—existed long before the Revolution, and that they also will remain a motive force in history. Especially we Americans of the last third of the twentieth century who already have an extensive experience

of the problems of technology and race and who, for all our
defects, errors, and crimes, for all our innocence, ignorance,
and enthusiasm, for all our misused power and wealth, for
all our bewilderment at finding ourselves *la grande nation* at
this point in human history, are perhaps the only people in
the world today that can look forward to 1989 instead of
1984.

Americans today are the only people in the world who can
dream, as the Frenchmen of 1789 dreamed, of remaking
human society from scratch, and not only society but the
human condition. Some Americans have been doing that for
a long time—it is, after all, what the New World has always
meant. You will find them everywhere, if you look, in either
conventional or bizarre disguises. The experience of the
Frenchmen of 1789 should serve as a warning of the hazards
of the enterprise; there may be a guillotine waiting in the
wings. Our own history urges us to take advantage of the
opportunity. But it, and all those histories we have fallen
heir to, also warns us that if we confine our dreams to the
inherited definitions of the word "revolution" we shall certainly be doomed from the start. A New American Revolution, if it is to be something more than a dreary rerun on the
Late Show, will have to be so revolutionary that it is not a
revolution at all, but something new on the stage of history,
as yet unnamed.